To Pat
The Greatest
From
Muhammad
Ali
Peace
May 15, 1975

PAT COOPER

HOW DARE YOU SAY HOW DARE ME!

PAT COOPER

HOW DARE YOU SAY HOW DARE ME!

As told to
Rich Herschlag and Steve Garrin

SQUAREONE
PUBLISHERS

COVER DESIGNER: Jeannie Tudor
FRONT COVER PHOTO: Jeffrey Hornstein
BACK FLAP PHOTO: Robert Weidenfeld
INTERIOR PHOTOS COURTESY OF: Pat Cooper
EDITOR: Marie Caratozzolo
TYPESETTER: Gary A. Rosenberg

Square One Publishers
115 Herricks Road
Garden City Park, NY 11040
(516) 535-2010 • (877) 900-BOOK
www.SquareOnePublishers.com

Lyrics for "Mack the Knife," "Who's Sorry Now," "Five Foot Two, Eyes of Blue,"
and "Volare" are used by permission of Alfred Music Publishing Co., Inc.

Library of Congress Cataloging-in-Publication Data

Cooper, Pat, comedian.
  Pat Cooper : how dare you say how dare me! an autobiography of a life in
comedy / Pat Cooper ; as told to Rich Herschlag and Steve Garrin.
    p. cm.
  ISBN 978-0-7570-0363-9 (6-x-9-inch hardback)
  1. Cooper, Pat, comedian. 2. Comedians—United States—Biography. I.
Herschlag, Rich, 1962– II. Garrin, Steve, 1954– III. Title.
PN2287.C594A3 2011
791.45'028'092—dc22
[B]
                                                            2010032168

Contents

Acknowledgments

Throughout my life—both personally and professionally—I've been surrounded by many wonderful people who have cared about me and have always been there for me. I would like to acknowledge them now. If I have forgotten anyone, please forgive me, and realize that it is a mistake of the head, not the heart.

I want to acknowledge Mrs. Tannenbaum, my teacher from Manual High School in Park Slope, Brooklyn, who encouraged me to pursue my talents as a performer. I also want to thank the Safari Club in Queens, the 802 Club in Brooklyn, and the Silver Edge in the Bronx for giving me the chance to perform when I was first starting out. Thank you to my managers Willie and Stu Weber, who got me my first big break with a booking on the *Jackie Gleason Show,* and then continued to keep my early career going from The Copacabana in New York to the casino-hotels in Las Vegas.

I am grateful for my close friends Anthony Bruno of Anthony's Runway 84 restaurant in Fort Lauderdale (the Best!), Dr. Calvanese, Tom Cantone, Clem Caserta, Rosemary Clooney, Judge Jerry Crispino and family, Ann and Charles Cumalla, Frankie C, Terri C, Joe D'Amico, Contessa DelaPasta, my pal Tony Delvecchio, Uncle Pete and Aunt

Marion Gargiulo, "The German," the Jamison family, Jimmy Labriola, Julius La Rosa, Barbara Lerman, Jerry Lewis, Tony and Pat LiCata, Frank and LuAnn LoDato, Dean Martin, Tony Martin, Al Martino, Jim Migliori, Tony Monte, the Pinetta family, Joey Reynolds, Dr. Ribolotti, Nick Rotundo, the Ruhls family, Danny "The Baker" Samela and family, Lenny Schwartz and family, George Sklar, the Slumowitz family, Jack Sugar, the Tanaglia family, Carl Thomas, Lou and Ann Tulinello, Peter Vardas, Mello Viscussi, Tommy and Mary Zarella, and singers Theresa Brewer, Lillian Briggs, and Patti Page. I also want to acknowledge my agent Billy Claire; my accountants Orland & Orland; my publisher Rudy Shur; my editor Marie Caratozzolo; my co-author Rich Herschlag; and my promoter, co-author, and friend Steve Garrin.

In addition, I'd like to mention some of the talented entertainers I have worked with throughout my career who, in my opinion, should have been superstar headliners: Kenny Adams, Peter Anthony, Toni Arden, Sid Bernstein, Lillian Briggs, Dick Capri, Norm Crosby, Jack Fontana, Carol Fredette, Mickey Freeman, Goumba Johnny, Vicki Lane, Maureen Langan, Mal Z Lawrence, Marilyn Michaels, Bunny Parker, Patti Prince, Freddie Roman, Joey Reynolds, Sal Richards, Saverio Saridis, Lonnie Starr, Stewie Stone, Lou Tully, Nelson Sardelli, Peter Vardas, John and Frank Tanglia, Vicki Taylor, Carl Thomas, and Floyd Vivino.

Finally, to my Uncle Vito, you made me proud to be your nephew. And to my beautiful wife Patti—my partner and the love of my life—you always brought out the best in me. How lucky I was to have you.

P.C.

There are many people who have been major influences in my life, and to them, I am very grateful. I would like to thank Moya Phillips, my teacher at Announcer Training Studios where my career began;

Joe Tarsia, founder of Sigma Sound Studios and my mentor; Ira Cirker, for showing me how to get a great performance from an actor; Alice and Milt Schwartz, who referred me to Anson Shupe; and Joe Franklin, a great friend who has opened many doors for me. I'd also like to acknowledge my lifelong childhood friends Lenard Dumoff, Marc Goldman, Barry Green, Richard Levin, Ed Nemore, and Rick Weiss, as well as my great friends S.B. Albertis, Terry Berland, Jon Conde, Alan Crandall, Lisa Musco Doyle, Ira Ellenthal, Sandy Fagin, Mark Goros, Forrest Hill, Abe Hirschfeld, Tom Lake, Jackie Martling, Dennis Riese, Simon Rosen, James Rosenzweig, George Simms, Lindsay Smith, Billy Terrell, Gary Trimarchi, Steven Van Zandt, and Giuseppe Vicari.

I would like to thank my family: my grandparents Betty and Nick Giarrizzo, who introduced me to the humor of "Pasquale Caputo" as I was growing up; my moms and dads—Claire and Stanley Weinstein, and Joan and Don Deutsch; my sister Janice, a talented and gifted photographer; my cousin Joan Golub, a loyal supporter and friend; and my brother Paul, an artist and visionary who took on "the man." A very special thank you to Debra, my wife and best friend, for her neverending love and support. And last but not least, thank you, Pat Cooper, for allowing me into your world.

S.G.

Dad, you're with me every step of these epic manuscript battles. Judy, you're a role model, voice of reason, and someone who has made helping others a profession and way of life. Now enjoy. Suzanne Israel-Tufts is officially my cousin and unofficially my sister. Having you and Bob a phone call away is a privilege I will use till we run out of phones. Danny Herschlag and Yonason Herschlag are the other half of the equation—cousins and brothers. I'm part of an amazing *mishpuchah,* and I never forget it for a day. Charles and Marianne Mann begat my lovely wife (not so) many years ago, and what they've done for all of us would fill a book of its own.

I have so many good friends, but I'll just mention a few who were instrumental in keeping me on the field: Mark Barseghian, Doug Bellicose, Jim Craner, Keith Goellner, Hunter Gordon, Peter Green, Brian Harris, Gabriel Lamstein, Marc Landis, John Mann, Frank Petrello, Steve Schoeffler, Danny Seitler, Matt Selton, Rick Spear, Billy Staples, and Russ Wellen.

Steve Garrin is a can-do individual I am lucky to have been introduced to by the great Joe Franklin and even luckier to have worked with for so many years. Pat Cooper, I'm proud to call you a friend. At the core, you are a tower of strength and a sage. I hope in my own way I have helped bring that out.

Elise, cats and spirits follow you around for a reason. You are a shining light. Rachel, you've blown us all away with your academics, filmmaking, and sense of humor. But who you are blows all that away. Sue, we're closing in on a quarter century. I owe you bigtime and will gladly spend the rest of this life and the next and the next paying you back.

R.H.

Foreword

For as many years as I can recall, a comic called a "comedian's comedian" was nice, but didn't always fit. This is certainly not the case with Pat Cooper, simply because he has this fantastic capacity to challenge the art form, and has done so with an exquisite approach to the human condition. I've seen Pat demolish pomposity and snobbery and take it to the level of excellence known as "down and dirty" comedy. He was and still is one of the funniest men working in our industry today. I'd love some of today's younger comics to watch and learn from Pat Cooper—a true master of comedy. Go ahead—read his book and see if I'm right.

I'm quite proud of being a small part of this exciting time for Pat.

—Jerry Lewis

1

The Battle
of Brooklyn

My father took no shit. One night when I was about four, we were sitting at the dinner table and my mother was giving my father a hard time over nothing. It was as if after his working all day as a bricklayer, she still didn't respect his masculinity or his right to eat in peace. My father almost never raised his voice, so when he suddenly stood up from the table, my big sister Gracie and I knew something dramatic was about to happen. We just didn't know what.

My father walked over to the wooden chest, opened the top drawer, and pulled out a piece of paper. It was their marriage license. He walked back slowly to the table, looked at my mother, and said, *"Are you Louisa Gargiulo Caputo?"*

"What are you asking that for?" my mother said.

"Answer the question. Are you Louisa Gargiulo Caputo?"

"Yes."

"Very good. Because a that's a you name over here. And that's a my name, Michael Caputo. Show me a where on a this a license it says I gotta take you shit." My mother was silent. *"Not on a top. Not underneath. Nowhere."*

He put the license down on the table and we went back to eating our macaroni. No one said anything for about five minutes. But in my mind I said, *Wow!* He could have yelled, he could have screamed, he could have threatened. Instead, he did something that would not only get everyone's attention and make his point, but something that none of us would ever forget as long as we lived. It was worthy of an Academy Award for the way he timed it. *That* was how to make an impression.

My father had a strange saying that he used all the time. *"You know,"* he would say, *"you are a some cute article."* None of us knew exactly what he was talking about, but we were always told, *"You are a some cute article."* Apparently, my father was the cute article. He was a handsome man. So handsome that if people looked at my father and a picture of Cary Grant, they'd have torn up the picture of Cary Grant. When my father was laying bricks, women would walk by and try to start a conversation with him. He wouldn't have it. *"Please,"* he would say. *"I'm a married. I have a to do my job. I have a no time for this a bullshit."* He told us he was a sixth-generation bricklayer and I, his son Pasquale, was going to be the seventh.

The first five generations lived in Mola di Bari, a small city on the Adriatic Coast of Southern Italy. Like so many Italians, he immigrated to New York in search of a better life. In those days, the 1920s, a bunch of Italian men would get together and rent a one- or two-room apartment. Each would have his own bed or couch in one corner or another, and they would come and go at all hours, depending on what shift they were working. My father, his brother Viduche, and a few of their friends had that arrangement until my father married my mother and moved out.

I was born in Kings County Hospital on July 31, 1929. I don't remember my height and weight, but I had both. We lived in the Midwood section of Brooklyn, a borough that was famous for, among other things, the Battle of Brooklyn. In 1776, at the very beginning of the American Revolutionary War, the British controlled New York

Harbor, and General George Washington and his troops got a foothold in Brooklyn at the Gowanus Canal. But the British attacked from the rear and sent the Patriots running.

My own Battle of Brooklyn began in the summer of 1934 when I was five. We were living on the third floor of a four-story apartment building on Coney Island Avenue and Avenue P. One afternoon, I was downstairs on the sidewalk because I didn't want to watch my mother taking the wax out of my Aunt Rosie's ear. They had a strange way of doing it in those days—they used an ear candle. They took a rolled-up tube of paper that was soaked in wax and lit one end. Then they put the other end into the person's ear and let the tube burn. Within five or ten minutes, the hot air would draw out the wax from the ear. You needed a wet towel on your shoulder and someone standing by watching the whole time. Whenever I saw them do this, I would think, *Aunt Rosie's gonna catch on fire!*

It was hot down on the pavement that day when a man around my father's age came up to me and said, "Son, I want to talk to you."

"No," I said. "My mother told me not to talk to strangers."

But the guy grabbed me by the shoulders and started to pick me up. I screamed as loud as I could, and then the guy got me around the waist. I struggled with him and then he started running, still holding me. Suddenly, running right behind him was my Aunt Rosie. She didn't have the tube in her ear, but flames were coming out of both ears, her eyes, and her mouth. "You put him down, you son of a . . ."

My Aunt Rosie caught up to us, drew back, and punched this guy in the face like Jack Dempsey. He dropped me and dropped to the ground. Aunt Rosie got on top of him and started pounding on him. People stopped. Vendors in the street stopped. But before the ten count, the guy managed to get up and run away.

Then Aunt Rosie went from screaming at him to screaming at me, "What's a matter with you? Don't we always tell you not to talk to strangers?" And the Battle of Coney Island Avenue was won. But the Battle of Brooklyn went on.

We had very few things that ran on electricity, and what electricity we had was controlled by a box. If you wanted lights, you put a few pennies in the box, and an hour later you did it again or ate your gnocchi in the dark. Plenty of apartment dwellers put slugs in those boxes. The electric company would come in, open a box that was full, and find not one penny in there. That's when the utilities said no more boxes. They took complete control and metered everything.

We had an icebox like everyone else. A good piece of ice could last two or three days until it melted into the pan underneath. My mother got every cent she could out of it and more. All day long we heard the icemen down in the street, "Ice! Ice!" My mother would open the window and call down for a ten-cent piece, which was pretty big. When the poor guy got up three flights of stairs with the ice on his back, my mother would hand him a nickel.

"Hey," the iceman would say, "you called down for a ten-cent piece of ice." "Well," my mother said, "it melted five-cents worth when you were coming up the stairs." She always got her way. There wasn't an ice cube's chance in hell he was carrying that thing back down.

Winter was my mother's favorite time of year because she got ice for nothing. We had a box hanging outside our window, and it was better than a freezer. It froze the chicken, the macaroni, and the sauce to perfection. We lived like kings. In fact, in King's County everything came to the door. We had fishermen passing by every Friday. We had butchers coming down the street on horse-drawn wagons almost daily. If you waited long enough, everything you could possibly want passed in front of our door.

The woman who lived next door to us was from Sweden. She had a son who had black hair. I on the other hand, son of dark-haired Italian parents, was born with blonde hair. I figured maybe somebody switched babies and I should have been walking around going, "Sve, svee, svum." There were times when I wished someone would switch us back.

When I was six years old, the Depression was in full swing, but I can't say my sister and I were aware of it. We simply understood that there were tough parents in the world and we had two of them. At dinner, if we asked what the second dish was, my father would say, *"You put a you hands underneath the spaghetti, and if a you find ice cream, then that's a the second dish."* My father had an answer for everything. He would never say, "I don't know." This is the man who told me that Jewish people sit shiva because they're cold.

My mother decided to save some money on clothes. So she put me in one of my sister's dresses. She sewed a seam down the middle so it looked a little more like pants, but it was still, without a doubt, a dress. I used to sit on the fire escape all day because I was ashamed to go downstairs looking like that. But eventually I wanted to play, so I would go down and people would say to me, "You know, you're not bad for a guy who looks like a girl." The truth was, at that time, with money hard to come by, it wasn't the first time people saw a six-year-old boy dressed like a girl. But my father did them one better and stuck the knife in. He'd say, *"You know, you woulda been a better off if you were a girl."*

He might have been right about that. As the boy in the family I should have been the king, but I wasn't even a queen. Gracie wanted piano lessons and she got them. She wanted voice lessons and she got them, too. Me? I got her dress. Every night at the dinner table, my mother and father would say that she was going to be great. But she was terrible. "Sing?" I said. "She can't even *hum*." My father gave me a little smack and said, *"Sonny, you outta order!"*

When I was seven, we moved to a three-family house on Avenue T and 8th Street. We lived on the top floor and the roof leaked every time it rained. The Scorcia family, who owned the house, wouldn't fix the leak no matter how much my mother yelled at them. My father came home tired from laying bricks and refused to pick up another tool. So my mother plugged the hole in the roof from the underside with a piece of tar. Three days later it rained and the water came right through again.

We had a black cast iron wood-burning stove that sat right in the middle of the parlor. People died from smoke and fire all the time from stoves like that one, but my father loved it. The stove was the one place in the house he would use a tool—a spatula. He was a better cook than my mother, hands down. He made the world's best chicken scarpariello on that stove. He made music on that stove.

We got a radio around that time, and then we had real music—my father's music and nothing else. The radio was always on the same station, the Italian station. This was Italian music from the old country. He would come home, turn on the radio, sit down, and all we would hear for three hours was "O Sole Mio!" He blasted it. This was a *parent* playing the music too loud. And if I ever tried to turn it down, he would have thrown me out the window, and the last thing I ever heard would have been "O Sole Mio!"

There were a lot of programs and a lot of great music on a lot of other stations that I wanted to listen to, and when my father wasn't around, I did. I listened to Bob Eberly with Jimmy Dorsey's orchestra. I listened to Dick Haymes. And then there were the comedians. The comedians! Fred Allen, Jack Benny, Red Skelton, Abbott and Costello. There was a whole new world right in my parlor, and I would have stayed there to listen to Milton Berle on *Stop Me If You've Heard This One* even if the rug went up in flames.

One time when my father came home, he noticed that the dial was changed from the Italian station. So he got two rubber bands and wrapped them around the dial to keep the Italian station in place. In the summer in our neighborhood, everybody had the window open, and they all had the Italian station on. No matter where you were on the street, you would hear "O Sole Mio!" That's how they invented stereo.

Saturday was my mother's day off, which meant I was sent to the babysitter. The babysitter was the movie theater. My mother would drop me off at ten in the morning and say she would be back for me at eight o'clock in the evening. I would tell the usher to let me know when it was eight. It was usually ten cents to get in, and if we didn't have the money, I'd sneak in.

All of us kids brought sandwiches, and the placed smelled like an Italian deli. We watched cartoons like *Popeye* and *Betty Boop* and serials like *Captain Marvel*. There were features with James Cagney, Humphrey Bogart, and Edward G. Robinson. I learned to imitate everyone I saw. I loved the movies. It was a lot better than sitting on a fire escape wearing a dress.

If my mother could pick up a little something extra, she would. I wasn't supposed to come back from the movies empty handed. She would hand me a ticket that was redeemable for a dish at the movie theater. The complete set of dishes numbered 250. Nobody on the planet ever collected the whole set, but my mother came very close.

When my old man couldn't take my mother, he would disappear for two or three days. "Disappear" meant he would go to sleep at his brother's apartment with all the longshoremen sleeping on sofas. Every one of them was a better cook than the other, so my father was right at home and never went hungry. But when I was around ten, my father walked out and stayed out for months. Eventually he and my mother made up, and he moved back in. Over the next couple of years, there were three trips to the hospital—one when my sister Carol was born; one when I had my appendectomy; and one when my sister Marie was born. I now had a total of three sisters and no appendix.

Around that time, we moved to an apartment in Red Hook, Brooklyn. My father found something that got him just as excited as his one-station radio—the telephone. We were one of the first families on the block to get a phone, and my father made an epic out if it. The thing was installed, and he insisted that we all had to be there for the first phone call. It wasn't exactly Alexander Graham Bell calling Watson in the next room. It was Michael Caputo calling his brother, my Uncle Viduche, over on Avenue X.

We all sat there at the table. My father stared at the telephone and said, *"This is a very big a moment."*

"Pa," I said. "You can't call Uncle Viduche."

"Why do you interrupt a this a big moment?" he said.

"I interrupt because Uncle Viduche got no phone.

"Shaddap! I throw you outta the window!"

"Pa, no phone, no phone number, no phone call."

"I kill a you."

"Go ahead, call him. How the hell can he pick up the phone if he don't got a phone? You're gonna have to go over there and tell Uncle Viduche to get a phone. Then you get the number. That's how it works."

I didn't win many arguments in the family, but this was one I couldn't lose. My father got a hold of his brother and talked to him the old-fashioned way. A couple of weeks later, Uncle Viduche had a phone. My father reassembled the troops, picked up the receiver, dialed his brother, and we waited with bated breath. This is how the conversation went:

"Hello. Can a you hear me?"

"Yes. I can a hear you. Can a you hear me?"

"I can a hear you. This is a you brother Michael. Is this Viduche?"

"This is a you brother Viduche."

"I can a hear you. This is a you brother Michael."

"Pa," I said. "We're all falling asleep here."

"Shaddap," he said. *"I kill a you."*

And if my father had killed me that day, Uncle Viduche would have been among the first to know.

In Red Hook, you can walk out your door, look out at the harbor, and see the Statue of Liberty like it was across the street. Liberty was what I wanted. Being the only son with three girls in the family, I should have gotten my fair share of the spotlight. In most Italian families that's the way it would have been, but for some stupid reason, not in ours. Everything was about the girls, the girls. I was practically an outcast.

I ran around imitating Peter Lorre or whoever I could. The kids at school loved it, but I had no audience at home. My father gave me no encouragement whatsoever. I was dealing with a man from Italy who was cemented in his ideas. He couldn't understand how doing a scene from *The Face Behind the Mask* would help me get into the bricklayer's union one day. My schoolteacher, Mrs. Tannenbaum, told my father, "This boy is special. He's gifted. Pasquale puts out energy. He puts out *electricity.*" My father could care less. *"Electricity? How come I no can a pay my bills?"*

So I took my act to confessional. Just about all the Catholic priests were Italian in the neighborhood. I would slip into the confessional booth and the door would open. Usually I would smell booze wafting in. From behind the screen the priest would say, *"All right, Pasquale, what a kind of a sin you make?"*

"You dirty rat," I said. "I ain't gonna tell you nothin'. Nothin', you hear?"

"Pasquale, you come a in here and do a James Cagney in a front of Jesus Christ? I'm a gonna tell a you father."

"You dirty rat! You tell my father, Father, and I'll have to rub out my father, Father. See, Father?"

"You get outta my church. Now!"

The next stop for me was the local bar. At least I got a little respect there. I would sit at the end of the bar, and the guys would give me a soda and tell me to do a couple of impressions. So I would do Clark

Gable: "Frankly my dear, I don't give a damn." Or whatever popped into my head. They called me Dr. Cyclops because I had big eyes. Sometimes it was Cy for short. "Hey, Cy," they'd say, "why don't you do Cagney for us?" That was a tough room. Most of the men were drinking and talking, and there I was trying to work.

When my mother found out about my barroom performances, she wasn't interested in my impressions. "Sonny," she said, "if you're going to the bar, you're getting free ice for me." My mother was my first agent. She took a hundred percent off the top. The ice melted all over the place and she rooked me even worse than she rooked the real iceman. But at least I was getting paid.

On weekends I would go to theaters like The Strand, The Roxy, and The Brooklyn Paramount and see big bands like Tommy Dorsey and Harry James. I would leave the theater imitating the music. I could sing like Eddie Cantor. I could move my mouth to sound just like Benny Goodman's clarinet. I could do Tommy Dorsey's entire theme song, "I'm Getting Sentimental Over You." Down at the bar they would say, "Ay, Cy, do Tommy Dorsey." On the street corner the old guys would say, "Ay, Coop, give me Louie Armstrong!"

Then I made it to a stage, sort of. I was at a wedding and the best man asked me to get up and do some imitations. So I unloaded everything—Cagney, Gable, Lorre, Robinson, Cantor, Goodman, Dorsey, Armstrong. It was like a Best of 1942. It went five or six minutes. I put it all out there, and the people at the wedding loved it.

My mother and father thought maybe there was something wrong with me. My father said, *"You sound a like a retardo, making a noises with a you mouth!"* They didn't know from Tommy Dorsey. They wanted to know why I didn't go out and get a job, even though I was thirteen and still going to school.

Then came the watershed moment in the history of entertainment in the Caputo family. Gracie came to the dinner table and announced she was entering the *Fox Amateur Hour.* That got my attention. The

Fox Theater was on Flatbush Avenue, right in the center of my world. Next door was RKO's Albee Theater. Across the street was the Brooklyn Paramount and down the street was The Strand. I spent my life in those places. The *Fox Amateur Hour* was the biggest thing on the radio Monday nights. I actually wanted my sister to do well. So did my father. *"Okay, Gracie,"* he said. *"That's a good. You show them what a you can do."*

The following Monday night I was with my mother and father in the Fox Theater. They showed movies during the first part of the evening, and then the amateurs went on around nine o'clock. The MC was Joe O'Brien, a very classy guy who had the aura of a boxing ring announcer.

Suddenly I saw Gracie running up the aisle. We were looking for her, but here she was looking for me. "Sonny!" she said. "Mr. O'Brien wants to talk to you."

"Talk to me?" I said. "To *me?*"

"Shhh. Sonny, you gotta come backstage."

Backstage, Joe O'Brien took me by the shoulder. "Sonny," he said. "Listen, we got a problem here. One of the acts didn't show up. We need about five or six minutes to fill up the hour. Your sister here told me you do something funny with your mouth. You do Tommy Dorsey impressions and things like that."

"You want me to go out there?"

"Yeah. Can you do it?"

"Yeah. Okay."

"Okay," Joe O'Brien said. "When your sister finishes singing 'Ave Maria,' you go on."

I was surprised. I was nervous. But the funny thing was that I had the balls to do it. I *really* had the balls.

My sister walked out on stage in a white dress looking like the Virgin Mary. In her hands was a big bouquet of flowers my mother and father had given her. She sang "Ave Maria" better than I ever remember her singing it. There was applause, and then Joe O'Brien made an announcement.

"Thank you. And now we have an added attraction. Here is Gracie's little brother, Sonny Caputo, with a bit of comedy."

I went on like a torrent. Noises were coming out of my head like a jukebox on amphetamines. I did Harry James's "Flight of the Bumblebee," and I sounded like a swarm of horns. I did Tommy Dorsey. I did Skinnay Ennis. I did Charlie Barnett's "Cherokee" sounding like an invading tribe. I was a wild man up there. I thought the faster I did these little bits, one after the other, the faster I could get off the stage.

I was a nervous wreck. And now the people in the audience were yelling and waving their hands. *Jesus Christ. Maybe they're telling me to get the fuck off the stage.* But somewhere between Louie Armstrong and Jimmy Cagney, I realized something. They were applauding.

The director gave me a hand signal and that was it. I never got backstage, because Joe O'Brien came right out with the scorecards. On the *Fox Amateur Hour,* the audience was the judge. There were eight contestants. My sister was the seventh and I was the eighth. The first six got decent applause. When O'Brien walked over to Gracie, she got a hell of a hand, and she deserved it. I stood there like a schmuck. I was a deer in the headlights, but that was okay. My mother and father were going to be very proud of their little opera singer.

When O'Brien got to me, the entire audience stood up and applauded. Actually, the entire audience minus two. A standing ovation! "Oh, there is no question tonight, ladies and gentlemen," Joe O'Brien announced. "Sonny Caputo wins the prize!"

Holy shit! My old man's gonna kill me.

When I got backstage my father said nothing. He looked right through me. My mother was screaming. "I paid six dollars for the flowers!" she said. "Six dollars!" One of the producers gave Gracie a wristwatch for second prize. Then he gave me a check for twenty-five dollars. I knew my mother would be taking her usual cut.

My night was far from over. A middle-aged man came up to me backstage and said, "Hiya, I'm Joey Adams." I didn't know who he was, but I had the feeling I was supposed to. He explained that he was the MC for the *Loews Amateur Hour*. They were putting together a tour of four theaters in the Loews circuit—the Bronx, Brooklyn, Queens, and Manhattan. Joey Adams wanted me to do my act at each of the shows for ten dollars apiece.

"You just do what you did," he said. "I'm going to give you a little song to do so the act will go a little longer. Are you in, kid?"

"Yeah. I'm in."

So I had a good night. I got a nice hand, I won twenty-five bucks, and I booked four more shows. And I became "public enemy number one" in my family.

I did the four Loews shows and made forty dollars without laying a single brick. My old man couldn't have been less happy. *"You make a fool of a yousself,"* he said. *"You don a understand what a you do is a bullshit with a you mouth. You talk out of a turn at a the table, an a you talk out of a turn on a the stage. And a you make a fool. An a you sister is a saint, an angel. She's a gonna go to heaven. Where a the fuck a you gonna go? Where a the fuck a you gonna go with a that poopadee-poopadee-poopadee shit?"*

My father was ashamed to go to work. The other guys said, "Hey, Mike, I hear your kid won the amateur show."

"Don a remind me!" he would tell them. *"He's a making a noise with his a mouth. He's a retardo. He's a fucking nuts!"*

I never went looking to upstage my sister. It just happened that way. But my father wouldn't let me forget it. He should have been proud of me. Instead, he refused to even accept a simple compliment from his friends. But that was okay. I decided I wouldn't take any shit either.

2

Powderhead

I dropped out of Manual Training High School to do manual labor. I was a longshoreman for three days. They were three of the longest days of my life. Next stop was laying bricks. That lasted a lot longer than three days and I hated every minute of it. But I figured I might as well buy the right tools, so maybe it would go faster. I bought a level for a dollar. What I didn't realize was that when I left the level sitting on a brick wall, the acid in the cement would rust it out.

I wasn't that good with a level, and without it I was even worse. I could never get anything straight. My joints looked like waves at the beach. You could always tell the part of the wall that Sonny Caputo laid. It was like part of the wall got drunk. It was my signature.

When I was fourteen, I got a job on weekends as an apprentice furrier with Ender and Kaufman, two wonderful Jewish men. They had big plans for me. They taught me how to wash the fur. They showed me how to be a cutter. They showed me how to be a nailer. And then they showed me Valerie.

Valerie worked in the back. She was maybe fifteen years older than me. When she said, "Hiya, honey," I figured she liked me, but I had no idea she'd be showing me *her* fur. I barely had my pants down when she hugged me, and that was all she wrote. I really didn't understand how all this worked. I knew more about cutting and nailing, and I knew almost nothing about cutting and nailing. When I walked back into the front of the shop, Ender and Kaufman looked at me and said, "*Mazel tov!* You are now a man!"

"What man?" I said. "I didn't get bar mitzvah-ed. I came in my pants!"

When I got home that night, my father looked at me and said, "*Something a different. You know, you have a spark in a you face. Something a nice happen to you?*"

"Nah, Pa, it's nothing. I just worked for Mr. Ender and Mr. Kaufman. They were teaching me how to nail and I hit my finger."

Naturally I brushed it aside. You didn't mention sex, and if you did, you didn't mention it to your father. And if you mentioned it to any father, it wouldn't be *my* father. Getting laid was better than laying bricks, but that wasn't something you learned from your parents. We learned about sex on the street.

The streets were where I was comfortable—I was out of the house and not laying bricks. The streets were my stage. In 1946, I was sixteen and *The Jolson Story,* starring Larry Parks, had just come out. The movie reignited interest in the great entertainer Al Jolson, who was one of the greatest stars of stage, screen, and recordings for many years. In 1927, Jolson starred in *The Jazz Singer*—the first ever full-length talking motion picture. In it, his character had a story to tell that was a little like mine. He played a Jewish kid and the son of a cantor, who wanted his son to follow in his footsteps instead of performing popular music on the stage. In the end, he managed to do both.

My life wasn't a movie. But I performed scene after scene from the Jolson movie on the street corner. I got down on my knees and sang "Mammy," and the people who gathered around loved me. At night I slept fast. I could hardly wait to wake up the next day and get back on that corner and perform again. There were actually people waiting for me when I got there. And when I left, they said, "Sonny, you coming back tomorrow?" Of course I was.

But not if my mother could help it. When I did "Mammy," all my mammy cared about was the fact that I came home with blood spots on the knees of my pants. She wanted to kill me. "You are not in Hollywood! You are not Al Jolson! You don't get another pair of pants!" Maybe I was due for another dress. Everything she put me in was a problem.

My whole life she made me wear shoes that didn't fit. There was a store in Brooklyn called Flagg Brothers. When there was a sale at Flagg Brothers, my mother's world lit up. Walking in a pair of Flagg Brothers shoes was like putting your feet in a pair of steel cages. As if that wasn't bad enough, the shoes that were on sale were never my size. But that didn't bother her. If I was a size seven and the shoes on sale at Flagg Brothers were a size five, she would get three pair.

"Ma, these shoes are too tight."

"They're on sale! They were only a dollar a pair!"

"What am I supposed to do?"

"Fold your toes a little."

So I folded my toes and walked with a limp. I could barely walk. And now she wouldn't even let me kneel. So, like Al Jolson, I took after my father. I left.

A friend of mine had a cousin who had a farm in Exeter, Pennsylvania. Exeter was a little town outside of Scranton. I was given ten cents an hour to pick tomatoes and pull weeds. There I was, six-foot-two and about a hundred pounds, easily confused with the tomato vines. I was on my knees all day, but not like Jolson.

The owner reminded me of my father. He had a thick Italian accent and everything I did was wrong, even before I did it. *"You know,"* he'd say, *"you not a fast enough."*

"Hey," I said. "I'm a kid. What the hell do you want? I'm just learning."

"You gotta speed a up. Otherwise you only gonna get a nickel an hour."

I figured pretty soon I'd be paying *him* ten cents an hour. In the meantime, he figured he'd train me at another job—planting. He handed me a hoe and said, *"You make a de hole, and you take a dis, and you digga de dirt up."*

"Okay," I said. "I digga the fucking dirt."

I lifted the hoe and took a swing, and for a rookie I didn't do that bad. It was a home run. I hit the owner's foot, which was bare at the time. I never heard a scream like that in my life. The cows were mooing like it was the end of the world. And the owner, who reminded me of my father, gave a speech like my father, only louder and with a bleeding left foot.

"You gotta no direction. You gotta no life. You getta offa my fucking farm before I kill a you."

He meant it. So I headed back to Brooklyn. I didn't belong at home either, but the reality was, I had to eat. My mother barely noticed I was back. She was very money oriented and wrapped up in her button business. A button company would drop off six thousand buttons and a thousand cards. She had to take each card and put six buttons on it. That was worth a penny. When she had a thousand cards done, the company would come by and pick them up. My mother worked like a one-woman factory and did it all without my father knowing.

There was nothing for me at home except bricks and buttons and parents who thought I was crazy. So I decided I'd show them. I was going to join the Air Force. I thought, *I'll come back to Brooklyn one day in my uniform, and to hell with the family. I'll become a fucking pilot!*

This was sort of a back-door plan, but it was all I had. My mother's brother's wife's brother, Sal, was a heck of a nice guy. Sal had a job as a civilian working at the Air Force base in Tampa, Florida. He told me if I could get down to Tampa, he would take care of everything else. I would start off as a volunteer, but he would sneak me into the base overnight, so I wouldn't have to stay at a hotel and I could eat for free.

I took whatever money I had and got on a Greyhound bus. It was about twenty-six hours from New York to the Gulf Coast of Florida, and I got twenty minutes of sleep here, ten minutes there. I was a zombie by the time I got off the bus in Tampa and called Sal from a pay phone. He drove down to the bus depot, picked me up, and paid a friend to stick me in a bed at the base. Sal told me to get some sleep, because in the morning I would have to get through a physical.

In the morning, I lined up for an examination. I was thin as a rail. I thought maybe that was good. Maybe I would use less fuel when I flew a mission. As long as I didn't break in two when they pounded on my back during the checkup.

"Caputo!" the lieutenant said. "Caputo!"

"Yes sir. That's me."

"Caputo, you have got to get some meat on your bones if you want to serve your country. You have to start eating more. Do you understand?"

"Yes sir." I had no problem with that. The food was free.

I thought the coast was clear, but a few minutes later the lieutenant came back. "I'm sorry, son," he said. "You can't be in the service. You have hammerhead toes."

"Hammer what?"

"Hammerhead toes. Son, your toes are permanently bent. That's an automatic disqualification."

"How did this happen?" I asked.

"Your mother probably bought you the wrong shoes."

There I was, somewhere on the outskirts of Tampa with no money, nowhere to go, and ten hammerhead toes. I didn't want to ask Sal for money because he had already done more than enough. I called home from a pay phone. "Ma, I got hammerhead toes. You gave them to me. I'm stuck down here. I got no money for fare to get home." She put my father on the phone, and I knew that was the end of that.

"Listen a to me, Sonny. You gotta earn a you way back."

"How am I gonna do that? I can barely walk!"

"You gotta figure it out."

Fortunately, my Uncle Viduche didn't take after his brother with things like this. I called him, and he sent down nine and a half dollars, which was just enough for a bus ticket from Tampa back to New York. There was no money for food, but maybe this time I would sleep better.

I boarded a Greyhound early the next morning and got myself a decent seat not too far from the front. About two hours into the ride north, a black lady got on the bus. She looked tired, so I automatically stood up and offered her my seat. No sooner did she thank me and take the seat when the bus driver slammed on the brakes. I almost landed on an elderly couple.

"You nigger-loving motherfucker!" the driver yelled.

"Are you talking to me?" I said.

"You see any other nigger-loving motherfuckers on this bus? Get off my bus, you fucking Yankee!"

"Get off where?" I said. "I'm in the desert here. Where am I gonna get off?"

"Get the fuck off my bus."

So I got off the bus. I was on a dirt road in the middle of nowhere with no money and hammerhead toes. I walked in the direction of the bus, and it took a half hour before I saw a house. But the house wasn't any good to me. I needed another bus stop. That took another hour. I waited there until finally another Greyhound bus pulled in.

I showed the driver my ticket stub and explained that the last driver threw me off the bus.

"What for, son?"

There was no way I was going to tell him the truth.

"He said something bad about the USA, and I told him to take it back."

"Get on the bus, son."

I got on, took a seat, and wouldn't have given it up to the Pope. I spent another twenty-four hours on the bus without eating and got back to New York even skinnier than when I left.

Another twenty-four hours and I wanted to get out of my mother and father's house again. I figured this time I would try the Marines. The armory where you enlisted was on Whitehall Street, all the way downtown in Manhattan. I took the subway, walked into the armory, and spent the morning filling out forms. One of the questions on the form was: "Have you ever volunteered for another branch of the military?" I wrote down the truth about the Air Force and my hammerhead toes.

"Who's Caputo?" the drill sergeant said.

"I'm Caputo."

"Caputo, let me ask you something. Do you know anything about the Marines?"

"Yeah, this is them."

"The Marines, Caputo, are the elite branch of the United States military. It says here that the Air Force . . . the *Air Force* turned you down. Well then, if the *goddamned Air Force* turned you down, how in hell do you think the Marines are going to take you?"

Another couple of days under my mother and father's roof reignited my love for my country. The Navy was next. I couldn't swim. The only thing I knew about water was that it came out of the tap. The enlistment officer for the Navy asked me directly if I had volunteered for any other branch of the service. Before I answered, all I could think was that an American sailor was an honest man.

"Yes, sir. Air Force, Marines, hammerhead toes, sir." At least this time, I didn't have to fill out as many forms.

Next was the Army. I said to myself that no matter what, I wasn't going to mention the toes. I loved my country enough to lie for it. I would limp through drills if that's what it took. I'd crawl on my hands and knees and get hammerhead fingers. Anything to get the fuck out of that house.

It didn't matter. The sergeant looked at me and said, "You're a little anemic, son. Why don't you go home and fatten up a little? Maybe come back in six months." There were no branches of the service left, so I went back to Brooklyn to lay bricks. Slowly I built myself up to the point where I could see my shadow against the wall. My joints got a little less crooked, but by then I decided, to hell with joining the service.

And then I got drafted. The Army called me back down to Whitehall Street. "You Caputo? Go stand in line and see Dr. Gatz!"

"Listen," I said. "I don't need to see any doctor. This is all a waste of time. I'm in no shape to go in the service. You're gonna turn me down anyway. So why don't you just let me go home now?"

The entire Department of War knew I had hammerhead toes. Harry S. Truman knew it. General MacArthur knew it. That was my ace in the hole. The doctor looked at my arms. He looked at my legs. He looked into my eyes and saw no fear, because I knew I was going home.

"Caputo, 1-A!"

"Wait a second. There must be a mistake."

"The Army doesn't make mistakes, son."

"The Army did this fucking time. I got hammerhead toes!"

"Hammer what?"

"Hammerhead toes," I said. "My toes are like hammers. Hammerhead toes. Hammerhead toes!"

"We don't care about your toes, son. You're going to learn to march like a soldier, shoot like a soldier, and follow orders like a soldier. 1-A. You're drafted."

"You sons of bitches," I said. "You can't do this to me. I volunteered for the Air Force and the Air Force turned me down. The Marines turned me down. The Navy. Even you guys turned me down. Now I don't want to go, and you go and draft me. Nope. No. Uh-uh. This is not fair. I want to fight for my country on *my* terms."

Getting drafted is not negotiable. That's why they call it getting drafted. I knew I was getting shipped out soon, but I hoped somehow they would forget about me. My mother, however, couldn't wait. She explained that some forms were mailed to the house and she filled them out to make sure every month, the twenty-one dollars I made would be sent directly to her.

"So that's what I'm worth?" I said. "Twenty-one fucking dollars? For twenty-one dollars a month you're counting the minutes till I get out of here?"

"*Sonny, listen to a you mother,*" my father said. "*The army will make a you a man. It's a good for you.*"

"It's good for *you*. It ain't good for *me!*"

A month later, I was shipped to a big camp in Boston along with a few hundred men. They called out names one by one: "Jones, you're going to Jersey. Porter, you're going to Minnesota. Goldberg, Los Angeles." I could certainly live with Jersey. Minnesota was the land of ten thousand lakes. Los Angeles was where Cagney and Lorre and Jolson were.

I stood there all day until there were about ten of us left. Finally I heard my name. "Caputo, Fort Jackson, South Carolina."

One word came out of my mouth, "Why?"

"Because that's where the Army wants you, son. You leave tomorrow morning on the seven o'clock train. Do you understand?"

About twenty-four hours later, I was standing in the yard of Fort Jackson, South Carolina, alongside hundreds of men from the North. We were all in our civilian clothes and all dead tired. The sergeant walked back and forth and barked at us through a thick southern drawl.

"I got some news for you. You goddamned Yankees are now in the Army. There ain't no bullshitting around here. We own your sorry Yankee asses, and if you don't believe me today, you will sure as all hell believe me tomorrow. I'm not from New Yawk or New Jersey or some fucking fairy place like that. I'm from Mississippi where we eat faggots like you boys for lunch."

He started to call out names: "Harper, Gerlitz, Davis, Mayberry, McMann . . ." I didn't hear my name and I started to drift off. Suddenly the guy standing next to me says, "Hey, I think that's you." I listened up, but it didn't sound like me.

"Pascal Capa-tutio! Where's Pascal Capa-tutio?"

"You calling me?" I finally spoke. "My name is Pasquale Caputo."

"That's what I said, soldier. Pascal Capa-tutio! Are you deaf, son?"

"There's been a misunderstanding," I said. "I don't belong in the Army. I got hammerhead toes."

"You got what, son?"

"Hammerhead toes. I can't march. My toes are bent like that." I demonstrated with my fingers.

"Son, your *balls* are going to be bent like that when we get through with you. You hear me, Capa-tutio?"

In the morning, they issued me the worst boots ever made in the history of mankind. They were like blocks of steel with laces. These boots made Flagg Brothers shoes seem like bedroom slippers. A week in these things and my hammerheads were going to have hammerheads. So I decided I would never walk a mile in them. I went back to the barracks, crawled into my bed, and refused to leave. The sergeant kept sending his men into the barracks to tell me to get the hell out there now and march. And I told each one of them to go fuck off. Finally the sergeant walked in.

"So, you goddamned Yankee cocksucker, you think you can pull some shit? Not on my watch, son. Listen to me, Capa-tutio. You get your sorry Yankee ass out there this instant! You hear me, boy?"

"I ain't going out!" I said. "I don't care if you kill me. I'll serve anywhere but here. Get me a transfer to the Air Force! The Navy! The Marines!"

The next morning at dawn, five guys grabbed me and dragged me out of bed. They took me to the barber shop, held me down, and cut off every last hair on my head. They shaved me like a cue ball, and to add insult to injury, they put talcum powder all over my head. Then they gave me a nickname—Knobby. I knew who they meant. The comic strip character Joe Palooka was a boxer, and his manager was a bald-headed guy named Knobby Walsh. And from that moment on, everyone on the base said things like, "Hey, Knobby!" "How's tricks, Knobby?" "Go fuck yourself, Knobby!"

A couple weeks later, I was sitting in bed and the sergeant walked in. I was still bald and still called Knobby. They kept me shaved and powdered at all times.

"Tomorrow is a big day, Capa-tutio," the sergeant said. "We're having a parade for the general. I don't want you fucking this up, you hear me, Capa-tutio? You haven't marched with this company one time, you fucking Yankee piece of shit, and you sure as hell aren't going to start tomorrow. Do you understand me? You're an embarrassment. I want you to remain in this fucking barracks."

"You don't have to worry about me, Sergeant," I said. "I'll be right here. And to tell you the truth, I could use a little more powder."

The next day was a gorgeous Saturday. The sun was shining brightly, and it was a perfect day for a parade. I was in the barracks in my shorts and my shaved head, listening to the bugles and the drums from the other side of the base. I decided it was too nice to stay indoors, so I went outside and started walking toward the parade grounds. As I got closer, I started running. There on the review stand were the general and his officers watching the soldiers march. And then suddenly there was confusion. The band stopped. The soldiers broke their stride. And the military brass looked over and saw me in my boxers and my skinny legs and my white head full of powder coming toward them like a ghost.

"What's going on?" the general asked. "Who is this man?"

"That's Pascal Capa-tutio," the sergeant said. "He's confined to the barracks. He's not supposed to be here. He's trying his damndest to get a Section 8." The soldiers were doubled over laughing.

"Look at what they did to me, General," I said. "I am legally in my rights. I can't march because I got hammerhead toes. I cannot serve my country under these conditions. And look what they did to me. They took all my fucking hair. I got no fucking hair. They put powder on my head. And now they're calling me Knobby Walsh!"

"Son," the general said, "you can't be out here during this march. You'll have to take this up with your commanding officer."

"But he's the one who put the powder on my head!"

"This is the last time you'll ever pull this kind of shit with me or anyone else in this army, Capa-tutio," the sergeant yelled. "Get the MPs and arrest this kid. Put him in the brig with the niggers. They'll tear his Yankee balls off."

The cell was about eight feet by ten. In it were a dozen well-built black guys and a skinny Italian kid from Brooklyn with a shaved, powdered head. The guys were giving me strange looks, and I thought pretty soon the Army was going to send me home in a long, narrow body bag. One of the guys looked at me real hard and said, "I hope you don't mind me asking, but what the hell happened to you, man?"

"First of all," I said, "I'm from New York. That's two strikes right there. Second of all, I should never be here in the first place. When I tried to explain that, they shaved my head and called me Knobby Walsh. Third, I got hammerhead toes."

"Hammer what?"

"Hammerhead toes. Here, I'll show you." I took off my right shoe. "See. How the hell can I march with those? And they gave me shitty boots."

"Jeez, those are some funny-looking toes."

"You know something," I said. "Just between you and me, they're expecting you to kill me."

"Man, you already look dead."

The MPs pulled me out of the brig the next day and took me to the general's office with the sergeant there. "Now, Private," the general said, "I've just spent the last three hours trying to get to the bottom of this. Can you tell me exactly what the problem is?"

"General, I volunteered for every branch of the service and got turned down. Even the Army turned me down. I had hammerhead toes. I was too skinny. So I went about my business. Then you draft me and give me these boots, and you make my hammerhead toes even worse, so I can't even walk to the bathroom. Then, because I can't walk, the sergeant shaves me, puts powder on my head . . ."

"Son, slow down. Slow down."

"And then they call me Knobby. Knobby Walsh. Like from Joe Palooka. And this guy calls me Capa-tutio. Capa-tutio! My name is Caputo, do you understand me? Not Knobby Walsh! Not Capa-tutio! And I got hammerhead toes!"

A few weeks later, I got a general discharge from the United States Army. They packed my bags, gave me a one-way ticket, and put me on a train back to New York. I took the subway back to Brooklyn, walked to our apartment on Clinton Avenue, went up the stairs, and knocked on the door. When my mother opened the door and saw me, she reminded me of the general, because she looked like she had just seen a ghost.

"Hey, Ma. I'm home."

"You on leave?"

"Permanent leave," I said. "I'm out. I'm no longer in the Army, Ma. I got a general discharge."

"You mean I don't get my twenty-one dollars a month?"

"That's right, Ma. I don't get it and you don't get it."

"But I only got it four months!"

"Well, I hope you didn't spend it all in one place," I said. "And thanks for rolling out the red carpet."

My father was convinced I got a Section 8. *"You always a crazy. And now you crazy getta thrown outta the Army."*

"General discharge, Pa. I'll show you the papers right here. It's all legal." The only thing crazy was coming home.

3

Crawling with Aunts

Not that I got along with my father, but you could depend on him for certain things. Like you could depend on him, once in a while, moving out on my mother and then moving back in. Until one day, when he skipped the part about moving back in. He filed for divorce. Suddenly, in my early twenties, I was the man of the house, which was strange because my parents never let me be the boy of the house.

Being the man of the house was not any fun. I went out and worked, brought home the mortgage money, and gave it to my mother, who was money-driven and very down on me. She now had a small brownstone on 4th Street in Brooklyn. My sister Gracie and her husband were renting out the first floor.

Before I went into the army for a whopping one hundred and fifteen days, a good friend of mine named Joe Colombo introduced me to his wife's sister. Dolores was a sweet girl about four years younger than I was. During my cup of coffee in the army, I wrote Dolores letters. It was probably the one normal thing I did as a soldier. And the good thing was that Dolores wrote me back.

When I got back to Brooklyn, we started going out. Everything was nice and romantic between us. We got along. At the same time, when I arrived home every night and got the business from my mother, I began to think, *If I don't get out of here I'm going to kill myself.* So I did what millions of nearly suicidal men did every year—I decided to get married.

Dolores and I were happy about it. My mother was dead set against it, and she wore her frustration on her apron. It wasn't so much that she was losing me. She was losing a check every week. She called me selfish. Maybe I was selfish. The marriage did serve my purposes, and I just wanted to get on with my life.

The marriage was a quickie for that time. We rented out a hall and arranged for a short church service. My father came to the wedding and handed me an envelope with two hundred dollars. I was glad he came and thanked him for the gift. But then he said something that ruined it. He said, *"Make a sure you protect the money I gave a you. Itsa hard-working money."*

"Well," I said, "that's nice, because I know you gave Gracie a thousand dollars when she got married. Was that hard-working money, too? Or was that easy money you found somewhere? The last time I checked, I was your only son."

He didn't say a thing. He just walked away.

Right away, Dolores and I went looking for an apartment, and right away my new in-laws found one for us. My wife was the baby of the family. She had a couple of brothers and six sisters. The apartment they found was a studio on St. Marks Avenue in Brooklyn. It was fifteen dollars a week, which, at the time, was a lot of money. But we had to start our married life somewhere. This somewhere was a few doors down from her mother's house.

I wasn't exactly sure what my young bride wanted out of life. We never discussed it. We got married on a shoestring and went right to the business of living day to day. Financially, we were down in the dumps, but I had a good sense of humor that bailed me out of all sorts of ugly situations that might have gotten even uglier. I thought it would bail out Dolores and me, too.

I knew what I wanted out of life beyond survival, but I never discussed it with Dolores. There was no talk of show business at the time. It wasn't just out of the question, there *was* no question. I had to make a living. I laid bricks. I hated it, and I was terrible at it. Fortunately, in the winter there wasn't much work. Even if there was, I wouldn't work, because I froze my ass off. So I drove a cab.

I loved driving a cab because I was on my own and I made my passengers laugh. I was a stand-up comic who happened to be sitting down at the time. Sometimes I did a five-minute set down Flatbush Avenue. Sometimes I did a thirty-minute set across the Williamsburg Bridge into Manhattan. I could get up bright and early and work a twelve-hour day behind the wheel and it went by like a matinee.

I was in no rush to get home. Dolores was not a bad person. She just didn't understand that when you get married, your husband is your husband. Her brothers interfered a little and her sisters interfered a lot. These people wouldn't back off. They would show up at the apartment and turn a little thing into a big thing. Any time my wife and I had a real confrontation, it was because her sisters turned a simple disagreement into the Battle of the Bulge. I told them to mind their own business. I told them we were struggling as it was, and it was tough enough without a third wheel. Or a fourth, fifth, sixth, seventh, and eighth.

I started doing comedy for a few bucks here and there, but it was strictly on the QT. In those days, in that situation, people looked at you like you were a jackass. People would say, "What the hell's the matter with you? Why are you so bullheaded? You got a family. Don't be stupid." But this thing inside was driving me. I wasn't driving it. It's not a cop-out to say that it was like having a disease. And there was no cure. There was only medication. When I stepped out in front of an audience, it didn't matter if it was only six or eight people. I felt good. Something good was happening.

I couldn't blame my wife for not understanding. She didn't come from show business people. She came from people who understood that you get married, you make children, you buy a house if you're lucky, and you die. But I had more important things to do. My first truly professional job was at the State Theater in Baltimore. I was working with a guy by the name of Lou Handman. Lou Handman wrote songs like, "Are You Lonesome Tonight?" and "My Sweetie Went Away (She Didn't Say Where, When, or Why)." I, on the other hand, told everyone where I was going.

The agent I was working with was trying to get me some real work—something better than playing to a handful of people in a dive for twenty bucks. I had no real track record, so his pitch to the manager at the State Theater was, "Hey, he's a funny kid." That effort got me booked for four shows on a Friday and four shows on a Saturday. As for the format, first they would show a movie—a western like a Stephen McNally movie or something like that. Then they would do a live show for an hour or so, show another movie, do another live show, and so on.

The pay was decent, and the people seemed nice. There was one problem though. I had no fucking act. I had bits and pieces of things, but nothing continuous that flowed. Nothing you might call a routine. I just pulled things out of a hat. And I didn't wear a hat.

When I went backstage, the manager asked me what my name was.

"Caputo," I said. "Pat Caputo."

"Cooper?"

"No, Caputo."

"Okay, Cooper, here's what you're gonna do. You're going to MC. What you do is you do about three minutes to open up, then you bring on the Cordays. The Cordays do about fifteen minutes. Then you come back on and do ten minutes, and then bring on Lou Handman. Lou does about a half hour, and we're out."

"That's fine," I said. *Okay,* I thought. *I have James Cagney. I have Jolson.* I had basically my bag of tricks dating back to the street corners of Brooklyn. As I was doing a rundown of material in my head, Mr. Corday of the Cordays came up to me. He looked concerned and he had a thick Italian accent.

"*Listen a to me, son,*" he said. "*You gotta help a me and a my wife. See a the dog?*"

"Yeah," I said.

"*Well, when me and a my wife go on, you stay a backstage and a you wait. And a you look a for my signal. And when I give a my signal, you let a the dog out. And a the dog goes a between my wife's legs and a my legs when a we dance. And the audience, they a love it. That's a how we close a the show.*"

"Okay," I said. "What's the signal?"

"*The signal is,*" he said, "*I give a snap a the finger. You understand? Not a one second too early, and not a one second too late. The dog, she knows. She's a smart a dog. She's a Yorkie.*"

I got through my opening three minutes okay and then introduced the Cordays. They went on and danced this way and that, doing the mambo and the samba and the tango and whatever else it was they did. Meanwhile, I had my hands full backstage with the Yorkie. She was about four pounds, and three-and-a-half of that was hair. She was shaggy and somewhere beneath were two nervous little eyes. I supposed she was practicing running through mommy and daddy's legs by running through mine. I really thought she was going to piss on my legs. And with all the commotion, I missed the snap.

All of a sudden, Mr. Corday, in the middle of doing a dip with Mrs. Corday, was looking backstage at me and making motions with his head. I knew those motions very well. They were Italian for *Ay, whats a matter you?* So I let the dog out from behind the curtain.

But it was too late. The dog got trampled. There was a Corday leg over here, a Corday foot over there, and lots of cursing. It was like an Italian carwash with a dog going through. And the Yorkie was barking like she was being run over, which she was. Mr. Corday screamed at me in Italian, *"Ay, figlio di puttana!"* I knew that one, too. He was calling me a son of a bitch, which was kind of funny because he was the father of the bitch.

The audience was on the floor laughing. They were practically paralyzed. I was paralyzed, too. I didn't know what to do. When the curtain came down on the Cordays and their trampled Yorkie, I started running, and Mr. Corday started chasing me. I didn't know who made the first move, but I knew he was serious.

"You come a here! I'm a gonna kill you!"

The wife wanted to hit me, too. With one arm she was holding the dog, and with the other she was waving a fist around. Luckily I had someplace to run—back out on the stage. It was kill or be killed out there. I had ten minutes to live. As I grabbed the microphone, I thought I could do Cagney in Spanish. Then Cary Grant in English. Then Cary Grant in Spanish. Then anyone in the world in Spanish. I could do the fucking Cordays in Spanish if I had to. And the fucking dog.

But it didn't matter. The audience was screaming with laughter before I said a word. I was out of breath. If I caught my breath, I thought it might be over for me, so I just rambled.

I was about nine or ten minutes in. I felt the clocking running down and the number of well-known American actors who could be mimicked in Spanish running down, too. So I delivered the only line I had left: "Thank you, ladies and gentlemen. And now, here's Lou Handman!"

And a voice came down from the rafters.

"I ain't ready, yet!"

"Why not?" I said.

"I'm ironing my shirt!"

"Well, what the hell do you want me to do?" I said. "That's it! I'm finished!"

"Can you give me another five?"

"I ain't got another five!" I said.

The audience was screaming. I never heard roaring like this in my life, not even at the zoo. Even their screaming when the Cordays trampled the Yorkie didn't compare. Then some guy in the audience yelled out, "Do Cagney in English!"

"Oh, yeah," I said. "I only did Cagney in Spanish." So I went right into that. "You dirty rat. You killed my mother. You killed my father." I got two or three minutes out of that, then I yelled up again, "You ready yet?"

"Hang on! I'm almost there! I got one more sleeve!"

Roaring. I glanced to my left and saw the manager standing backstage. I could read his lips clearly: "Fucking kid. I'm gonna kill you. I'm gonna fucking kill you"

Lou Handman finally walked out on stage adjusting his tie. He was like the Messiah to me. Now I had two, maybe three people backstage looking to kill me. The audience didn't even stop to catch their breath. Lou sat down at the piano and went right into "Are You Lonesome Tonight?" Lonesome, no. Dead, maybe.

Backstage, the manager's face was red. He looked me in the eye and said, "Just answer me one question, son. One question. Is this your first job?"

"Well," I said, "the first job like this one. But I gotta break in somewhere."

"Why did you pick my theater, son? Out of all the theaters in the world, why did you pick mine?"

"It seemed like a nice place."

"Don't you have any more material?" he said.

"I have a Clark Gable I could do in Spanish."

"That's not what it's all about, son. You gotta have material. Real material. Twelve, thirteen, fifteen minutes, bare minimum. Otherwise you're not going to get laughs. You're going to be a joke."

The manager looked around, and I looked down for a moment and said nothing. Then he looked back at me and said, "All right, I'm going to give you some jokes to tell for the next show. Just to stall. These are good jokes. I have a file. And tell Lou to be ready. Tell him to iron his shirts beforehand."

So I was given a reprieve, but then I remembered this was double jeopardy. Mr. Corday was still lurking around backstage. *"Stay away from a me, son,"* he said. *"Because if I get a hold of a you, I will a go to the elec-a-tric a chair. I would a fucking kill you! You trying to kill a my fucking dog! This kid, he's a fucking retardo!"*

The manager let me stay through Saturday, which meant another four shows. I used some of the jokes the manager gave me, but not all of them, and the ones I did use I switched around. I was still all over the place, and I was still terrified about filling up the ten minutes. So I let the audience in on it. I talked to them like I was on trial and they were the jury.

"How am I doing here? Because I really don't know how much time I have left to fill. Anybody here got a watch?" This was not an act. I was nervous and needed to know. But they yelled: "Two-and-a-half left, kid!" "Two to go!" "Another minute twenty!"

When it was all over, the manager came over to me backstage and paid me a hundred dollars. Then he said, "You know, son, I gotta tell you, I have never laughed like this in my life. What could have become a tragedy was okay. You're a ballsy young man. But you gotta learn your craft, son. You can't go flying an airplane without a license. You were the talk of the town. Everybody and his kid sister came in here to see you fuck up. And when you fucked up, you were hilarious."

"I wasn't trying to fuck up," I said.

"You're a professional fuck-up, son. You're a natural."

As for the Yorkie, I heard the dog would never do a show after that. The dog would never so much as go near a curtain.

My son, Michael, was born around this time. I was proud to have a son. It was a wonderful thing, but not in the cliché Italian way. People came up to me and said, "Congratulations, it's a boy!" The thought behind it, at least from what I thought, was *Thank God it's not a girl*. A son was supposed to be something special. That was all bullshit to me. I was a first-born son, and I got *ugats*—balls! Nothing! Anything my first son got from me was not going to be because he was a first or a son. It would be because he was my child.

I went back to driving a cab where I came up with twelve hours of material a night. Sometimes more. I had an extra mouth to feed, and it was the most important mouth in the world. But things at home were getting worse. For my wife's sisters, it was as if our son being born was an excuse to yell more, scream more, and interfere more. They were aunts now, and our little apartment was crawling with aunts.

One Saturday afternoon the pot boiled over. There was an unwritten rule that whenever my wife's mother cooked beans, we ate beans. When she cooked macaroni, we ate macaroni. Today it was beans. From a few doors down, the mother ran the show, right down to our menu. I had enough of it. I told my wife what we had here was our own individual family and we would make decisions for ourselves. I told her the truth, which was that her mother was a lovely lady, but this particular thing had to go.

Within minutes the scene in the apartment was like a four-alarm fire. The mother called us and started yelling on the phone. Before I could get her off the phone, one of the sisters was in the apartment yelling. Then another. I looked out the window and there were two more on the pavement. It was like they landed on Omaha Beach. So I grabbed a broom and started swatting at the two sisters in the apartment. I chased them out the door and down into the street. I was in my underwear, but I didn't give a shit. And I started whacking them in the ass with the broom, one after the other. They were screaming, "He's crazy! He's crazy!"

"At least I'm not a ball-breaker like you people!" I said.

"Help! Police! Get the police!"

"Go ahead! Get the police!" I said. "They should arrest you for ruining my fucking life! What is wrong with you people? Can't you just mind your business? I wanna do what I wanna do, and that's what the fuck I'm going to do!"

The cops did show up, and what they saw was a grown man in his underwear whacking a bunch of know-it-all, pain-in-the-ass, ball-breaking women with a broom. The cops were laughing. They knew me from the street, and they knew what I was capable of, though in this case, I did their expectations one better. They calmed me down. I went back inside, put my pants on, and ate my beans.

About a year later, we moved from the apartment into the first floor of my mother's brownstone. I figured living near my mother would be better than living near Dolores's mother and the killer bees. But it turned out we had a new problem even before we moved in. The first-floor apartment was available because my sister Gracie and her husband decided all of a sudden to move to New Jersey. In fact, they left in the middle of the month and paid only half of the forty-dollar-a-month rent. Since Dolores and I agreed to pay a whole month's security, I figured if we moved right in, we would start paying rent after the first two weeks were up. But I was wrong.

My mother demanded the security and the twenty dollars for the two remaining weeks. The shit hit the fan. Every money-driven thing she did, from putting me in Gracie's old dresses to the Flagg Brothers shoes that gave me hammerhead toes to her complaining about losing my army paycheck came into play. There was screaming and yelling and fighting and hard, sad feelings. It was just like old times.

But we moved in anyway, and staying there was worse than moving there. By the time I had the couch moved in, I knew I made a big mistake. My wife broke my balls and my mother broke my balls. My wife's sisters broke my balls, too. Distance was no obstacle for these girls. Not only could they scream and yell and interfere, they could walk and run and take a subway.

Then things got even worse. My wife accused me of going out with another woman. It didn't take an Einstein to figure out who put that idea in her head. It was absolutely not true, but that didn't matter. It was unimaginable to any of these people, my own mother included, that I was going out and polishing my craft as a comic. I had my own track, and I wanted to pull into my own station. That drove them crazy, so they accused me of whatever they wanted to accuse me of without any evidence whatsoever. I plunged myself into my cab and my stand-up. Somehow, I was home just long enough for my wife to be expecting another baby.

One evening, I pulled the cab up to my mother's brownstone. My mother happened to be standing out in front. As I got out and closed the car door, a window opened and clothes started flying out. They were my clothes—my pants, my shirts, my shorts, my socks, and my suits—being thrown out by my wife.

"So you're throwing me out of my own house?" I yelled. "Okay, now I got you by the balls. You want to get legal? Okay, we'll get legal. I'll tell the fucking judge you threw me out. Which is what the fuck you're doing. What did I do? Nothing! And what are you gonna get? Nothing!"

I started to pick up my clothes from the sidewalk. I was going to need them, especially my suits. I was performing that week, and I had to get practical in a hurry. Very practical. My baby girl, Lou-Ann, was born two weeks earlier.

The first practical decision I made was not moving in upstairs with my mother. Even she knew that if I lived there, this would become a big fucking war. Between me and Dolores, her sisters, and my mother, there would be no end in sight until what got thrown out the window was a body. The fact that I had no other place to stay was beside the point. So I moved into a one-bedroom apartment in Greenpoint, Brooklyn, for eight dollars a week. And from that day on, my life started to change.

4

And Away We Go

There I was, separated, in my early thirties, living in an eight-dollar-a-week hotel. The rooms were furnished. There were five guys living on the same floor, each with a different bedroom, all sharing the same bathroom. The place looked and smelled like an eight-dollar-a week hotel, but the people who ran it, the Hallorans, were the nicest people in the world. Anyway, what was I going to do? I had to support my kids, and that was another forty dollars a week.

I did whatever I could to make a few bucks. I laid bricks. I drove a cab. I worked at a hot dog stand in Greenpoint that also served breakfast. The owners were George Sklar and Jack Sugar. God love both of them. They were two of the nicest men I ever met. They thought I was hilarious, and I ate for nothing there, which was a big help.

They gave me the keys in the winter, because when it snowed, they needed somebody to get up at four in the morning and shovel the sidewalk for the people coming out of the subway. Sometimes I'd light the stoves before George and Jack came in. I was getting a dollar an hour. Whatever they gave me was fine. I was just looking to make the eight dollars to pay the rent.

There was no one around now to stop me from making a few extra bucks doing stand-up. There were hole-in-the-wall places all over the city. I met Patti Del Prince at a little club in the Bronx called the Silver Edge. I was her opening act. Patti was petite, pretty, and sang her ass off. It so happened that I used to close with a song called "Has Anybody Seen My Gal?" that went, "Five foot two, eyes of blue . . ." It might as well have been about Patti. I worked with her a couple of times. She was a nice girl. But I was a skinny kid with no sex appeal. Absolutely none. And my hands were covered with blisters from laying bricks with a goddamned trowel. At least I no longer peed on my hands. Not many people believed me, but when I was still living in my parents' house, my father told me what to do in case of a blister. He said, *"Well, whadda you gotta do, you gotta blister on a you hand, you gotta pee on it."*

"What?" I said. "You pee on it? Are you kidding me?"

"No, I'm a serious. Because a the ass-acidity, its a gonna make a the thing go down."

This was real old time shit—the peeing and the sulfur water. These were the same people that would get out the brown Octagon soap when you had a boil on your ass. They would put the soap on your ass, and the infection would come out of the boil. And you walked around with half a bar of soap bandaged to your ass so that you couldn't sit down. This was that generation. This was my parents.

There was no question that I had feelings for Patti, but she was going out with a very nice man from Queens. And, of course, I was having all sorts of trouble with Dolores. I didn't want to start more problems, so I turned around and let it go.

I had visitation rights to see my son and my daughter once a week, and every time I went to see them, it got ugly. I wanted to take them out and spend time with them *without* Dolores, but she wouldn't allow it. One Sunday, my lawyer even came to the house with me, because he didn't believe that I was telling him the truth. But that Sunday was no different from the one before, and my lawyer told Dolores that she wasn't supposed to be there. "It doesn't matter," she said. "These are my kids, and I'm not letting my kids alone with *him.*"

It seemed like every month Dolores dragged me into family court and tried to embarrass me. I tried to be understanding and not get angry. She was a mother. She needed money. By this point, I was moonlighting quite a lot doing comedy. I tried to take her aside and give her some extra money, but she wouldn't have it that way. She forced me to go through the court just for the sake of humiliating me. And by doing that, she actually got less. The most hypocritical part of it all was that she was the one who threw me out. She was the one who threw my clothes out the window.

One day, I dropped by my agent's office and ran into Patti. I was glad to see her and we wound up going out for coffee. As the weeks went by, I saw more of her. We didn't start anything, but it was really nice to have someone to talk to.

Around that time, my agent booked me to do three weeks at a jazz club opening for Matt Dennis, who wrote "Angel Eyes" and a whole bunch of other great songs, and was a wonderful man on top of that. I got a hundred dollars a week, minus ten percent for my agent.

My first show was at eight o'clock, and I got there at seven. In my suit bag was a tuxedo. In another bag were my trowel, my jointer, and all my other bricklaying tools. For my act, I did Cagney in Spanish and all the old jokes: "The horse was so slow they arrested the jockey for kidnapping." The people giggled a little bit while they waited for Matt Dennis. We did three shows a night, and I did basically the same set in the second and third show. This went on for a few nights, until the manager came up to me.

"Pat," he said, "listen to me. You've gotta have two separate shows. The first show and the third show can be the same, but during the second show, people stay over from the first show."

"Well," I said, "I don't think I got a second show."

"Look," he said, "get up there and try something different."

I didn't want to try and sing. Not on the same stage with Matt Dennis. So I pulled something out of a hat. It was a bunch of observations about every Italian wedding I had ever been to. And the audience loved it. They were literally screaming. A guy named Willie Weber happened to be in the audience that night. He came over to me after the third show and said, "Who's your manager?"

"I ain't got no manager," I said.

"You mind if I ask what's in the bag?" he said.

"It's my jointer for brick work."

"You're telling me," he said, "that you come here with your fucking tools?"

"Well," I said, "I got kids to support. I finish at five o'clock, come over here, and take a shower."

"Wait a second," Willie said, looking at me like I was nuts. "You mean you come from work? Every day?"

"Yeah," I said. "Every day."

"But why do you have to bring your tools with you?"

"You see," I said, "I don't last long on these jobs. I don't want to have to go back there and get my fucking tools."

Willie laughed. "You gotta put that in your routine."

We talked some more the following evening, and Willie made me an offer flat out. "Look," he said, "I'm your manager. Would you trust me?"

"Sure," I said. "Why not?"

"Okay," he said. "From now on, anybody calls you, you call me. Son, I'm gonna be like your father, but not like the father you got. I'm going to put you on the *Jackie Gleason Show*."

"Really?" I said. "You gotta be fucking kidding me."

"No, no," he said. "I'm not kidding you. But first," he said, "I'm sending you to St. Louis."

"Why St. Louis?" I said.

"Because you're gonna bomb!" he said. "Your material won't go in St. Louis. I'm going to teach you what it means to bomb. And I'm very interested to see how you react."

In St. Louis, they had me working with a dance team. I thought I would be opening for them, but they were opening for me. They did about fifteen minutes, and then I went on with the routine now known simply as "The Italian Wedding." It took less than a minute for me to find out that the audience didn't know what the fuck I was talking about. Either they had never been to an Italian wedding or the ones they had been to were completely different.

It didn't matter. I bombed. I did one more show like that and the manager and his staff had a meeting. They decided to have me open for the dance team because they couldn't close the show with a disaster like that. It didn't matter much. I bombed anyway. It was a long slow death that started all over again every night.

I was ready to take the next train back to New York, lay some bricks, and piss on my hands. I called up Willie Weber and told him there was no doubt about it, my career was over.

"What?" he said. "Your career ain't over. It's just beginning. This was a valuable experience. You just don't know it yet. Now you'll learn to just be who the fuck you are. Don't you see, son, I'm trying to put a callus on your career. You're gonna need it. And next, we're gonna teach you another important lesson. Fuck stardom. You hear me, son? Fuck stardom. *Get the money.*"

"Where the fuck are you gonna send me for that lesson, Willie? Detroit?"

"No," he said. "I need you back in New York when this engagement is over. I didn't get a chance to tell you. I got you an audition for the *Jackie Gleason Show.*"

"The *Jackie Gleason Show,*" I said. "What am I going to do on the *Jackie Gleason Show* in front of the whole country?"

"The Italian Wedding."

Back in New York, I went with Willie Weber on a Saturday afternoon to CBS Studio 50 on West 53rd Street in Manhattan. They
brought us into a small room with the producer, who took a seat. I
stood up and tried to pretend the room was packed and did about five
minutes of "The Italian Wedding." Forget about laughter. I didn't get
so much as a smile from the producer. It was St. Louis without the
audience. The producer said "Thank you," and I walked out of there.

Three hours later, I was back in my room in Brooklyn thinking
that I'd be laying bricks and selling hot dogs for the rest of my life
when someone down the hall said I had a phone call. It was Willie
Weber.

"Okay, Pat," he said. "We're taping Tuesday."

"What?" I said. "That can't be. I didn't get one fucking laugh."

"Are you kidding me?" Willie said. "He fucking loved you. You
have to understand. He never laughs. The situation doesn't call for it.
He would have to force it."

When Tuesday came around, I was working at the hot dog stand
in Greenpoint. Patti came and met me there, and until a few minutes
before it was time to go to the studio, we weren't sure how we were
going to get there. But the guy who delivered baked goods to the
stand had a truck and offered to give us a ride to Studio 50. I had my
tuxedo in a bag and said, "What do I do with this?" He said, "Put it
in the back."

On the way over the 59th Street Bridge, I looked out the window
and had that marvelous view of the Manhattan skyline. Right then I
realized how nervous I really was. I was practically shitting in my
pants. I didn't know if Jackie Gleason was going to like me. But when
we pulled up in front of Studio 50, at least I knew I was the only comedian ever to arrive for the *Jackie Gleason Show* in a big white bakery
truck with a tuxedo in a bag in the back.

I was still nervous as hell inside while I was waiting to go on. Putting on the tuxedo didn't help much. There were a lot of people out

there. But the bandleader, Sammy Spear, was great. He walked up to me and said, "You're gonna be fine, son. You'll be fine." Then Jackie Gleason walked out of his dressing room wearing a big smile. He said, "Pat, if you weren't the greatest, you wouldn't be on my show." I just stood there in awe. Then the producer came over and gave me a hug. And with one vote of confidence after another, I went out and I did "The Italian Wedding."

"You recognize me? Clark Kent?" I pointed out my thick black glasses and neatly combed hair. "The original Superman? It's not easy looking like Clark Kent. I got a seven-year-old boy. I take him for a walk, I pass a phone booth, I gotta get undressed. That's not so bad. My wife tells the kid, 'Tell Superman to take out the garbage!' Soon as he opens the window, I gotta jump right out. Thank goodness I live in the basement.

"You know what I went through to get this seven-year-old genius? On my twenty-first birthday, my mother—and I have a genuine Italian mother—four feet eleven. If they're five feet, they're Turks. She has a bun over here, knitting needle over here, gold tooth over here, beauty mark over here. She says, '*Your daddy wants a to talk a to you.*'"

"Papa says, '*I thinka it's a time a you gotta married. And I gotta the girl picked a for you.*' He called up SICILY-6-3720 . . . and they shipped in a genuine Italian goil—four feet eleven, with a bun over here, knitting needle over here, gold tooth over here, beauty mark over here. Black dress, black stockings, black shoes. I says, 'Papa, why they wear black?' He says, '*In a case anybody dies, they ready.*'

"And we had a beautiful church wedding. Fourteen ushers. Fourteen bridesmaids. And my best man was a Puerto Rican. I didn't even know the guy. We're walking down the aisle and this guy's singing, 'A cinco-cuando-a-cinco a-la-baca-de-cuando . . .' I ran to my father, I said, 'Papa, you're embarrassing me. You're a genuine Italian. I'm an Italian-American. I don't have purple feet.' He says, '*A shut up and a keep a you mouth shut. I'm a you father. And a remember, a tonight is the reception.'*

"What a reception. What a reception we had. An Italian football wedding. What's an Italian football wedding? Simple. Two Italians get together to get married. They rent out the hall, then they rent out the sandwiches. And everybody jams in, and one guy yells out, 'Hey Nadal. Throw out the capicola!' And a sandwich goes flying across the room. Another guy yells out, 'Angelo, the provolone.' And another sandwich flies across the room. And all night long, the sandwiches are going *fata-ton a fata-ting, fata-ton a fata-ting.*

"We had a band. Uncle Dado's band. Three pieces. Two mandolins, one guitar. That's not so bad. All they knew was one song. For six hours, this is what they played: *Lada-be-da-bada-ting-ta bada-teeta-tata-bada-ting da-dee-da-tata-bada. . . .* And the sandwiches are going *fata-ton a fata-ting . . .*"

And the people were laughing. That was music to my ears. The show aired on Saturday night, and before I knew it, I was hearing from my ex-brothers-in-law. They told me that at first they didn't think it was me. "It looked like you," they said. "But it can't be you because this guy on the TV is not a retardo, and you, of course, are a fucking retardo."

And then my father got a hold of me and said, *"Why you open a you fucking mouth telling a everybody about our a personal life?"*

"What are you talking about, our personal life?" I said. "I'm talking about a wedding."

"No," my father says, *"You making a fool of us! A fucking a fool!"*

The next thing I knew, I was hearing from the Italian Anti-Defamation League. They wanted to sue me. But the wonderful thing was, I was getting hired. Joe Scandura was managing me part-time along with Willie Weber. They got me a great job working at a place in Brooklyn on Ocean Parkway. Then they got me an engagement opening up for Neil Sedaka, who had hit songs like "Breaking Up Is

Hard to Do." Unfortunately, opening up was hard to do, too. Neil was not happy with me, because I was the new kid on the block and was taking his audience away from him.

But Dolores was a lot more upset than Neil Sedaka. By this time, I was giving her a hundred-something a week under a court order. And I still thought she was getting screwed. I was starting to see somewhere in the area of six hundred to seven-fifty a week. Dolores, however, convinced herself I was making millions. She kept hauling me to court and quoting insane numbers to the judge. "Your Honor, he's making nine thousand a week, forty thousand a week . . ." Whatever crazy figures popped into her head.

The judge didn't buy it for a second. He said, "We have all the information we need regarding Mr. Cooper's income through his lawyer. So please, don't you tell the court what you think he's making. We won't have any of that nonsense here."

For that reason alone, Dolores was convinced I had the judge paid off. The truth was, the judge was an honest, intelligent man. Meanwhile, her sisters—my ex-sisters-in-law—were always raising their voices and generally making a scene in the courtroom. It was the last thing in the world I wanted to listen to, but in terms of the judge, it couldn't have hurt my case.

In the middle of all this, I still wanted to give Dolores a couple hundred extra dollars a week above and beyond what the court had ordered. The judge and my lawyer said that it was allowed, but only if she gave me a receipt. That seemed simple enough. I made the offer to her in person, but she turned it down. She would take the money, but she refused to give me a receipt. "What the hell is that all about?" I asked her. "You say the kids need the money, and then you have the nerve to turn it down like that?"

I was going to slip her the money anyway, but my lawyer told me not to. "Back away, Pat," he said. "Back away. Just do what the law says. No more, no less. Unfortunately, that's how you have to handle this." Meanwhile, my mother and my father were on my ass constantly. They told me I ought to be ashamed of myself.

Patti and I were seeing each other more often, and soon we were going out. She had a knack for pacifying me, especially with my family situation. She also brought up the possibility of getting married. My only concern was that although things had been going pretty well since I did the *Jackie Gleason Show,* I didn't know how much longer this success would last.

Eventually I went to Ashtabula, Ohio, to meet Patti's family. They were wonderful, and very religious. When she brought up the subject of marriage with her parents, they were against it. Her mother said, "You can't marry this man. This is a divorced man with kids to support. You'll be starting off your life at a big disadvantage, and you don't know what his future holds." I sat there and told Patti, "You know something, your mother's right." And there was one other thing. I wasn't even divorced. So I decided that I would at least take care of that.

I booked a flight on a divorce junket to Juarez, Mexico. With a few hundred dollars in my pocket, I boarded the American Airlines flight out of Kennedy Airport. The plane was loaded with men and women who, for one reason or another, were having some difficulty getting a legal divorce in the United States, and I was one of them. We had a stopover in Chicago, where more wannabe divorcees got on the plane. We took off for the border and I was a bundle of nerves.

I calmed down a little when our guide stood up in the middle of the flight. "Hello, my name is Juan," he said. He looked like Anthony Quinn in *Viva Zapata!* and sounded like him, too. "I am so sorry to meet ju under deese conditions. We are going to Juarez, because you are going to get dee-boors."

We landed in El Paso and were taken to a motel. At five the next morning, three buses came by the motel to pick us up and take us across the border to Juarez. Three busloads of people thousands of miles from home looking to shake their other half like a newspaper stuck to their shoe.

We crossed the border, drove for a while, and got to a little farm on the outskirts of town. They had us waiting in a fucking barn. They explained we would each be called one by one to go see the judge. "Okay, now," Juan said. "When you go into the courtroom, you gonna go by alphabetic, A . . . B . . . C . . . Ju understand? And de judge going to call you, and ju going to get dee-boors."

They did the A's, then the B's, and soon it was my turn. "Paqua Caputo!" Juan yelled.

I said, "Here!"

"Paqua Caputo," he said. "Ju gonna get de-boors."

It was still early in the morning. I walked across the yard to a little shed and heard a rooster crowing, "Errrrrr-errrrrrrr!" I couldn't believe it, but it was true. I was on a farm in Mexico getting a divorce at dawn.

"Paqua Caputo!" Now it was the judge calling my name. He looked like he was stampeded by a herd of cattle, and the bailiff looked worse.

"Yes, your honor!"

"Paqua Caputo, ju come from the United a States?"

"Yes, your honor."

"Ju wanna get de-boors?"

"Yes, your honor."

"We gonna get ju the paperwork. Ju take the paperwork back a the United a States. Ju have any problem, ju tell you ex-wife she wan to contest this dee-boors, she got to come to Juarez. Ju unnerstand?"

"Yes, your honor. I understand."

He handed me a book the size of the Manhattan Yellow Pages. I could have gotten a hernia carrying that thing. I flipped through it for a second, and it was all in Spanish.

"Okay, now," the judge said. "Ju unnerstand?"

"Yes, your honor."

"Good. Now ju a de-boors!" He smacked his gavel on the desk. And I heard the rooster crowing, "Errrrrr-errrrrrrr!"

Later in the day I got back on the bus, and the next day I got on the plane with my suitcase and the Spanish version of *War and Peace*. There was a strange kind of camaraderie on the plane ride back to Chicago. On the way down, we were all married. On the way back, we were all divorced. Except for two couples. Two of the guys had married two of the girls while they were all down in Juarez getting the divorce. It was one-stop shopping for these people, and now on the plane ride back, they were bombed out of their minds. Having ended one mistake, they couldn't wait to start another one.

Back in New York, I called my lawyer and asked him what to do next. He said, "Nothing. Go about your life." New York wouldn't accept the divorce, but some other states would. In the meantime, the divorce was uncontested.

About a month later, I got a call from my ex-wife. "I heard about what you did," she said. "You and I can't get a divorce! It's illegal. My lawyer says it's illegal!"

"If it's illegal," I said, "then you go to Mexico and un-illegal it. Be my guest. I will gladly pay all the expenses. But you won't even go on a trolley car, let alone a fucking airplane."

A few weeks later, Patti and I got married in Connecticut. Not long after, I got a call from my ex-wife's lawyer, Mr. Fusco. "Mr. Cooper," he said, "we have a problem."

"I have no problem," I said.

"I understand you got married," he said.

"Yeah. But it's none of your business. What are you gonna do?"

"Well," he said, "first of all, there is the matter of your children."

"Listen," I said, "you have no right talking to me. Talk to my attorney. Then the two of you make a convenzione or whatever the fuck you want to do. That's what we have lawyers for."

"Mr. Cooper . . ."

"Talk to my attorney. You understand?" With that I hung up the phone. My lawyer told me I did the right thing. He would handle it, and I should continue to go about my business.

A few weeks later, I got another big career break—two weeks at the Copacabana on East 60th Street in New York opening for the Four Seasons. The group was led by Frankie Valli, but still called simply the Four Seasons. They were four kids with about the best vocal harmonies anyone had ever heard, and they were hot as hell in 1964 with hits like "Sherry," "Walk Like a Man," and "Big Girls Don't Cry." Tell me about it. My first night, as I was getting ready to go on with what seemed like every friend of mine waiting out in the audience. I stood backstage, took a peek out front, and said to myself, "Jesus. I just can't believe it."

At that moment, a guy in a suit who I had never seen before tapped me on the shoulder and said, "Excuse me, are you Pat Cooper?"

"Yes. Pat Cooper," I said.

"This is for you."

By the time I opened the envelope and saw that it was a summons, the guy was gone. It was in regard to my divorce, but I hardly understood a word of it in the few moments I had. I got about two-thirds of the way down the first page when I heard my name called again. "Ladies and gentlemen, the Copacabana proudly presents Mr. Pat Cooper . . ."

I walked out to the front of the stage still reading the summons without ever really breaking my train of thought.

"Ladies and gentlemen," I said, "you'll have to forgive me. I just got a summons. Just a few minutes ago. And I'm having a little trouble understanding this thing. 'The party of the first part requires the party of the second part to appear on said date in order for the party of the second part to respond to a plea made before this court by the party of the first part in regard to motions filed by the party of the second part . . .' Ladies and gentlemen, do we have any lawyers out there? Any divorce lawyers? Because I cannot for the life of me figure out whether I'm the party of the first part or the party of the second part. Maybe I'm the party of the third part. I really don't fucking know!"

The audience was howling. They loved it. For all I knew, they had just gotten back from Juarez. I went on with the rest of my act, and everything blended well. The second show also went well, but I didn't do the bit about the summons. When I got off the stage, I went to the kitchen to get a bite and in stormed Jules Podell, the owner of the Copa.

"Where's my comedy star?" he shouted. "There he is, my comedy star! Mr. Pat Cooper! Everybody, three cheers for Pat Cooper!"

"Thanks a lot, Mr. Podell," I said.

"Let me ask you something, Pat," he said. "What happened to that routine about the party of the first part and the second part and the third part? They loved that, then you didn't do it the second time."

"Well, Mr. Podell," I said, "I didn't plan that. I got served a summons right before the first show."

"What? You got a summons? In *my* club?"

"From my ex-wife's lawyer."

"What?! No one gets a summons in my club. No one! Carmine! Carmine!" He snapped his fingers and his head manager came running into the kitchen.

"Yes, Mr. Podell."

"You see this man? This is Mr. Pat Cooper, my comedy star. How on earth does my comedy star get a summons? How the fuck did they get past security? Can you tell me please?"

"Mr. Podell, don't worry about . . ." I tried to interject a few words, but the guy was on a roll.

"Shut up! Shut up! Nobody gets a summons in my place! And by the way, Mr. Pat Cooper, my comedy star, you're coming back in September with Tony Bennett. And make sure you do the thing about the party of the first part and the party of the second part. Always do that thing!"

Jules was nice to me. He would turn around and throw me some extra work here and there. One afternoon, he told me to walk over a couple of blocks to the Plaza Hotel. A friend of his was hosting a wedding, and it would be nice if I would do ten or fifteen minutes. I said, "Sure." When I got there I realized the friend was Joe Colombo, a boss in the Profaci family. I said, "How are you, Mr. Colombo?"

"Pat, Jesus," he said. "Thanks. Jimmy Roselli don't want to come."

"Well," I said, "I don't speak for Jimmy. It's not my business." Jimmy Roselli, a great Italian singer, had a thing against most wiseguys, but I wasn't going to be the one to explain that to Joe Colombo. I did my ten minutes and got off. It went over well, and I walked back to the Copa. When I got there, Jules told me to go into the kitchen because he just had one of the cooks make me some coffee. When I walked into the kitchen and looked at the table, there was five hundred dollars under a coffee cup.

Patti and I had moved into a nice apartment on 63rd Street and Third Avenue in Manhattan. We had a gracious Jewish doorman in his fifties who absolutely loved me. "Uy, vat a vunderful Yitalena! Vat a vunderful Yitalena!" It took me a couple of months to figure out that "Yitalena" was Yiddish for "Italian." His hat never fit him. His jacket never fit him. But he took a lot of pride in his job. He jumped to open the door on my way in, and he jumped to open it on my way out. I tipped him a dollar every time, whether I felt like it or not. On a typical day, it cost me twenty dollars to walk in and out of my apartment.

One morning, it cost me a lot more than a twenty to walk out the door. As I stepped out onto the sidewalk, I saw my ex-sister-in-law coming at me from the side. Before I could say a thing, she punched me in the face. My Clark Kent glasses went flying off.

"What do you think you're doing to my sister?"

She was screaming. And I was screaming, too.

"Who the fuck are you to hit me? How is this any of your business? I'm divorced. Stay the fuck out of it."

Seeing me hit like that, the doorman went into hysterics. He blew the little whistle he carried with him and shouted. "Call de cops! Ve van de cops! To hit this man is a terrible thing. A shanda. Vut gives her the right to hit this vunderful Yitalena?"

My nose was swollen, my eyes were tearing, and I realized I was in shock. Patti came downstairs and ran over to me. And then the cops came. The doorman was all over them.

"This terrible woman hit this vunderful man! Lock her up! Put her avay! Hang her! Give her the 'lectric chair! She's a terrible person to hit this vunderful man."

The cops quickly decided to arrest my ex-sister-in-law. They cuffed her and put her in the squad car. Her body language changed real fast. She looked scared and her face was white as a sheet. I was still in shock.

"Good," I said. "Good! Look at you now. You deserve to be locked up."

But Patti had other ideas. She was a fucking saint. She told me we couldn't do this. It was just plain wrong to arrest someone who was part of your family, even if what she did lacked any respect. So instead, I agreed to call my ex-sister-in-law's husband with his wife still sitting in the back of the squad car.

"Your wife just punched me in the face," I said to him.

"Pat," he said, "you gotta be kidding me."

"No, I'm not kidding you." I was getting pissed off again, "She waited for me outside my building and punched me in the face. It was no fucking accident. And I'm gonna lock her ass up! You hear me? I'm gonna lock her ass up!"

But once again, Patti talked me down. She was great at that, and this time it took all her abilities. I told the cops to let her out of the car. We wouldn't be pressing charges. We would work it out. I knew in life you had to go through a lot of shit, and I wasn't stupid enough to think that now, because I was enjoying a little bit of success, that any of that would change.

I tipped the doorman five dollars for calling the cops. And somewhere I heard a rooster crowing, "Errrrrr-errrrrrrr!"

5

The Chosen Comics

When I was coming up in the comedy ranks in the '60s, ninety percent of the people in the business thought I was Jewish. It didn't matter that I was doing routines on Italian weddings, Italian mothers, Italian fathers, and Italian food. What they heard was a sharp Jewish comedian who figured out that the next big thing was going to be Italian-American humor. And although that "Jewish" comedian was actually one-hundred percent Italian, people believed what they wanted to believe.

First, there was my name. They figured Pat Cooper was a stage name, and my original name was Paul Cooperstein. Or Kappler. Or Keppler. Or Saul Rosenberg. When they finally learned that I changed my name from Pasquale Caputo, they still didn't believe it. They thought, sure, Italians are great singers. They're great plumbers, butchers, and carpenters. But there are no Italians with a comedic flow like that.

They believed that the skinny kid with the horn-rimmed glasses davened in the morning, did his routines on garlic and saints at night, and said the Shema before going to bed. He was circumcised, not baptized. He was bar mitzvahed, not given Holy Communion. He dropped out of law school, not trade school. And when he left comedy, he'd be going into upholstery, not bartending. The only thing they'd give him is that his mother yelled.

At some point, people couldn't deny I was the real thing, but that still wasn't the end of it. They didn't understand why I would change my name from Pasquale Caputo and then do routines on being Italian. For the hundredth time, the only jobs I could get with "Pasquale Caputo" involved docks, mortar, or catering. Then they said I took on the name Pat Cooper because I was protecting myself and my fellow Italians in case I bombed. In that event, they said I could quietly go back to making pizzas without bringing shame on my heritage. That was quite a scenario.

Under that scenario, I was even sharper than the Jewish comic they accused me of being. Under that scenario, I was an Italian who took on a stage name that was just middle-of-the-road enough, so that when I did my Italian routines and succeeded, people would think I was Italian. But when I did those same Italian routines and failed, people would think I was Jewish. One problem—only a Jewish lawyer could pull that off.

Then I got sued by the Italian Anti-Defamation League. They said that, as an Italian, I was an embarrassment because I was hurting Italians. I told them that wasn't me up there. It's a Jew up there named Morty Stein. And watch out—he's got a great Italian lawyer.

My parents didn't like it either. My father said my stage name was a disgrace. My mother said she wasn't impressed. "You'll always be Pasquale Caputo," she said, and she didn't mean it in a good way. But when I wrote her out a nice fat check and signed it "Pat Cooper," she cashed it right away.

Everybody has a theory. Everybody's insulted. They say, how *dare* you. Really? How dare *me*? How dare *you* say how dare *me!*?

When all the smoke cleared, two things were for sure. One, I was not the first Italian-American comic. Two, I *was* the first Italian-American comic to go out there as an Italian-American. Comics with an Italian heritage like Pat Henry and Jackie Vernon (not their real names!) started to realize, "Hey, we've got a pretty entertaining culture. Hey, my father's from Genoa. My mother's from Sicily. We're part of the in crowd now. Meatballs are as funny as matzah balls." That's right, folks. Come on in, the water's fine.

But if there is one insult in the world that is the highest form of flattery, it's being mistaken for a Jewish comic. I don't know whether it was the forty years wandering in the desert or the fifty years living on the Lower East Side. I don't know whether it was running from the Egyptians three thousand years ago or running the studios in the 1930s. I don't know if it was arguing over lines in the Talmud or fighting over punchlines for *Your Show of Shows*. The Jewish people have an affinity for entertainment in general and comedy specifically. There is no doubt about that. The question is, is this a matter of genetics or culture? The answer, without a doubt, is "yes."

It's in the Jewish DNA somehow. For the details, you'll have to ask Watson and Crick. It's in the culture, too. For those details, you'll have to ask Groucho and Harpo, and Harpo won't give you an answer. What I know is that no matter where I've gone in my life, Jewish people have always had an appreciation for entertainment, whether it's performed on a street corner or the mezzanine of the Imperial Theater on Broadway.

Jewish people understand rhythm and flow—and that's comedy. They question things no one else questions—and that's comedy. They know life's horrors can be beautiful and life's beauties can be horrible. Most of all, they know life's horrors can be horrible, and they'll tell you the whole story and more. They know the more you know, the less you know—and the less you know, the more you need a good lawyer and a better accountant.

The Jewish culture of comedy starts early. When a cute little Jewish kid says something funny at the dinner table, the father says,

"Another Milton Berle!" When I said something funny at the table, my father said, *"Why don a you shutta you fucking mouth?"* So I did what any smart Italian comedian would have done in those days— I followed the chosen people. And that led me right to the Catskill Mountains.

The Borscht Belt, as it was known back then, was Jerusalem for entertainment during the '40s, '50s, and '60s. At the turn of the twentieth century, working-class Jewish people built little bungalows in upstate New York and took in boarders. Some of the bungalows became bungalow colonies, and some of the bungalow colonies became little hotels. Some of the little hotels became big hotels. Every summer, these places attracted tens of thousands of people and some of the biggest names in entertainment, present and future.

The Catskills were a training ground for young comics, and I'm proud to say that I trained there, too. It lasted a lot longer for me than the army, and the pastrami was a lot better. It wasn't all about entertaining a room. There was talent pushing its way through every corner of these places.

Around 1949, an aspiring young comedian and writer named Mel Kaminsky—who you may know as Mel Brooks—had a job at the famous Grossinger's hotel entertaining the guests by the pool during lunch. One afternoon, he walked out onto the diving board wearing a business suit with an attaché case chained to his ankle. *"Oy gevalt!"* Brooks yelled. "I'm going *benkrupt!* I don't vanna live another day!" With that, he tossed the attaché case into the pool, and the rest of him followed. As Brooks tells it, this got yelps of delight and upchucks of kreplach from the lunch crowd. But no one came to save him.

You were on your own up on stage, too. If you died up there, you were buried quickly and the next act was up there before anyone could sit shiva. You couldn't get cute up there. You had to be a performer. You had to have a real act. You started out working a bungalow colony and tried to work your way up.

Which is not to say these were the minor leagues. These were the major leagues as far as the owners were concerned, and if you wanted to succeed as a comic, you had better think the same way. Jewish people were stereotyped as being afraid to fight. That was total bullshit. These owners were tougher than the Mafia. Surviving pogroms in Russia and building a place from scratch in the middle of nowhere will make you tough. There were fights all the time—backstage, in the kitchen, in the office. These people took no shit.

At the same time, they were wonderful. You were not only a performer, you were their guest. They were proud of everything, and that included their entertainment. They wanted you to do well. You learned your craft there. If you bombed, you could put the pieces back together another night. They may have been Jewish, but there were a lot of resurrections in the Catskills. Comics talked about what went right and what went wrong, and if you could put aside your ego for a few minutes, you became a better performer. These people wanted to see talent rising, especially theirs. That was what they called real *nachas*—real pride and joy.

From the bungalow colonies, you worked your way up to a place called the Raleigh. Next was Brown's. At the top of the heap was the Concord, which was like the Copacabana of the Catskills. Making it to the Concord was like making it to Broadway and getting bar mitzvahed on the same day. This was a three-thousand seat venue. The entertainment managers and agents would all talk the same language. "Is Pat Cooper ready for the Concord? Yes? No? Maybe it's too early. Then where are we gonna put Pat Cooper? I know, we'll put him in there opening for someone, and we'll see."

The performers you opened for, or the ones who opened for you, might be legends or legends in the making. Among them at one time or another were, to name just a very few in no particular order, Woody Allen, Milton Berle, Shelly Berman, Lenny Bruce, Sid Caesar, Rodney Dangerfield, Phyllis Diller, Estelle Getty, Buddy Hackett, Alan King,

Robert Klein, Carl Reiner, Don Rickles, Joan Rivers, Freddie Roman, Jerry Lewis, and Jonathan Winters.

And there I was, Pat Cooper, a *Yitalena,* playing the Concord. Or, according to some people, a Jew playing a Yitalena playing the Concord. When you were up there with a microphone performing in front of a great audience like that, it didn't really matter which. It didn't matter much backstage either. You were welcome. You were family.

There were other proving grounds in America, and other places you could learn from great Jewish performers. The first time I worked a casino was in the early '60s in Sparks, Nevada. I was hired to open for the legendary singer Tony Martin. I was so nervous, I flew out three days early to get comfortable in my hotel room and look around. I wanted to dress perfect. I wanted to fit right in. I even had a bow tie. Part of my anxiousness came from not knowing anything about a casino crowd. The other part was the idea of opening for Tony Martin.

Tony Martin was one of the great voices of the twentieth century. I remembered sitting in a movie theater as a kid watching him sing and act opposite the Marx Brothers and Margaret Dumont in *The Big Store.* He appeared in movie after movie for MGM starting in the late '30s and had a string of top twenty hits through the '50s. He was also about the most handsome son of a bitch you could ever meet, and women loved him. That included his wife of many years, the beautiful dancer and actress Cyd Charisse.

Tony Martin dressed impeccably and sang romantic songs. Perhaps his most famous song was, "There's No Tomorrow," which climbed all the way up to number two on the pop charts in 1950. The melody and lyrical theme were borrowed for the song "It's Now or Never," which produced a number-one hit for Elvis Presley in 1960. But both songs came from the classic Italian melody, "O Sole Mio."

I figured Tony Martin's real name was Tony Martino. Or Di-

Martino. Or Martinelli. By the way Tony Martin looked, dressed, sang, and even by the songs he picked, he was one sharp Italian. It was going to be an honor to perform with him for a three-week engagement no less, and for all I knew, maybe a little bit of his class would rub off on me.

The first full day I was in town, I got a call in my hotel room from someone who said that he was George Burns. He told me he had a problem.

"I have a problem, too," I said. "I just got into town and I got someone on the phone telling me he's George Burns."

"This *is* George Burns. And my problem is that I have four hours to go before my show, and Dorothy Provine just cancelled out. So son, could you come down and give me fifty minutes?"

"I don't have fifty minutes," I said. "You want me to borrow it?"

"This is no time to be funny. Do you know who you're speaking to?"

"Well," I said, "you're telling me you're George Burns. Can I ask you why Dorothy Provine left the show?"

"None of your fucking business. Now, if you don't think it's really me, I'll give you my room number at the hotel where I'm at, and you can call me back. But in the meantime, I'm up against the wall. I need fifty minutes."

"Well," I said, "there's one other problem. I'm supposed to start an engagement opening up for Tony Martin in three days as his comic. I'm happy to come down, but I really couldn't do it unless I got clearance from Tony Martin."

There was a long pause on the other end. By this point in the conversation, I knew it really was George Burns. The legend. He had started in vaudeville at age ten after his father died, and he knew he didn't want to make a living shining shoes and selling newspapers. In vaudeville, he made a living, but that was about it. When he met Gracie Allen in 1923, he tried to make her his straight man, but she was the one getting all the laughs, even when her lines weren't funny. George Burns was smart enough to realize *he* was the straight man.

So he wrote for Gracie's bewildered, illogically logical character, and Burns and Allen shot to the top of the stage, radio, and television for four decades. In reality, George Burns was no straight man. When asked about his good fortune in meeting his stage partner, he said, "All of a sudden, the audience realized I had talent. They were right. I did have talent—and I married her."

And here he was, George Burns, apparently dumbfounded by a schmucky kid from Brooklyn who thought he was someone making a prank phone call. By someone who didn't have to put on an act to seem stupid. By someone who maybe didn't have fifteen minutes, let alone fifty. By someone who was going to make a legend sit around and wait. I didn't want to hear what was coming next.

"You know something, you'll never have trouble making a living. You're a classy young man."

"I am?" I was frozen.

"You certainly are," Burns said. "That's exactly how I would want to be treated if you were on my show and someone gave you a call like this one. Go ahead and give Tony a call. Take my number. I'll be right here."

I left a message for Tony Martin, and he called me back about an hour later.

"That was a good thing you did, "he said.

"Thanks, Tony. Can I call you Tony?"

"You can call me anything you want, Pat" he said. "I'm happy to have a guy like you on my show. Go ahead and work with George. Go right ahead. It's my pleasure. And do yourself a favor. Don't get nervous. You're what they call a 'disappointment act.' There was no advertisement. You're filling in. No one expects a damn thing from you, so if you make one person laugh, you're ahead of the game. And if

George likes you and he doesn't have anyone, you might as well work the next two nights."

"Listen, Tony, I want to thank you."

"I want to thank *you*. Pat. We haven't met yet, but I'm in a hurry to meet you. We're going to have a drink together."

When I met George Burns an hour later, he shook my hand and puffed on a cigar. This was real. I was in the company of greatness. I was an uneducated man blessed by God. I went on, did twenty minutes, and realized I wasn't even halfway through. So I pulled things out of a hat. It could have been the State Theater in Baltimore all over again. It could have been the corner of Flatbush and Avenue L. But I did okay. I created sparks in Sparks and the fire wasn't even started yet. George had me back the following two nights.

On opening night with Tony Martin, I was dressed to the nines. When I went out on stage, however, I didn't feel a hundred percent. I was nervous. I didn't bomb, but I wasn't getting through to the audience either. I left the stage telling myself the only good thing was that the local press wasn't there that night.

Tony Martin was backstage doing a couple of throat exercises just before going on. He was such a handsome man you wanted to bite him. The problem was that he looked like he wanted to bite me, and not because I was handsome.

"Pat," he said, "I want to talk to you when the show's over."

This was like when the teacher wanted to talk to you after school. Ninety-nine percent of the time it was bad. In my case a hundred percent. It only took twenty minutes to kill all that good will. The stage manager was very sick, and maybe that had something to do with Tony's mood. I really didn't know. I just hoped Tony Martin had a better show than I did.

It was normal for a main act to have a nice dressing room. But Tony Martin also had his own valet. As we sat down, Tony told his valet to bring a bottle of whiskey over.

"I'm going to have a drink with this young man. And then I'm going to read him the riot act."

The riot act for not being a riot. Now it sounded less like a teacher after school and more like a sit-down with the boss. I was beginning to think this might be my last drink.

"Pat, let me tell you something. I am the sex symbol here. Do you understand?"

"Yes, sir."

"I sing the romantic songs."

"Well," I said, "I didn't sing no songs. You gotta give me that."

"But you did everything else," he said. "You were overdressed. And it hurt your act. That's what people were looking at. You confused them and you confused me. You don't come out with patent leather shoes and a tuxedo. You don't come out with a cummerbund. And the bow tie. Give me a break with the bow tie. That thing was practically touching your ears."

"You don't like the bow tie?"

"Get rid of the fucking bow tie! Where did you get that fucking thing? Shoot it!"

"With all due respect," I said, "what exactly should I wear?"

"Have you ever heard of a suit? Wear a suit tomorrow night. That way they know you're the comic. And when I come out, they know I'm not closing for you. They were all looking at your clothes, you dumb Guinea!"

"What do you mean dumb Guinea?" I said. "I'm Italian, you're Italian."

"I'm Jewish."

"You're Jewish?" I said. "You're kidding me."

"You want me to prove it to you?"

"I just didn't think a Jew could sing that good."

Tony Martin, it turned out, was born Alvin Morris. I went back out on stage the next night in a suit and I got laughs. It was the first dress-down Friday in history. I kept the suit the next night and the next night after that. For the rest of the three-week engagement, we killed. A Jewish guy hit the high notes and an Italian guy made them laugh, even though everyone thought it was the other way around.

About fifteen years later, I was booked for a week in Miami. I didn't know for sure if it was the peak of my career, but I was doing really well. But that wasn't why I was excited. The reason I couldn't wait to get down to Florida was because I was appearing with the legend, my mentor and dress consultant—the great Tony Martin.

But the minute I saw the marquee, my excitement ended. There in big letters was the name "Pat Cooper." And underneath, in smaller letters, were the words "Special Guest Star, Tony Martin." I walked right into the theater and told the manager to turn it around.

"What?"

"Turn it around!"

I couldn't let them do it. I understood that in their minds Pat Cooper was the bigger name at that moment in time. But in my mind, Tony Martin was the bigger name for *all* time. To forget about all those movies and hit records was an absolute disgrace. So I watched as the theater crew redid the letters. When they read "Tony Martin. Special Guest Star, Pat Cooper," I was satisfied. I had a couple hours to kill, so I went out and had a late lunch.

When I got back to the theater around six o'clock and checked the marquee, I almost went berserk. The letters were back to where they were before I got there the first time. So Pat Cooper, the headliner who wanted to be a special guest star, ran backstage and found the manager. The manager explained to me that while I was out, Tony Martin came in and demanded that they switch the names back. I was going to get up on a ladder and switch it back myself, but instead I found Tony Martin and read *him* the riot act.

"Tony," I said, "this isn't right."

"Pat," he said, "let me ask you something. Is success bothering you?"

"Not at all, Tony. It's a matter of respect."

"Look," he said. "I was once a saxophone player. Then I became a singer. Then I became a headliner. Now I'm a singer again. And if I have to play the saxophone, I will. It doesn't matter to me. I want to work."

"You're gonna work," I said. "And I'm going to open for you. In a suit."

"No, Pat. You're hot property. I'm going to open for hot property. You can even wear that fucking bow tie."

"Tony," I said, "would you just do me a favor? Plain and simple. You close."

"Still afraid to follow me, Cooper?"

"I'm afraid to open for you, Tony."

We hugged. I got my way and we got to talking. I found out that all those years ago when we worked together in Nevada, the stage manager, who had been sick, needed an operation. And Tony paid for it out of his own pocket. A man like that deserved top billing, and he got it whether he wanted it or not. And for that week in Miami, sparks flew again.

There were other Martins with golden voices who really were Italian. Dean Martin, who was born Dino Crocetti, was the best of them. The first time I saw Dean Martin in person was around 1946. I was walking down the street in Manhattan and ran into singer Sonny King. I knew Sonny because we were both born in Brooklyn and raised around Fifth Avenue. With Sonny that day was an agent by the name of Lou Perry, and with him was a young singer named Dean Martin. At the time, I was just starting to poke my head into show business, but I had next to nothing going on. We said hello, and that was that.

Not long after, I saw an ad in the *Daily Mirror* for a show at the Loews State Theater on Broadway and 45th Street in Manhattan, and

I decided to go. In those days, you could lose yourself for an entire day for the price of one ticket. First, I saw the movie *Kismet,* starring Ronald Coleman and Marlene Dietrich. Next was the comic Johnny Burke, who dressed in a World War I uniform and told army stories. The special guest star was Dean Martin, who sang for about twenty minutes. I thought the guy I had run into with Sonny King and Lou Perry was pretty good. Then Dean Martin finished, walked off the stage, and I watched *Kismet* again.

Three short years later, I went to the Paramount Theater to see the comedy team of Martin and Lewis, which was all the rage. As a mousy 130-pounder, I was able to sneak into the theater as people were coming out. Inside was one of the most exciting shows I had ever seen. As the story went, when Dean Martin and Jerry Lewis had first started as a team, Skinny D'Amato almost kicked them out of his 500 Club in Atlantic City because their skits in the first show fell flat. For the second show, Jerry and Dean threw caution to the wind. Dean tried to sing and Jerry broke tables and chairs around him. They pulled bits out of vaudeville and out of thin air, and the audience loved it.

I loved it, too. At the Paramount, I could see they had a rhythm. Dean had a nice quiet rhythm. Jerry had a big rhythm. It was rhythm you couldn't buy. It was the rhythm of someone who couldn't turn it off, someone who kept creating even when he went to sleep. Together they had the rhythm of a big band, and it was unstoppable. You could feel something huge was happening and you were happy to be a tiny part of it. After the show, it was chaos. The audience gathered outside Dean and Jerry's dressing room window. In a gesture that was as natural and rhythmic as their act, they opened the window and threw autographed pictures down to the crowd. You could see the world being turned upside down.

You have to be born with rhythm like that. You cannot buy it. You cannot go out in the street and take it off someone. The rhythm was deep in Jerry Lewis's DNA, and it continued for him, as it did for Dean, even after they broke up the act.

Jerry Lewis was beyond special. He had every tool a performer could possibly have, and was so smooth, you never saw the tool chest. He could turn typing on a typewriter into a concert. He could conduct an orchestra for real, as he did in *The Bellboy,* to the point where you thought he wrote the music himself. He could eat a plate of spaghetti and turn it into a high wire act. He could dance like Fred Astaire, as he did in *Cinderfella.* I once saw Jerry Lewis on television have a showdown on the drums with the great Buddy Rich and hold his own. Talk about rhythm.

There was hardly ever a better showcase for this man's incredible range of talent than *The Nutty Professor,* and that's why it became a classic. The movie was based loosely on *Dr. Jekyll and Mr. Hyde,* and Lewis owned both ends of the spectrum. He had the gawky buck-toothed professor in one pocket and the supercool playboy in the other. He could switch pockets and switch back again right before your eyes like he was tuning an instrument. On top of it all, he wrote, directed, and even innovated the way movies were shot. After the split, Dean went from star to superstar. Jerry went from star to giant.

One day many years later, he came to my home. It was hard to believe, but after all, we were neighbors in Las Vegas. He brought along his manager Joe Stabile and Joe's wife, Claudia, who managed Joe's brother, the bandleader Dick Stabile. Dick was the bandleader for Dean and Jerry, and was still part of the family. Patti made *pasta pizzelli*—peas and macaroni—for all of us.

I became part of that family, but only on the outskirts. I got to know Jerry, but I never got very close. I didn't hang out with him much. That was not for me to do. And that was okay. Like the burning bush on Mount Sinai, if you got too close, you could go blind from the brightness. When I got to play the Westbury Music Fair with Jerry

Lewis, I stood back and thought about the Paramount, and Dean and Jerry throwing pictures out the window, and said to God, *Dayenu*—it's enough! It was more than enough. I was in awe and as close as I wanted to be.

Awe usually fades over time. New performers come along who make the old footage seem grainy and irrelevant. But with Jerry Lewis, the awe I felt grew. Jerry had what seemed like all the tools, but there was one more great tool he saved for the right time—his heart. As national chairman of the Muscular Dystrophy Association, he could have made an appearance here and there and said the blessing over the bread. Instead, he did for fighting disease what he did for entertainment—he redefined it.

Of course, he raised hundred of millions of dollars to fight muscular dystrophy. I could only imagine the empathy he must have felt having made a living with perfect control of his body and having to see innocent kids lose theirs. But the Labor Day telethons reinvented giving. When you saw Jerry Lewis year after year, fighting off sleepiness on the national day of rest, you opened your own heart and your checkbook. If you were an entertainer, you wanted to do more. You wanted to be a part of it. I certainly did.

It took quite a few years before I got the call. I was living in Las Vegas, but I was in New York at the time. So I had to fly out to Los Angeles, which was fine because a little jetlag made you fit right in. I was excited. In an effort to save lives, I was going to kill. I had my Italian mother, my Italian father, and my Italian wedding. I had the saints. I had bits and pieces of albums and more bits and piece of things I thought up when we hit turbulence and I almost got someone's dinner on my lap. I was going to be performing in front of forty million people, and for all the right reasons.

They sent a car to pick me up at the airport and take me to the studio. Everyone was very gracious, and lines were flying through my head. I walked over to Jerry and thanked him for having me. Doing the telethon was an honor. Then Claudia, who was producing the show, walked over to me and said, "Pat, maybe four minutes."

"Fine," I said. "Whatever you say."

Four minutes wasn't much, but it turned out to be even less than that. As I walked out, the band played. And played. And played some more. By the time they were done I was down to two-and-a-half minutes. I said a little about my Italian father and less about my Italian mother. There were no saints and no wedding and absolutely nothing about the plane ride. The band began playing again, and there was turbulence in my stomach.

How could they do this? Between the trip to California and the one back to New York, it was six thousand miles. Who travels six thousand miles to do two-and-a-half minutes? That was more than two thousand miles per minute. To do twenty, I would have to go to the moon and back. It wasn't as if they had no time. This was a fucking telethon. They had nothing but time!

Then, backstage, right there with a bunch of groggy volunteer telephone operators taking a coffee break, I realized something. Just being there was the right thing. I had heard stories of celebrities at these telethons demanding all sorts of perks. For them, it was all about first-class flights, limousines, and caviar in the dressing room. Jerry went along with it because of his kids. I didn't want to be a problem for Jerry. I couldn't be. I was blessed, and I wasn't a kid.

Then I remembered something else. In the Jewish religion it is said if you saved a single life, it was as if you saved the whole world. Jerry Lewis has saved countless worlds. He was well on his way to becoming the first Jewish saint. As for me, I was an Italian. But on this day I was something else. Today I was a *mensch*.

Pasquale Caputo, age five. What a handsome kid!

My father, Michael Caputo, in our Brooklyn backyard.

Basic training—before they shaved and powdered my head.

"Pascal Capa-tutio" is in the top row, fourth from left.

At the Copa with Patti.

Aunt Rosie and her friend (at left), Patti, me, and my mother, Louise Caputo.

I argued with Patti about which way to wear the flower on our wedding day. She let me win.

Me and my girls—Patti and Patti Jo.

Working at home in Vegas.

40 years together

Patti helped design this party invitation for our fortieth wedding anniversary.

6

Opening for Legends and Opening My Mouth

I opened for some of the greatest names in the history of show business. People would say to me, "Pat, wouldn't you have preferred to headline?" The answer was no. Not at that point. First of all, I was making good money, and one thing my manager Willie Weber explained to me very early on was not to worry about being a star. He said, "Always remember, make the fucking money and you'll never be sorry."

Second, the people I opened for were legends. I'm not just thrilled to have worked with them as I look back—I was smart enough to be thrilled by it then. Why would I want to follow someone like Frank Sinatra or George Burns? But in spite of my good fortune, some of these people could be a pain in the ass. What made me different from other opening acts was that I didn't take it.

In 1964, I had an engagement to open for Bobby Darin at the Flamingo in Las Vegas. Bobby was like me in that he was from an Italian family in New York and not born well off. Like me, Bobby's given name, Walden Robert Cassotto, was a little too Italian for show business. But he had a couple of extra strikes against him. He had rheumatism when he was a kid, and it left his heart in a weakened condition. He wasn't even supposed to live past the age of sixteen.

Meanwhile, he eventually found out that his older sister was actually his mother, and the woman he thought was his mother was really his grandmother. He never found out who his father was. My mother, father, and sisters gave me a lifetime case of *agita,* but at least I knew who the fuck they were.

The bottom line though was that Bobby Darin was talented. He sold millions of records with hits like "Mack the Knife" and "Beyond the Sea." He wrote and produced great songs for other performers. And he had a voice as smooth as silk. He had looks, timing, and unbelievable stage presence. When he walked out in his tuxedo, you just stopped whatever you were doing. Sammy Davis, Jr. said Bobby Darin was the one performer he never wanted to follow.

When the engagement began, I went backstage and knocked on Bobby Darin's dressing room door. "Bobby," I said. "What can I tell you? It's a fucking honor to work with you. And it's such a nice thing to see an Italian enjoying the success he deserves." Bobby thanked me. He was a very nervous guy. But I liked him. I loved being around talented people, and I never got jealous of them. I got jealous of assholes.

The Flamingo was a huge pink art-deco building that mobster Bugsy Siegel built and then died for in 1947. Fortunately, I was not dying there. I was doing exactly twelve minutes opening up for Bobby Darin. I knew it was exactly twelve minutes, because every night, the clock at the foot of the stage right in front of me said, "11, 10, 9, 8, 7 . . ." and when it got to zero, I got off. Then Bobby Darin would come out and sing "Splish Splash," "Dream Lover," and "Beyond the Sea" for an hour and twenty minutes and tear the joint down.

A week into the engagement, there was a knock on my door. It was Bobby. He looked nervous and a little panicked. "Pat," he said. "I gotta drive out to the airport and pick up my wife. Can you do me a favor and stay on till I get back?" "Sure, Bobby," I said. "I'll stay on."

It seemed a little strange to me for the headlining act to be running out right before a show to pick up his wife. But I figured, what the hell, I'd stay on a few extra minutes. After all, his wife was the great Sandra Dee. When Bobby married her in 1960, it was a match made in Hollywood heaven. Sandra Dee was a pin-up girl and star of popular movies like *A Summer Place* and *Gidget.* On top of everything else, Bobby Darin was at the peak of his success. Not only was he a famous singer, he was also a respected movie star, having just earned an Academy Award nomination for best supporting actor in *Captain Newman, M.D.*

I was on stage looking at the clock: "3, 2, 1 . . ." and I heard the band start to play the overture: "Oh the shark, babe, has such teeth, dear . . ." I wrapped it up and said, "Well, ladies and gentlemen, it's been a pleasure, and enjoy Bobby Darin. There's no one like him." As I walked toward the curtain, I heard the stage manager's voice. "Stop! What are you doing, Pat?"

"What do you mean what am I doing? I finished my twelve minutes. I'm fucking done."

"He ain't here yet."

"Who ain't here yet?"

"Bobby Darin ain't here."

That's when it hit me—he really did go to pick up his wife in the middle of a show. I couldn't believe it. But now I had to believe it. So the band stopped, and I walked back out on stage and said, "Ladies and gentlemen, you gotta understand show business. This guy Bobby Darin, a huge unbelievable star, went to pick up his wife at the airport. You know his wife, Sandra Dee. Gidget. This big, huge star, God forbid he should send a fucking limousine to pick up his wife at the airport."

The audience was screaming and laughing. I did a couple more minutes on Bobby and Sandra Dee, then a couple of minutes of some other material, and then I started to exit again. "Ladies and gentlemen, you're gonna love Bobby Darin. I think they just dragged him off the fucking runway." The audience screamed, and once again, the band

started playing the overture: "Oh the shark, babe, has such teeth, dear
. . ."

And the stage manager waved at me from the wings and said,
"He's still not here! You gotta go back out there!"

"Wait a second," I said. "I came in here with twenty-four minutes
of material. I did twelve and don't remember the other twelve."

So I ran back out there with an update. "Ladies and gentlemen,
here's the latest information. We don't know where the fuck he is.
Maybe the plane is late. Maybe the plane arrived and Sandra Dee
wasn't on it. Maybe he took the first plane out of Vegas. Maybe he's
on his way. Maybe he's doing another show somewhere else. Maybe
he died. Who the fuck knows? Nobody here knows." Now the audience was screaming at the top of their lungs, and the band was laughing, too. And as I tried to get off the stage again, they could barely play
the overture: "Oh the shark, babe, has such teeth, dear . . ."

I did this for over an hour. Bobby Darin missed the entire show.
Afterwards, there was a knock on my dressing room door. It was
Bobby Darin. And this nervous guy—who had just missed an entire
show—was screaming at me. "How dare you get laughs at my
expense!"

"Bobby," I said. "What the fuck are you yelling at me for? Why the
fuck didn't you send somebody to pick up your wife?"

"Who are you to tell me how and when to pick up my wife?"

"I ain't telling you," I said. "But the reality is, you got a show to
do. You got people depending on you. The place is jammed, and I'm
over here with twelve minutes trying to stretch it into twenty-four.
Then I'm trying to stretch it into an hour. What the fuck did you want
me to do?"

"You could have done something else."

"The point is," I said, "if my wife tells me to pick her up in the
middle of a show, the answer is, 'Go fuck yourself. I have a job, here,
darling. I'm obligated.' Maybe she says, 'I don't want no busboy pick-

ing me up,' and my answer is, 'Then call a fucking cab or wait at the airport for a couple of hours.'"

"You're never going to work with me again," he said. "Never!"

"Fongool!" I yelled back. "I don't give a fuck! You shouldn't have done what you did. Ask anybody here!"

We didn't speak to each other for the rest of the engagement. I found out later that Sandra Dee had a drinking problem, an eating problem, and whole bunch of other problems. They got a divorce in 1967. For a year or two, Bobby lived in the woods, grew a beard, and wrote folks songs. During that time, I wrote to him. I heard his health wasn't good. They didn't give him long to live, and I felt for the guy.

Eventually the Copa bought his contract, but evidently they didn't know exactly what they were getting. Who do they ask to open for him but me? Before the show, I went up to him and said, "For Christ's sake, I thought I wasn't going to work with you no more."

"Don't worry about it," he said. "I ain't picking up my wife this time."

I did twelve minutes on the nose, and Bobby Darin came out on time. He should have been late. Everyone in that audience was shocked when they saw him, myself included. No more tuxedo. He had on a pair of jeans and an open jean shirt. He wore no makeup and no toupee. He sat on a stool with a guitar and started strumming some shit about flowers. He went right in the fucking toilet. The audience was silent. They looked like they wanted to cry. I wanted to cry, too.

About six months later, the Copa brought him back under the condition that he be Bobby Darin. He had to dress like Bobby Darin, wear a toupee like Bobby Darin, and sing like Bobby Darin. He did, and he kicked ass like Bobby Darin. It was great to have him back. Not long after that, he died coming out of heart surgery. He took an enormous amount of talent with him.

In 1963, I performed at a benefit for Dolly Sinatra, Frank Sinatra's mother. I guess she liked me, because the next thing I knew, I got a call to open for Frank Sinatra at the Sands in Las Vegas. The engagement ran from mid-December of '63 into January of '64.

Outside of anything I had ever heard about how generous Frank Sinatra was on the one hand and how spiteful he could be on the other, I loved Frank Sinatra the entertainer. There was no one better, ever. He took music and added more music.

There were a lot of singers, even some of the best, who sang along with the melody. Their voices were instruments, and as long as the instruments were in tune, the songs were great. Sinatra went beyond that. He made the songs his. He brought out elements of the music that no one knew were there. He gave the songs another dimension. When you threw in the fact that Sinatra's band at the Sands was the Count Basie Orchestra, this was about the best opening gig I could have ever hoped for.

Sinatra's manager, sidekick, bodyguard, and one-man entourage was Jilly Rizzo. Jilly was a New York guy around Sinatra's age and identified, correctly or incorrectly, as one of the last true tough guys. His voice was rough, kind of like Edward G. Robinson with something caught in his throat. Jilly was about five foot ten and built like a dumpster. He made his living for decades as a bar owner. Jilly's in Manhattan, originally on 21st Street and later on West 52nd Street, was the nightspot most closely identified with Sinatra. It was his off-hours and after-hours hangout, and over time, Frank and Jilly became best friends.

One other thing Frank and Jilly had in common was the women in their lives. Back in the day in Hoboken, New Jersey, Dolly Sinatra was a well-known abortionist. Honey, Jilly's wife, was a member of the same profession. She had green hair, a mouth like a sewer, and spent Jilly's money faster than he could make it. I felt for Jilly.

At the beginning of the engagement, Jilly came over and told me

Frank wanted me to do about twenty to twenty-five minutes. I said, "Fine. When you tell me to do twenty to twenty-five minutes, that's exactly what I'll do." Just to be on the safe side, I did about twenty-three minutes—not twenty, not twenty-five, but somewhere in between.

The gig was not easy. I was under a lot of pressure. Aside from the enormous audience of loyal Sinatra fans, some of the biggest stars on the planet were sitting up front. Names like Lauren Bacall and Cary Grant. They were all looking at me like *When the fuck is he going to get off?* They weren't even smiling at me. I pulled a line out of my ass here or there and got a reaction. The one thing that really helped me get through was that Count Basie and the guys in his band fucking loved me. Sometimes, theirs were the only laughs in the entire room.

After about the third night, Jilly came over to me and said, "Listen, Pat, Frank says that thing about the saint you talk about . . . Frank says take it out." He was referring to a story I told about my mother turning her statue of Saint Anthony upside down because he didn't answer her novena.

"What?" I said. "That's what you came over to tell me? That thing is one of the few laughs I'm getting. That's my line. It works. I'm happy getting a fucking snicker out there."

"Well, that's what Frank said."

I didn't want to argue with Jilly. That was a losing proposition. I wanted to see what the man himself had to say. So I marched over to Sinatra's dressing room and knocked on the door. "Frank," I said. "It's Pat Cooper."

"Yeah, kid, come on in. What's the problem?" He opened the door about halfway, and I took about a half step into the room.

"Frank," I said. "Did you tell Jilly Rizzo that I gotta take out that thing about the saint?" Sinatra stopped whatever he was doing and stared. It was strange, because he wasn't looking directly at me but past me. That's when I realized Jilly Rizzo was standing behind me.

The look on Sinatra's face seemed to say, *Why is this guy coming in here and saying this to me?* So I opened my mouth.

"Frank, no disrespect, but I don't tell you what songs to sing. Don't you tell me how to be funny. That's a tough room for me. I'm not exactly killing out there. They're killing *me*. They want to see you. They're in a hurry to get me off the fucking stage. I'm telling you, it gets so hot in there I wouldn't be surprised if it started to rain in that room."

Sinatra looked at me, then Jilly, then me, and didn't say a word. Nothing. Then he turned around and walked back into his dressing room. Jilly then said to me, "Pat, come on. Let's go." When we got a few steps down the hall, he turned to me and said, "Why the fuck did you say that to Frank Sinatra?"

"If I got one little bit that half works," I said, "how can he not let me do it?"

I finished the engagement. The saint thing stayed, and no one had the guts to hang me upside down.

A few days later, I was working downtown with the great jazz singer Joe Williams, who was giving me five thousand dollars a week. I had gotten only a thousand for the week at the Sands with Sinatra. When I mentioned that to friends, they usually said the same thing: "It looks good to have worked with Frank Sinatra. You should have done it for nothing."

"No way," I said. "I did a benefit for his mom. I ain't doing nothing for him for nothing." On top of that, Joe Williams was a gentleman, wonderful to work with and never told me what to do.

A couple years later, I wound up doing something for nothing again. This time it was a benefit at the Aladdin in Vegas. Among others on the bill were Peggy Lee, the Step Brothers, and Frank Sinatra. I would be introducing Frank Sinatra, who was working in town at Caesar's Palace. Before the show, Sinatra walked over to me and said, "Pat, I'm gonna do three songs and then I gotta get back to Caesar's." I said, "That's fine, Frank."

I got out on stage and told a couple of stories, then said, "Ladies and gentlemen, what can I say? He's here. Frank Sinatra!" He did the first song and blew the audience away. Same thing with the second song. By the end of the third song he had them mesmerized, so he began to launch into a fourth song. That's when I ran out and yelled, "Frank! Frank! You want to work with me again? I told you three songs. You can't do four songs. Now do you want to work with me again or not? Make up your fucking mind!"

I really didn't know what Sinatra was going to do, but the fact is, he literally fell down laughing. The audience was laughing with him. Out of the corner of my eye I saw Peggy Lee and the Step Brothers, and they were hysterical, dying. After the show, my wife asked me for the thousandth time what on earth makes me do things like that. And I told her my old man must be right. I'm a *stunad.*

A couple years later, I was invited to a celebrity roast in LA for Tommy LaSorda, who was still a coach for the Dodgers at that time, not yet a manager. We had a slew of names there—Dean Martin, Sammy Davis, Jr., Joey Bishop. I was waiting on the dais for my turn, when who starts making his way up to the microphone but Old Blue Eyes. He stopped at my seat, tapped me on the shoulder, and said, "Can I do that fourth song now?"

This time, I was the one who fell down laughing. No one else knew why. It was our little private joke. Sinatra had a look in his eyes that said, "Hey, you're a nice kid." That was an amazing smile. It was like an oil painting.

In the early '70s, I got a gig opening for Shirley MacLaine. She co-starred with Jack Lemmon in *The Apartment* and appeared in many great motion pictures, but before her movie career, she wanted to be a dancer. More recently, she was also known for speaking and writing about her spiritual beliefs, like reincarnation and out-of-body experiences.

The engagement was at the MGM Grand. Before that, Shirley MacLaine worked at Caesar's for about two hundred thousand dollars. She didn't do spectacular business there. Not long after, MGM hired her for two hundred and fifty thousand dollars. So a few days before the engagement I went on a local television show and opened my big mouth. I said, "Jeez, it's amazing. She didn't draw that well at Caesar's, and the MGM gave her a fifty thousand dollar raise. I'll tell you what. Give me a ten thousand dollar pay cut not to show up and I'll save everybody some money."

I had no idea whether Shirley MacLaine heard any of this, but the day before the engagement, I drove by the MGM Grand, and there's her name on the marquee in huge letters: SHIRLEY MACLAINE. Right below is a silhouette of her in a dancing pose. And in tiny letters, right between her legs, are two tiny words: PAT COOPER. I went fucking bananas. I stopped the car, got out, ran inside, and started screaming for the entertainment director. And I fucking hit the ceiling.

"What the fuck do you think you're doing putting my name between this woman's legs?"

"Well," he said, "we had no other place to put it."

"How about putting it on your fucking ass?" I said. "You don't do that to me. I'm a fucking name performer. Are you sick or something?"

"Well," he said, "let me see . . ."

"No, no, let you see fucking nothing. Take it down!"

"How about if we move one leg?"

"How about you give her eight fucking legs, take off her arms, and spell her name in Chinese? I don't fucking care. This is wrong. You're not doing this to me!"

I went back home that day and got one phone call after another: "Ay, Patty, they put you in Shirley MacLaine's pussy." The MGM called Joe Scanduri, my manager, and then Joe called me. He started screaming at me, saying, "You can't talk to them like that. You'll never work there again! This gig is gonna end before it begins!"

"Well, if I don't work there, I don't work there," I said. "You shouldn't be worried about them. You should be worried about me. You've gotta protect me. I don't want to be between her legs. Not that way, anyway."

"Pat, I'll see what I can do."

"My contract says equal billing," I said. "Do you realize that?"

After some back and forth, they took my name out from between Shirley MacLaine's legs, made it bigger, and put it next to her name. I did the first night of the gig and went backstage to her dressing room. She was sitting there next to Pete Hamill, the writer. She was separated at the time, and Pete may have been her boyfriend. At that point, she might have heard what I said on the television show. And without a doubt, she heard all about how I hit the ceiling the day before. I took a seat right near the two of them, and Shirley MacLaine winced at me.

"Can I ask you something?" she said. "Where do you get your balls?"

"Miss MacLaine," I said, "let me say this. I can only respect your dignity. How fucking dare you not respect *my* dignity?"

At this point, Pete Hamill started laughing. Shirley MacLaine was a ballsy broad and wasn't used to this kind of response. It was like a showdown, and Pete was enjoying it.

"I guess you say what you want first," she said, "and ask questions later."

"And from what I've read," I said, "I guess you have out-of-body experiences. Let me tell you, if I had your body, I wouldn't go back in."

Pete Hamill was pounding the table so hard I thought he was going to break it. Then he went under it. "Cooper," he said, "you're out of your fucking mind!"

I did the next few shows and checked my name on the marquee every day. One night backstage, Pete Hamill grabbed me and said, "You know I've never laughed so hard in my entire life."

"Do me a favor," I said, "don't write this story for the newspapers. She'll have me killed."

"I don't think so," he said. "She likes you, because you've got balls. Almost as big as hers. She's just not used to an opening act talking down to her."

"If you notice, Pete," I said, "I never actually talked down to her. I took a seat in the dressing room that was low, and I was actually talking up to her. Will you tell her that for me?"

"Pat," he said. "Whatever you do, don't change. Don't ever change."

As far as trying to be fair, show respect, and tell things the way they are, I haven't ever changed. But through the '70s, I watched the entertainment industry change in ways that were not good. In particular, live performances with big-name entertainment started to collapse under its own weight. Egos got out of control.

As a comedian who often opened for name singers, I had seen the best and the worst of headliners. I had been taken advantage of, used, lied to, and disrespected, all without ever doing the same thing to another human being. I had seen other performers—particularly other comedians—suffer the same treatment. The difference between me and them was that I never took it. Whether or not I could afford to fight back wasn't the point. The point was self-respect. The point was character.

I had been in show business as a professional for over two decades and had made a very good living. I wasn't a superstar, but I had a good reputation for working hard and putting people in the seats. One thing I understood from the beginning was how lucky I was to be in this business. Especially during the hard economic times toward the end of the '70s, there were people in America and all over the world who were struggling to make a living and crying for a decent job—literally crying.

What millions of these people saw were so-called big-name entertainers demanding more and more money, with more and more contract clauses that pampered them like babies—all without bringing in much business. When I saw a place struggling, I would offer to take part of the door so there was no way the owner could lose money. I knew that by taking more than I should up front, even though I might walk away with more money, I would be hurting the venue, the audience, the next comedian who had to play there, and ultimately the business itself.

All this came to a head for me in early 1981. The Sands Hotel gave me an eight-week contract. I never asked for it. They offered a hundred and sixty thousand dollars for the eight weeks, and I accepted. Walter Kane was running the Sands. He was a gentleman, and I never had a problem with him. For the first week, I would be opening for Tony Bennett. At the time, hard as it might be to believe, Tony Bennett's career was in the toilet. He wasn't drawing, period. In a room with seven hundred seats, eighty people would come and he'd argue that there were actually eighty-one. That's where his brain was.

A few days before the engagement, I got a call from Walter Kane, who sounded unhappy and resigned. I asked him what the problem was. He explained that Tony Bennett's contract allowed him to pick who he wanted to work with, and he didn't want Pat Cooper. Fred Travalena was in and Pat Cooper was out.

I was shocked. First of all, there was no reason in the world for Tony Bennett to disrespect me. Second, the hotel was doing this to me with virtually no notice. Third, the hotel had a contract with Pat Cooper before it had one with Tony Bennett. So I went to see Walter Kane in his office. I asked how he could do this to me, especially right before an engagement. He tried to blame it on Tony, but I wouldn't accept that. I had the date. The hotel could have chosen to honor my contract instead of Tony Bennett's.

"Well," Kane said, "looks like we owe you the date."

"No disrespect, Mr. Kane," I said. "You don't owe me the date. I don't want to work here no more. You can't do this to me. You can't control me. And you can't tell me this is acceptable, because it is not."

And with that, I cancelled the eight-week contract and effectively gave back a hundred and sixty thousand dollars. That was unheard of from a comedian or just about anyone else, at least until then.

Naturally, I had feelings, and that was part of the reason I did what I did. But it was more than that. In a way, I was watching my business—the business that I loved—commit suicide. Half-famous ego-bloated singers were like the knife, and misguided hotels were sticking it in. The little-guy comedians who sometimes couldn't even get their names on the marquee were often the ones bleeding the most, and they were afraid to say anything. I said to myself, *Someone should do something about this.* And that someone was me.

Right after that, I happened to get a call from a guy who wanted to be my manager and who told me that he could get me on *The Tomorrow Show* with Tom Snyder. When I said I would be happy to do the show, he wanted to know what he should tell the producer I would talk about. "Tell him I'm pissed off," I said. "And I'm going to talk about people I don't like in the business."

"Well," he said, "I don't think that's going to work."

"Tell them that anyway," I said.

I wasn't sure what business this guy had being my manager or anyone else's manager. I knew Tom Snyder would jump at the chance to have a controversial show, which is exactly what happened. My agenda was not to bash a bunch of performers, but to make a point about the state of show business. At the same time, some of the run-ins I had over the years and some of the things I had said would definitely come up.

For instance, years before, when Tony Orlando had a huge hit with "Tie a Yellow Ribbon," I said it was a disgrace when bodies were coming home from Vietnam in boxes to have to hear a fucking song like that. I knew those comments and dozens of others I had made were waiting in the wings, but I was going to do the best job I could under the circumstances to get my story, and the bigger story, out there.

The Tomorrow Show followed Johnny Carson on NBC week-nights. The show aired at one in the morning on the East Coast, but filmed at five in the afternoon. I was informed that before putting me on, the producer had called Walter Kane to check out my story. It was hard for them to believe that Tony Bennett would toss someone off the bill for no good reason whatsoever, and even harder to believe that anyone would promptly return a hundred and sixty thousand dollars on principle. But to his absolute credit, Walter Kane backed me up a hundred percent.

In the studio on March 6, 1981, Tom Snyder gave the audience his introduction and we were off and running:

"First up, we have Mr. Pat Cooper, who has been a comedian for twenty-two years. And in 1980, he began saying things about fellow performers that they did not like. For example, he went on a radio program in Las Vegas one night last year after Helen Reddy had appeared on the same show the previous night. In discussing show business and fortune, Helen Reddy was quoted to have said that being successful in our business is ten percent talent, eighty-five percent ambition, and being in the right place at the right time. Well, the next night Pat Cooper came on and said, 'You know, Helen Reddy was right. That's what she's got—ten percent talent.' And a whole great big fight started. And since then, he has been zinging other performers in show business, and he has gotten himself few invitations to Helen Reddy's house, among other things. Mr. Pat Cooper is our first guest tonight to take a look at the other side of comedy and to talk about why he is very unhappy about the way things are going in his business."

The studio audience gave me a rousing applause, which felt good. The studio was a little like theater in the round, with a raised stage in the middle. The set was basically Tom Snyder in a chair sitting directly opposite the guest. There was no big desk in between. It was just you and Tom face to face having a frank conversation with the country listening in. Tom threw the first pitch:

"Now I told that little story at the top about you going on a radio program in Las Vegas and making that remark about Helen Reddy."

And I swung:

"I think she's a hundred percent wrong when she says it's ten percent talent. It's more than that. It's a hundred percent talent. You gotta lay it down on that floor. She's from Australia, she's got a couple of hit records, now she comes to this country and dictates policy, and I say she can't do that."

And Tom threw a curveball:

"All right, then you had an episode with Tony Orlando. What did you say about him?"

There it was. Bringing up things I once said about Tony Orlando or Helen Reddy was not why I was on the show. I needed to get this thing on track:

"Let me tell you what's bothering me. These are the people who dictate who works with them and who don't work with them. I have a contract with a hotel for eight weeks, and they say you're going to go on with Tony Orlando. I say fine. You're going to go on with Tony Bennett. I say fine. Now Tony Bennett turns around and says to the hotel, 'I don't want him.' I ask the hotel why. They don't answer. 'Well, I have a right to work, and I want to know why you're doing this to me.' At least give me an answer.

This happens again and again. I open at the Hilton ninety-nine percent of the time. I'm booked to open for Steve and Eydie and suddenly they don't want me. I want to know why. The hotel says, 'Well we like you, but they want to go in another direction.' I say, 'What direction?' Steve and Eydie say, 'Tell Pat it's nothing personal, but we want to have Jack Carter.' Fine! 'Cause we love Jack Carter.' Fine! Now I go see the marquee, it says STEVE AND EYDIE in huge letters and Jack Carter's name is an eye test. And I say, 'If you love this guy, why didn't you put his name up there so people can actually see it?' So I think they're hypocrites. It's always *nothing personal*. And I say to myself, *Why doesn't somebody do something about this?* So what do I do? I decide that *I'm going to do it.*

I worked with Jack Jones up in Albany, right. I'm talking about people who don't bring the business in. Now, if you bring the business in, you deserve the money. You deserve the accolades. If you don't bring the business in . . ."

"Now you're saying that Jack Jones doesn't bring business in?"

"No, he doesn't. Absolutely not."

"All right."

"Steve and Eydie bring the business in, so they're dictating policy. If you bring the business in, I say you should dictate some policy. Okay, I'm up in Albany with Jack Jones. This man surrounds me with the band—twenty-eight men. I'm in the center. I gotta work. There's all these music stands around. I say, 'Can you move the band?' I can't work. It's unfair to me. Jack Jones doesn't budge. He thinks, *I'm the star. I'm the boss.* But I think, *No you're not the star, and you're not the boss.* I'm asking you now to please do me a favor and move it. Still no. I offer a thousand dollars to management to build me a platform. They refuse to do that, okay? I say, 'Jack, I'm unhappy.' He still refuses to move the band. What am I gonna do? Three days later, I quit the job. Now they say about me, 'Well, he's getting too big for his britches.' I say, 'I can't work under these conditions. Who are you to do this to me, Jack? I'm a human being.'"

Tom Snyder says, "Except, isn't it a fact that in show business, the headliner gets to call all the shots, including who his or her or their opening act is?"

"Sometimes."

"And don't Tony Bennett, Jack Jones, Steve and Eydie, whoever, have the call as to who they want to open for them?"

"Yeah, but tell me why you don't want me."

"If they would say to you, 'Hey, listen, we don't think you're very funny, we don't like your humor, and we don't happen to like you very much,' that would be jake with you? That would be okay?"

"Then say that to me. Say, 'Pat, we don't like the way you operate.'"

"What if they're trying to spare your feelings? What if . . ."

"No, no, no, they don't spare feelings. If they don't like you, they tell you right in front of your face, because they're swinging. They're doing great. They don't care. There's no feelings involved here. It's the ego. It's an ego trip here. I got a great reputation. I do a great job. I work hard. I got feelings. I care about my business. I put into the business. And so I say to these people who don't put into the business, 'Hey wait a minute, who are you to tell me? When did this happen? I'm in this business twenty-two years. I've built up something and you push me aside?'"

Some hotel corporation gives me eight weeks work. Didn't want it, didn't ask for it, but I signed a contract for it. All of a sudden I got *no* weeks work. I had to give back the contract because I said you can't push me around. You tell me Tony Bennett is my next show, and all of a sudden Tony Bennett says I don't want him. And I say to Tony, 'I don't understand you. You didn't do this to me before.' But I know why he did it. All of a sudden, these headliners start getting panicky because they're not bringing in the business. They need an opening act that will at least fill the room, so that they can get the credit."

Tom Snyder said, "All right now, then it's your contention that there are some people in the industry who are fading stars and who don't bring in the business, and to save their own egos, they'll go for someone who is hotter than you to fill the room to satisfy their egos."

"Absolutely."

"Now let me ask you something. Are you gonna get a lot more work by talking this way on television?"

"Yes, because I have a built-in business. I go around this country. I work all the time. I don't know who works more than I do. I'm a good man because I worry about bringing more business in. I'm the kind of man where if a guy can't afford me, I take the door. I say forget about it. You give me so much of the door. If nobody comes in, you don't lose anything. I'm trying to keep my business open, Tom. My business in Vegas now is starting to close. There's no more name-policy. It's going now to revues. Atlantic City now is going revues."

"I can't challenge your facts in Las Vegas, because I don't know what the receipts are at all the hotels. But I just can't believe for the life of me, sitting here, off the top of my head, that some of the headliners—including some of the people you mentioned—are not doing well."

"I promise you, Tom, that if they were doing the big business for the kind of money that they're commanding, they would never use a David Brenner or a Joan Rivers to open. They would hire a Harry Nobody. They don't want to share success. They give you nothing. But tomorrow, if Pat Cooper became the biggest thing in this country, they'd all fight to have me on the show."

"Let me try this theory on you. Pat Cooper is jealous of other comedians that may be more successful than he is."

"Oh, no, no, no, please don't. That's not right."

"But I have to ask you the question, because this sounds like sour grapes to me."

"No, no. I knew that was going to come out. I've had people say, 'Are you bitter?' I say no. I'm saying that if Rona Barrett said exactly what I said now, that would be called journalism. I say it, they say I'm bitter. I have no reason to be bitter. I'm a very wealthy man, Tom, because I worked at my business. I want to give back to my business. I want to put a stop to some of the nonsense of the stars in my business who think that they own a David Brenner or that they own a Pat Cooper. Joan Rivers and David Brenner right now are bigger names than Tony Bennett. They're bigger names than Lola Falana. They're bigger names than Dionne Warwick. Yet they turn around and they're nice enough to open for these people. So why not turn around and give them credit? They don't give them credit. Tony Bennett don't bring nobody in. David Brenner comes in, it's a sellout. And I don't see Tony Bennett thanking a David Brenner or a Joan Rivers. Come on, we're comics, we're not dogs. We're wonderful, what we do in our business."

"So what you're trying to do then is open up the business a little, to get rid of the hypocrisy and the hype, huh?"

"What happened to caring in my business? My business has been very good to me. What happened to caring?"

Before we wrapped up, I threw in a story about Jerry Vale. Some time ago, my wife had sent a fruit basket to me backstage. The card she wrote to me got lost. Jerry Vale automatically thought the basket had to be his, so he had it taken to his dressing room.

I also said, in a nutshell, what I came on the show to say:

"Life is short. With the millions of dollars we make a year, people are walking the street, can't pay their taxes, can't buy a sandwich, and we're gonna show the public that we're stupid? No. This is a great business. We should explain to the people that at least we're grateful."

"All right, but look at yourself! Here you are, a funny man."

"I'm hilarious."

"An hysterical man. You're getting yourself exercised. You're getting yourself all worked up."

"It's the Italian in me."

"What are you doing to yourself?"

"Do *you* know what I'm doing?"

"No I don't. But do *you* know what you're doing?"

"Yes. I'm not afraid. I have no reason to be afraid. I'm a good working man. I've always worked. I've always made a living. If tonight they tell me you're blackballed from show business, I'm okay, because I'm a hell of a guy."

"All right. Keep 'em honest. Thank you for being here tonight."

"Thank you for having me."

"My pleasure. All right. Mr. Pat Cooper. Good luck, my friend."

With that, Tom Snyder signed off giving a very quick but telling gesture. He winked, sort of with both eyes at once, as if to say, *Yes, good luck, my friend. And you're gonna need it.*

My friends all seemed to agree with him. About one-thirty in the morning on the East Coast, right after the segment aired, they started calling me one after the other to offer me their condolences. They all asked me what I was going to do now that I was out of show business. I told them I was going to raise my price a thousand dollars.

My beautiful wife agreed with Tom Snyder and our friends. It just took me a little longer to find out. She was at our home in Las Vegas, and the show didn't air out there until four in the morning. When I picked up the phone in my hotel room, I wasn't even sure where the fuck I was. All I knew was that Patti was on the other end of the line crying her eyes out.

"What's the matter, sweetheart?"

"You don't deserve this," she said. "What are you going to do now that you're not going to work?"

"What? Are you fucking crazy? I'm not going to work? Patti, I'm going to get more fucking jobs than you can believe from this."

"It's a terrible thing, Pat," she said. "They don't know you. They don't know all the wonderful things you do for people."

"And they don't fucking need to know."

In the little Ohio town my wife came from they all talk in a whis-

per. Even when there's a war on, they whisper, " . . . there's a war . . .
shhh . . . " So nobody fucking knows.

The next day I got phone calls, dozens of them, looking to hire Pat
Cooper. They didn't give a fuck about the "Italian Wedding" routine.
It was all about last night. Controversy breeds money. It was very hard
to get my wife to understand that, but the past twenty-four hours had
certainly helped. I got my point across and also wound up helping
myself. I killed two birds with one stone. I knew there was nothing
wrong with that, especially when one of those birds deserved to be
stoned. And I knew one other thing. It would be a long time before I
had to open for anybody.

7

This Thing of Theirs–
Part I

There are great Italians all around us, but they rarely get the credit they deserve. When was the last time you saw *The Great Caruso* starring Mario Lanza? Probably never. But we've all seen *The Godfather* a dozen times. When was the last time you saw *The Agony and the Ecstasy* about Michelangelo? You'd agonize trying to remember. But the average guy on the street can quote *Goodfellas* all day.

It starts when we're kids and, in the end, has very little to do with being Italian. Every generation loves gangsters—some tough guy throwing another tough guy through a window and sticking a boot up his ass. For my generation, the love affair started with people like James Cagney shouting, "Made it, Ma! Top of the world!" Gangsters are romantic, and unfortunately nobody turned out gangsters more romantic than the Italians.

Things are a lot different when you actually meet these guys. If you started in show business when I did, you were going to meet a lot of them. I did, or at least I assumed I did. I never asked. It was none of my business. Maybe you were with the underworld. Maybe you were with the overworld. I only knew if you were in *my* world. And if you were, I hoped to hell you had some class and dignity.

In the late 1950s, I was working a club in Rhode Island. I was a young kid "pumping oil," as they say, trying to make a name for myself. This was not an easy task. I was a stranger in a strange town, performing for a mostly Italian hard-nosed audience. The gig was for two shows Friday night and another two shows Saturday night, and the pay for the whole thing was about a hundred dollars. I was a skinny 130-pound comic living moment to moment by my wits on stage.

About the middle of the second show on Saturday night, I was starting to really loosen up. As I flipped the microphone from one hand to the other, it happened to drop. The mic bounced off the wooden floor and sounded like a truck backing into a flagpole. I scooped it up quickly and got right back on my feet. When something like that happens you can just let it go or, if the timing is right, make a funny remark. Before I could say anything, though, I heard a shout from the back of the room.

"You motherfucker! You dropped my baby!"

When I heard the word "baby," I thought someone in the audience had dropped a little kid. So I looked around, past the glare of the stage lights. I didn't spot any little kids or hear any crying, but the next thing out of my mouth, addressed to nobody in particular, was, "What is your kid doing in a fucking theater at this time of the morning?" There was another angry shout from the back of the room.

"You son of a bitch! You dropped my microphone! Get the fuck off my stage!"

"What?" I said. "Who the fuck are you talking to?"

The room was silent. Dead silent. I heard a gentleman in the front row calling me. "Son. Son."

"What?!" I asked.

He was calm, and from his seat, he looked me right in the eye, "Son, get out of here and don't look back."

"Why?"

"This guy is a mob guy. He's nuts. That's his microphone, and he's nuts. I'm telling you, get out of here now and don't look back."

As crazy as it was, it made sense. I had crossed some kind of line. I felt it in the room. I was no longer a kid scared of bombing. I was a kid scared of dying. I thanked the audience and put the microphone back on the stand . . . carefully. I walked backstage and found my way to the men's room, which I remembered had a window and an alleyway. What I didn't remember was how small the window was. As I put my hands on the tiles and pushed myself out, I was grateful I was only 130 pounds. At 140, I might have been stuck there long enough for this degenerate lover of microphones to sing me one last song.

Fortunately, I made it into the alleyway and onto the streets of Providence. I didn't know the name of the street or the next one or the next one. I hadn't been paid, so I had only a few dollars in my pocket. But it didn't matter. I kept running and running, knowing only that with each block I was one block farther away from this maniac and his microphone. I felt like I could run all the way back to Brooklyn.

As fast as I ran, I knew I wasn't running from a tough guy. I had already met a few tough guys—guys who could tear your tongue out before you opened your mouth if they really had to. But they very, very rarely had to. In fact, they didn't want to, and that's what made them tough. They were gentlemen. They were classy. They were not looking for a confrontation. If there really was some kind of problem, they were not going to hit you. They would say, "Can I see you outside? Listen, son, you're a young kid, and I know you didn't mean anything by what you said. Just do me a favor and don't do it again."

Frank Palumbo was that kind of man. He owned Palumbo's in South Philadelphia, one of the best and most important clubs in the country at the time for making careers in entertainment and, in some cases, breaking them. Frank Palumbo never came on like a strong guy, but nobody fucked with him. He was Frank Palumbo, and this was his territory. No one jerked him around, and every wiseguy in Philadelphia respected him.

Was he a wiseguy himself? There was a difference of opinion about that. Frank Palumbo was a man any aspiring politician in South Philadelphia would go to for support before an election. When he and Blinky Palermo managed middleweight boxer Billy Fox, they were accused in 1947 of throwing a fight against Jake LaMotta, the "Raging Bull." In 1951, Frank Palumbo was called in front of a Senate investigation into organized crime because known mobsters met at Palumbo's. He never testified and was never charged.

The bottom line was that it didn't matter whether or not Frank Palumbo was a wiseguy. He was a good guy. Period. He raised huge sums of money for children's charities and even bought animals for the Philadelphia Zoo. He turned his father's boarding house into one of the premier clubs in the world, and he became one of the great club owners of all time. He had dancing girls opening the show. Palumbo's was like Radio City in Philadelphia. His wife, Kippee, was a dream. She and her husband gave chances to countless unknown performers.

As a performer, no one treated you better, whether you were Mel Torme, Jerry Vale, Lou Monte, Buddy Greco, or just some struggling comedian from Brooklyn trying to get a job as an opening act. Frank Palumbo put you up at a first-rate hotel down the block, and there was always a bottle of wine in your room. He paid you top dollar and never looked to cheat you out of a dime. I never heard of a single performer who didn't want to go back to Palumbo's. Entertainers fought to go back there.

I was lucky. I never had to fight to go back, and I was treated like a son. Frank would say, "Pat, did you eat? Did you eat? Where are you going? Sit down and eat. *Mangia*. Come on, take a bottle home. Pat, did you get paid? Hey . . . did you get paid, Pat? Pat, thanks for working here. You did a great job last night. People here love you."

Palumbo's had multiple rooms including a couple of ballrooms downstairs. Once in a while, Frank would say, "Pat, I have two weddings going on. Could you just drop by and say hello?" It didn't matter if I was already doing three shows upstairs that same Saturday night. My answer was always, "Of course."

When I showed up, the MC would say something like, "Congratulations once again to the bride and groom. And now, Mr. Pat Cooper would like to say a few words." I would say more than a few. I would do complete routines and make the people laugh. Afterwards, Frank Palumbo would come up to me and say, "Pat, I asked you to say a few words. You didn't have to do twenty minutes. What are you doing?" And I would say, "Mr. Palumbo, that was easy. That was from the heart."

Hollywood should make Frank Palumbo's life story. He was the kind of guy who made you proud to be Italian. He was a great philanthropist and one of the truly great impresarios. But most of all, I was just proud to be his friend.

Another first-rate impresario with mob associations was Skinny D'Amato, owner of the 500 Club in Atlantic City. The 500 Club was an unassuming two-story building on the boardwalk, but, like Palumbo's, it was a hot spot near the center of the entertainment universe. Skinny D'Amato took over the club in the 1940s and later became legendary for breathing new life into Frank Sinatra when his career was in freefall.

In the early '50s, Sinatra's records weren't selling like they had been and he separated from Nancy, the mother of his three children, to go with the voluptuous actress Ava Gardner. By Tiger Woods standards, that might seem like nothing, but in those days it was a major scandal and a career killer. As is well known, Skinny D'Amato had Sinatra performing at the 500 Club when almost nobody else would touch him.

That break was a springboard for Sinatra to resurrect his career and go on to win an Academy Award for his unforgettable role as Maggio in *From Here to Eternity*. You can bet that for years after, Frank Sinatra never turned down an offer to play the 500 Club no matter how busy he was.

When I was booked to perform at the 500 Club in the early '60s, I had a vision in my mind. I saw myself opening for the likes of Dean Martin, Louie Prima, the Count Basie Orchestra, and, of course, Frank Sinatra. What I didn't realize was that I wasn't even prepared to walk into the building.

I went down to Atlantic City on a cold winter afternoon. I introduced myself to Skinny D'Amato, who was playing cards and twirling a matchbook cover. He asked me if I needed any rehearsal time and I said no. "Okay," he said, "you're going to be working the Five Bars." I didn't know from Five Bars. I didn't know if I could work one bar, let alone five.

"I don't mean to be rude or anything, Mr. D'Amato," I said. "But I've really never worked this Five Bars . . ."

"Okay," he said, "it's upstairs. The lounge. There's gonna be a platform up there where all the bars can see you. How much time can you do?"

"About twenty minutes."

"Twenty minutes?" Skinny said. He looked like there was some kind of mistake. There was. "You gotta be kidding me."

"I wish I was," I said. "Mr. D'Amato, I don't know what you want me to do."

"Get up there and talk. And keep talking."

That night I stood on the stage upstairs in the lounge and started talking. It was confusing up there, like theater in the round without a center. I couldn't tell if there really were five bars, but there were at least five people, and they were a rough little crowd. Everyone was talking as if I wasn't there, and I wished I wasn't. I heard a voice from somewhere shout, "Hey, kid, say something funny." Then another voice shouted, "How's your mother?" Then another, "Hey, kid, fuck you!"

I did twenty minutes and walked off. I walked up to Skinny and said, "Mr. D'Amato, I don't mean to be disrespectful, but this is not for me. I'm wasting your time up there. I feel so bad that I can't cut this."

"I understand, son," he said. He gave me a couple dollars and said, "Don't worry about it."

But I did worry about it. It was my fault for taking a job that I knew nothing about, but it was also the fault of the agent who booked it and told me absolutely nothing. It wouldn't have hurt him to explain to me that I wasn't going to be in the main room and that I wouldn't have a singer, a juggler, or a dancer batting behind me—just a bunch of old-time boxers with their gloves off sparring in a gym.

For every Frank Palumbo or Skinny D'Amato, there were ten wiseguys you were better off without. A lot of them wanted to give you things, and you wanted to decline. You knew you were going to pay one way or another. If they picked up your check in a restaurant, you were going to have to entertain at a party. They were great at making you an offer you couldn't refuse.

Sometimes the offer was a two-for-one. In the mid '60s I was working a club in Chicago with Al Martino. I liked Al and had a lot in common with him. He was a first-generation Italian-American from a working-class neighborhood in Philadelphia. He even laid bricks as a kid. But he stopped laying bricks before I did. He recorded a song called "Here in My Heart," which went to the top of the pop charts in both the US and England in 1952.

However, just as Al Martino's career was taking off, the mob bought out his management contract and told him he had to make a "down payment" of $75,000. He paid just enough of it to keep the wiseguys from following him across the Atlantic to England. He lived there, an Italian bricklayer with a golden voice, in exile for most of the 1950s. Eventually, a friend of the family talked to the mob on his behalf, and he was allowed to return to the States. By that time, rock and roll had broken big, and Al Martino was starting almost from scratch. But soon he picked up where he left off. He recorded a string of hits, peaking with "Spanish Eyes," which went gold and then platinum in 1965.

Considering what Al Martino went through, it was understandable that he tried to politely refuse the offer that he and I received in Chicago. A big local wiseguy had brought a lot of people to the show and asked us to appear the next morning at his granddaughter's christening. Al tried to explain that he had another show to do the next night and that trying to sing so early in the morning would jeopardize his voice.

"Don't worry about your voice," the wiseguy told him.

"It's the tool of my trade," Al said.

"You'll drink a little white wine and your voice will be fine. I'm sending a limousine in the morning. You and Pat will come down, and we'll have a nice time."

In the limo the next morning, Al and I were wondering what the fuck we were supposed to do at this christening. Hopefully just walk around, say hello, and mention how cute the little baby girl was. The limo pulled up in front of a mansion so large they could have held a christening in the bathroom.

The wiseguy was happy to see us, and we were comfortable enough walking around the living room shaking hands. Then came the crucifixion. The wiseguy walked over to Al and said, "Why don't you go over there and sing a lullaby to my granddaughter?"

"Excuse me?" Al said.

"A lullaby. Make the kid go to sleep."

"Well, I really can't sing much at this hour." I admired Al Martino. He had balls. Unfortunately he was going to have to use those balls to sing.

"You came here to my house," the wiseguy said. "And now you're going to insult my whole family?" The wiseguy was visibly upset. Al looked over at me for help, and all I could do was bite my lip. I wanted to crawl under a table.

Al walked to the crib like he was walking the plank. He leaned over and started singing the words: "Lullaby . . . end of night . . ." More like end of life. The kid started screaming. Maybe she wanted something more up tempo. Whatever the case, Al Martino, owner of a string of gold records, was failing the one audition you couldn't afford to fail. And the louder the kid screamed, the louder Al sang "Lullaby."

"Get the fuck away from my grandkid!" the wiseguy said. "Get the fuck away from her. I ask you to put her to sleep and the fucking kid is screaming. What the fuck is wrong with you? You sing too fucking loud. What am gonna tell the kid's mother?"

I knew what was coming next but I didn't want to believe it. In my mind there was still a slim possibility it wasn't going to happen. But it did. The wiseguy looked me right in the eye and said, "Make the kid laugh." The Italian women in the room looked at me like I was a marked man, and they looked at the baby girl like she was an orphan. I didn't know who they felt sorry for more.

It was my turn to walk the plank. I ran through every routine I had ever done, from James Cagney in Spanish to my mother hanging St. Anthony upside down. Some of these routines had really killed. Now one of them was going to kill me.

"Ay, goombah," I said to the wiseguy. "I don't think I can make the kid laugh. How about a song?"

"You know what?" the wiseguy said. "Get the fuck out of my house. Both of you. Get the fuck out."

"How do we get back to the hotel?" Al said. He still had his balls.

"You take a fucking cab," the wiseguy said. "I don't want you using my limo."

That was fine. I didn't want to get into the limo. It reminded me of a hearse. We hailed a cab. On the ride back I looked at Al, whose face was as pale as a communion host. I caught a reflection of myself in the mirror and saw that I was just as pale. We had a show that night. There would be no mob stories and no lullabies.

But if you were in show business at that time, you were going to run into people like that. If you were in a bar you might run into an alcoholic. But what I couldn't stand, from either a wiseguy or an alcoholic, was a cliché. Wiseguys had their own clichés, and they pulled them out when they wanted you to do something you didn't want to do. One time a wiseguy I had never met before told me, "We know the same people."

"We do?" I said. "Okay, let's see who you know." I hit this guy with a name. Then another name. Then another. I hit him with about seven Italian names altogether and he didn't know any of them. "Well," I said, "maybe we don't know the same people. I'm not even sure we know the same countries."

Another cliché' I hated was, "Come on, do the right thing." Usually the right thing was the wrong thing. And even if it seemed like the right thing, you still had to wonder. My answer to that cliché' was, "Tell me when the fuck *you're* gonna do the right thing. Because this isn't it."

Of course, a cliché, like a broken clock, can be right twice a day, or at least twice in a lifetime. One time in the late '60s, I got a call in New York from an FBI agent. Apparently, he and I knew the same people. He wanted me to pay him a visit in his office.

"I'm not sure exactly what you want me for," I said. "But I ain't going into no fucking office."

"What's the problem, Mr. Cooper?"

"The problem is, let's say someone sees me walking into your fucking office. Someone will think I'm squealing on somebody. Which I'm not going to do in your office or on the fucking moon. I don't need that."

"You've gotta be kidding me," he said.

"This is one thing I will never kid about," I said. "Think about what I'm saying."

"Okay, Mr. Cooper. Where exactly do you want to go?"

"Stage Delicatessen."

"Your tab?"

"My fucking tab."

At the Stage Deli, this guy ate like he hadn't eaten in three days. Between the first and second half of a corned beef on rye, he asked me about a friend of mine who had been linked to mobsters.

"You know," the agent said, "he's with the underworld."

"And I'm in show business. Arrest us both."

"The two of you went to a fight a couple of Fridays ago, isn't that right?"

"Look," I said, "one time I showed up at his kid's wedding. Another time I showed up at his cousin's wedding. I guess he wanted to reciprocate. Once in a while we have dinner. And yeah, the other day he called me up and said, 'Pat, I got tickets to a fight. Ringside.' And we watched the fights. Is that interesting to you? To me it sounds pretty fucking boring."

"Well, do you know anything about his background?"

"I don't know anything about his background," I said. "I don't know anything about his foreground. I know he doesn't eat like you. Nobody eats like you. Are we getting close to done yet?"

Strange but true, it was an FBI agent—probably one who knew the first FBI agent—who confirmed for me something I had long believed. He said the wiseguys who went around bullying were, more often than not, *gingerellas*. What is a gingeralla? A gingerella is a wiseguy who acts like a bully to cover his homosexuality. They figure if everyone knows they go around busting heads, no one's going to suspect they're gay. What's wrong with being gay? Obviously not a thing. But slapping people around to hide who you are is a disgrace. This FBI agent claimed it was true ninety percent of the time. Someone who spent years listening to wiretaps couldn't have been too far off the money.

If you're going to have any dignity in life, you have to be yourself and not let either side push you around. Sometimes that's like walking a tightrope. But if you're not breaking the law, you have a right to associate with whoever you want to.

I knew another wiseguy from Chicago, this one a sweetheart and a gentleman, who used to come see me when I was performing. He always told me about his boat. Patti and I had a standing invitation to come see his boat and spend the day with this wiseguy and his wife. I always told him maybe next year. I was really not a sailor. But eventually we agreed, and my friend sent a car to pick us up. We drove up Lake Shore Drive to the boat basin on Lake Michigan on a perfect spring day.

When I thought about my friend's boat, I pictured a thirty- or forty-foot motorized sailboat with a cabin and a nice little deck. The boat, however, was more like a ship, a hundred feet long with two decks and every convenience imaginable. It was parked in a dry dock. Patti and I got aboard and were shown to our seats by the maitre d'. My friend and his wife hugged us.

We sat down and a waiter served us coffee, fruit, wine, everything you could order in a restaurant. A maid scurried across the deck with some towels and disappeared. Boats almost as nice as the one we were on floated by and the passengers waved to us like old friends. What a life this was. I took it all in and wondered why we hadn't accepted the invitation sooner. And the day was just beginning.

"Tony," I said, "I gotta tell you, this is so wonderful. You really have it made here. Where are we gonna go?"

"Well," my friend said, "I don't put my boat in the water."

"You don't put the boat in the water? Where do you put it?"

"I leave it right here," he said.

"Why?"

"Well, first of all, I don't want those things on the bottom of my boat. Those things . . ."

"Barnacles?"

"Yeah, barnacles," he said.

"The boat is made to take barnacles," I said. "It's a fucking boat. Look, when was the last time you took it out?"

"I've got this boat here five years," he said. "And it's never been in."

"Five fucking years?" I said. "Then what good is having a boat?"

"I like to be near the water."

"Then get a fucking park bench," I said.

So we sat there for three hours with maids and waiters and a maitre d' running around and went nowhere. All we were missing was a captain. This time I was a fish out of water for real. Three months later, sadly, my friend was found shot to death in the back of a car. There was no burial at sea.

Some things have a way of balancing out if you live long enough and pay close attention, even in the so-called wiseguy world. A few years after I left the 500 Club with my tail between my legs, I was performing with Frank Sinatra at the Sands in Las Vegas. Of all people, Skinny D'Amato walked into my dressing room. He said, "Pat, you were great out there. Just great. I want you to know, you can work the Five Bars anytime."

"Skinny," I said, "I want to thank you. You could have been rude to me after what happened, and you weren't."

"No, no," he said, "you're an honorable guy."

"Well, I had no right taking that job in the first place. I always said when you can't do something, you don't do it. So that was my fault."

I did go back and work the Five Bars, and it was still rough. Fortunately, I was rougher. But strangely, I never got to work the main room. Broadway, yes. Carnegie Hall, yes. But never the main room at the 500 Club. I guess Skinny was waiting till I was seasoned enough. He might have waited too long. The 500 Club burned down in 1973.

By that time, Skinny D'Amato and Frank Sinatra had lost most of their closeness. It was easy to see how that could happen. People said Frank Sinatra was always there for these guys. The truth is, they were there for him. For every favor Sinatra did for them, they did Sinatra twenty. Sam Giancana and his friends helped Frank out time and time again. When Frank was up against a wall, all he had to do was pick up the phone and the wall went away.

One thing I couldn't stand hearing was how all those guys in Sinatra's dressing room were bodyguards. They were wiseguys. For the most part, Sinatra didn't need a bodyguard. Who wanted to hit Frank Sinatra? Nobody. The only physical dispute I recall was when Frank hit Lee Mortimer outside Ciro's for writing something about him in the paper. Sinatra threw one punch in his career, and it went a long, long way.

Things balanced out somewhat for my friend Al Martino as well. In 1972, he played Johnny Fontane in *The Godfather*. The character was loosely based on the life of Frank Sinatra when he was down and being shut out by Hollywood. When Fontane strolls into Connie's lavish wedding at the home of Don Corleone, the women swoon. As Fontane launches into "I Have But One Heart," the women's hearts break in two.

But upstairs, Fontane's heart is broken as he squeals to his godfather that show business isn't fair. One horse's head in a producer's bed later, and Fontane has his movie part. How ironic that my friend Al

Martino got to play Johnny Fontane. Al Martino achieved nothing because of wiseguys. He achieved everything in spite of them.

As for me, no matter how straight a path I walked, I tripped across a wiseguy somewhere along the way. It reminds me of Michael Corleone's line in *The Godfather: Part III,* "Just when I thought I was out, they pull me back in."

8

This Thing of Theirs–
Part II

I had a manager whose name I won't dignify with a mention. I was with him for years. During that time, I did a nice engagement that paid ten thousand dollars, and I was waiting on the check. The way it worked was that the venue would pay my agency, GAC. My agency would pay my manager, and my manager would pay me. A few weeks went by without my receiving the check, so I figured it must be hung up at the agency. When I called GAC, they told me they had sent the check to my manager, which he then denied. But a week later, the financial department at GAC called and asked me to come in. They showed me the cancelled check endorsed by "Pat Cooper." It didn't take us long to figure out that my manager had forged it.

I hired a lawyer the next day, and the lawyer recommended we press charges.

But I was so pissed off I couldn't leave bad enough alone. So I called my manager just to fire him and vent my spleen. "You garbage dump," I said. "How could you do this to me? Do you have any idea how much money you've made off of me? How the hell could you stab me in the back like that?"

A couple of days later, I got a call from a wiseguy who knew my now ex-manager. This wiseguy also knew my father and said what my ex-manager did to me was a disgrace.

"Pat," he said, "he can't do this to you."

"Well," I said, "he did it to me. And I'm pressing charges."

"Pat," he said, "you don't want to put this guy in jail."

"Jail is exactly where the fuck I want to put him. I can't think of a better place. The man committed forgery."

"We'll make good for it," the wiseguy said. "Don't worry about it."

The wiseguy arranged a sit-down at a restaurant on East 72nd Street in Manhattan. Against my lawyer's advice, I walked in, got a table in the back, and waited. A few minutes later, the wiseguy walked in with my ex-manager and my ex-manager's wife. They all took seats, and the wiseguy started talking.

"What he did was wrong, and he knows it. No two ways about it. I'm gonna take care of you for the ten thousand, Pat. But I want him to hear it and know that he's gonna pay me back." Then he turned to my ex-manager, "You understand?"

"Yeah, I understand," my ex-manager said.

What happened next was straight out of a movie, but unfortunately this movie was my life. The wiseguy took his hand and smacked my ex-manager across his face. Then he did it again. Then again. My ex-manager, who could no longer even manage himself, took it. He had on a white dress shirt that was now covered with the blood running from his nose.

"We're gonna make sure you understand," the wiseguy said, still issuing blows. "We're gonna make sure you don't forget."

My ex-manager's eyes were rolling in his head. His wife was screaming and crying. The staff and customers in the restaurant were like my ex-manager—they just took it. I had to do something but I didn't want to die doing it.

"Please," I said to the wiseguy, "do me a favor. I don't need this. You're scaring me, and you're scaring that woman."

"He's a prick," the wiseguy said. "He forged your name!"

"Please, he understands," I said. "We all understand. But we don't need to see blood."

I excused myself and went over to the bar. I ordered a brandy, and as I reached out to pay the bartender, I saw my hand was shaking. I didn't know where this was headed, but obviously it was not headed someplace good. Sure my ex-manager was a prick, but he didn't deserve to pay within an inch of his life. Whatever I could do to make this whole thing go away I decided I would do. My hand was still shaking, so I ordered another brandy. I was not a drinker, so I got drunk. And my hand was still shaking.

The next day I dropped the charges, and my lawyer said to me, "Wrong!"

"But as long as I get the money back," I said, "why press charges?"

"You're not going to get the money back," he said. "You can count on that. Going down there to meet with these people was the worst move you could have made. But given that you did, you should at least have gotten the money before you dropped the charges. Then you would have had them by the balls. Now they have *you* by the balls. And there's nothing I can do for you."

"Okay," I said. "But what if they held the money and threatened me to drop the charges."

"That's not as easy as it sounds," my lawyer said. "Were he to threaten you, we would go to the FBI. Then he's fucked. The most he's making from this is probably the ten grand. Do you think it's worth it to him to get involved with the FBI for ten grand? Definitely not. They know it, and we know it."

My lawyer was right. But I wasn't done making bad moves. When a few months went by and I didn't get the ten grand, I called up the wiseguy myself and asked him when I could expect it.

"After what I did for you?" he said. "You're lucky I didn't ask *you* to pay me."

"What exactly did you do for me?" I said. "If you don't mind me asking. Because I'm still trying to figure that out."

"Well," he said, "grow up, son. This is reality. We all have to live in reality. You want to put a guy in jail for a lousy ten thousand?"

"So now my money becomes a lousy ten thousand?" I said. "It wasn't a lousy ten thousand when that asshole took it. And it wasn't a lousy ten thousand when you held on to it. But now that I want it back, it's a lousy ten thousand."

This was a nice racket they had going. Whether my ex-manager paid the wiseguy the whole ten grand or they split it, everybody won, except me, of course. So I figured two can play this game. Or three. I called another wiseguy and explained the situation. He said he might be able to help me, but I would need to advance him three thousand dollars to talk to the first wiseguy.

Suddenly I was going to be in for thirteen grand. For all I knew, I would wind up calling a third wiseguy to deal with the second wiseguy, and a fourth to deal with the third. I did the math in my head and told the second wiseguy I would have to think about it and call him back. I never did.

Months and years went by and I never heard from the first wiseguy, which was no big surprise. My lawyer asked me why I didn't listen to him, and I told him because I'm a schmuck. "No," he said, "it's because you're a nice guy. That's really how they got you. Maybe next time, if there is a next time, you'll know." The truth was, we were both right. I was a very nice schmuck.

The problem with next time is that when it comes, you might overreact. And because the next time is never exactly the same, you may not even know you're overreacting.

While the Italians generally had the market cornered on great singers, they held only a small share of the great comedians. My friend—who

I will simply call "Lenny"—was an exception. He was a successful recording artist and a top-notch comedian. But this nice gentleman and World War II veteran had a gambling problem.

I was working with Lenny in Chicago in the fall of 1971. He was opening and I was closing, but sometimes he was late, and when he was, most of us in the show knew that he was at the track. In that situation, you don't go to the boss. You cover for your friend by opening the show, and you don't mention it. And that's exactly what I did.

When I went ahead to my next engagement at Palumbo's in nearby South Philly, I got a call from Lenny saying he wanted to meet me. He wasn't on the bill at Palumbo's. This was over a different matter. He needed a loan of fifteen hundred dollars because he was having big trouble with the Internal Revenue Service. How do you have a string of hit records, work constantly, and still have problems with the IRS? You gamble with Uncle Sam's share.

I told Lenny I would lend him the money. He came right down to Palumbo's and picked it up, and didn't even stay for the show. When I considered how many race tracks and underground betting parlors there were between South Philly and Atlantic City, I gave myself a swift kick in the ass.

Over the next few months, I made a point of not calling Lenny every five minutes to ask about the money, no matter what my impulse was. I didn't want to turn a friend into an enemy for fifteen hundred dollars. So I called exactly once, and I got the routine. The routine that everyone, including Lenny, used was, "Ay, goombah, I'll give you your fucking money!" Which made me wonder—which did I want repaid more, the *lousy* money or the *fucking* money?

The following summer, '72, I was hired to perform at the Democratic National Convention in Miami Beach. The Democratic Party was split between the old timers who were pro-union and concerned about bread-and-butter issues and the newcomers who were pushing for women's rights, ethnic rights, and gay rights. What united them all was a desire to see the war in Vietnam end. That, and Pat Cooper, who poked fun at everyone.

After the convention, I stayed in Miami for a while. The Republican National Convention was taking place the following month, also in Miami Beach. It was a rarity for both parties to hold their convention in the same city. But that was about all they had in common. The economy was pretty good. Nixon was cutting deals with China and the Soviet Union, while the Democrats were busy sniping at each other. The bottom dropped out for the Democrats when it was learned that their vice-presidential candidate had received electroshock therapy as treatment for depression.

I got a phone call from my good friend Dominic Bruno, who owned a hotel in Syracuse called the Three Rivers Inn. He suggested we go watch the show at the Republican Convention and say hello to a friend of ours who was performing there—Lenny. I told Dominic, with all due respect, that this guy owed me fifteen hundred dollars. I explained that it would have been one thing if he had said, "Pat, I'm in trouble right now. I can't pay it." Then I would have told him to forget about it. But he gave me the routine, and I deserved better than that. I told Dominic if I saw Lenny I might make a scene. But Dominic convinced me to go anyway.

We had fourth-row seats at the Miami Beach Convention Center. It was packed with well-groomed Chamber-of-Commerce types who ran the country. My old pal Lenny came out with a guitar and ran through a string of hits. Then he began his rendition of the famous Connie Francis tune "Who's Sorry Now." I tried to enjoy the show, but the more I watched, the harder it got. There he was, getting applause from the upstanding pillars of society. This had to be a decent gig for him. I, of all people, had some idea what a national political convention paid. He could have taken a tiny sliver of that fee and said, "Hey, Pat, I really appreciate what you did for me."

Then came the lyrics. Sometimes you hear exactly what you feel in a song and it's overwhelming:

> *Just like a friend*
> *I tried to warn you somehow*
> *You had your way*
> *Now you must pay*
> *I'm glad that you're sorry now*

Usually when I was upset, my mouth led and my body followed. This time my body led. I jumped out of my seat and into the aisle, and climbed up on the stage. Lenny was on the other side of the stage and looked like he had seen the ghost of Al Capone. I grabbed an open mic and started singing, "Who's sorry now, Lenny? Who's sorry now? I lent you fifteen hundred dollars. Now you must pay." It could have been the best comedy routine in the history of show business, center stage of American politics. Instead, Lenny turned white as a sheet, dropped his guitar, and ran off the stage.

"Who's sorry, now, Lenny?" I couldn't stop myself. I started to run after him, and in the process, stepped on his guitar. My foot went right through the hollow body, and I thought, "Shit. Well, take it off the tab." Before I got too far offstage, a bunch of Republicans and their bodyguards stopped me. One of them, who looked like he might have been a delegate from the Deep South, said, "'Scuse me, suh, what gives you the right to get up on that stage?"

"Lenny and I are friends," I said. "This is like a running fucking gag. It's okay, really."

But it wasn't. The gentleman was absolutely right. I was out of line. I asked to see Lenny backstage. I knew I could make all of this go away if we could just talk face to face for three minutes. But that wasn't going to be possible. My friend had collapsed in his dressing room. The ambulance was taking him to the hospital. *Who's sorry now, Pat? Who's sorry now?*

I learned that Lenny, who was on doctor's orders not to drink, was so shaken up backstage that he grabbed a bottle of whiskey and poured half the contents down his throat. This induced a stroke. Now he was lying in a hospital bed fading in and out of consciousness. What a shmuck I was for fifteen hundred dollars. I thought, *God forbid this poor guy dies, I'm going to the electric chair.* Talk about shock therapy.

Dominic was almost as upset with me as I was with myself.

"What were you thinking, Pat?"

"I wasn't thinking, Dom."

I asked Dominic for a favor. Since he was close to Lenny, did he know anyone at the hospital? I wanted to go over there and apologize to him in person. I would be quiet. I didn't want to cause any commotion. Dominic told me he would see what he could do.

On the way over to the hospital the next day, I felt like I had to explain myself again. "Dom, I really like the guy. It wasn't about the fifteen hundred. I'm not a heartless bastard. But the guy was practically spitting in my face." We walked right through the front entrance of the hospital. Security didn't say a thing. When we walked in the room, there was Lenny in bed asleep. He looked half-comatose. There was an IV tube sticking out of his arm and a couple wires running from his chest to a monitor. I thought, *Jesus Christ, did I do all this?* I pulled up a chair next to the bed, leaned over, and gave the speech of my life.

"Lenny . . . Lenny . . . Pat Cooper here. Are you there, Lenny? Lenny, I'm so sorry. I was out of order. You know how crazy I get sometimes. It's not even the money, Lenny. In fact, forget about the fifteen hundred. Forget about it. And I know I broke your guitar. I'll buy you another fucking guitar. Just please get well, Lenny. Can you hear me, Lenny? It's me, Pat. This thing has been eating me up inside, my friend. I just want you to get the fuck up and out of here and for us to go back to being *paisans*. So please, Lenny, can you forgive me? I mean, I love you and all of that shit."

He blinked a little and his eyes moved a bit. Other than that, Lenny was motionless. After about an hour of this, Dominic suggested we go. I dropped him off at his place, went back to my hotel room, and continued to fret. I felt like the other shoe was going to drop very soon. Whenever the phone rang, I thought it could be the police. Or a lawyer. Or, worst of all, Dominic informing me that Lenny had passed.

Two days later, I got a call from Dominic and braced myself. But he had good news. Lenny was awake and doing much better. Dominic had, in fact, gotten a call from him about me. "Dom," Lenny had said, "I just woke up from this terrible fucking nightmare. I dreamed Pat Cooper was in my room. He was whispering in my ear, 'Lenny, you son of a bitch, where's my fucking money? Where's my fucking money?! Fifteen hundred dollars, Lenny!'" Dominic was laughing as he was telling me this, but I didn't think it was that funny.

"Dom," I said, "what the hell did you tell him?"

"Don't worry, Pat," Dominic said. "I told him you were in the room with me, but you were apologizing the whole time."

"Okay, okay . . ."

"Yeah," Dominic said. "I told him, 'Listen, Lenny, Pat felt fucking terrible. He'll do whatever it takes to make it up to you. He said forget about the fifteen hundred dollars. And he'll buy you a new guitar.'"

"Listen," I said, "thank you for calling, Dom. I feel better already. How much does he want for the guitar?"

"Thirty thousand."

"Thirty thousand dollars? For that fucking guitar? Is he out of his fucking mind?"

"I'm just saying what he said, Pat . . ."

"I stepped on a guitar, not a fucking Rolls Royce. You tell him he can go fuck himself!"

Things calmed down for a couple of weeks. And then the other shoe dropped. I got a call from a wiseguy by the name of Sonny G. He wanted to know when I was going to pay Lenny for the guitar.

"None of your fucking business," I said.

"What?"

"You heard me," I said. "It's none of your fucking business."

"Well," he said, "that's a bad attitude. I have to figure out what I'm gonna do here."

"Do what you gotta do," I said.

I couldn't sit still after I got off the phone. I couldn't sleep, and I couldn't eat. So I called my old friend Frank Palumbo in Philadelphia. I explained the whole story to him and told him Sonny G. was threatening me.

"He's what?!"

"He's threatening me," I said. "Now I don't know what the fuck to do."

"Pat," he said, "he's not gonna threaten you no more. I guarantee it."

A few days later, I got another call from Sonny G. This time, *his* attitude was a lot different. "Pat, Jeez," he said. "I was only kidding. You had to go and call Frank Palumbo?"

"Well, you see," I said, "I was only kidding, too. And Frank Palumbo was also just kidding. We're all just fucking kidding."

Three days later, they found Sonny G. in the trunk of a car. He had been beaten to death with a hammer. *Holy shit,* I thought. *Is this a coincidence, or did all this really happen because I lent my friend Lenny fifteen hundred dollars?* I needed this like I needed tuberculosis.

For the next couple of years, I wondered periodically if I was a mental case. I got my answer at dog track in Hollywood, Florida. I was at the ticket window making a bet, and the guy in the cage said, "You know who's here, Pat? Your buddy Lenny."

"What? That fuck is still gambling?"

"I guess so. He's sitting over in Section B."

I stormed away from the ticket window and spotted Lenny leaning against the rail in Section B. "Lenny," I shouted, "you cocksucker! What the hell is wrong with you? You'd give a dog fifteen hundred dollars before you pay me back? You know, you really stuck it up my ass . . ."

He saw me and ran. It was like the Republican National Convention all over again without the guitar. I started to run after him, and my mind raced along with my feet. *How can he be this way? A person is dead because of him. There's a body! Where does this thing end?*

It had to end here, at a dog track in Hollywood, Florida. I stopped myself after about fifty yards and just let him go. Thank God Lenny could run that way again, even if it was from me in fear for his life. I didn't need to put myself back in the electric chair. Another collapse and I'm a two-time loser. There couldn't ever be a third time. Ever. This was out of my system, for good. And the strange thing was I really liked the guy. It was good to get off that merry-go-round before it became a ring of death again.

You learn in life that what goes around comes around if you're around long enough to see it. And the last thing you need to do is push it around faster. Believe me, it's going to go around with or without you. When you force it, you can go straight to jail without passing go and without collecting two hundred dollars. Or fifteen hundred.

Once, it came around in Rhode Island almost twenty years after the fact. I was working with the sensational singing duo Sandler and Young at the theater in the round just outside of Providence. There was a knock on my dressing room door. I opened it, and standing there was a tough-looking guy in his fifties or so.

"Pat Cooper! You recognize me?"

"No," I said, "I'm sorry. What can I do for you?"

"You owe me a microphone." I never had his face clearly in my mind. But when I heard him say the word "microphone," it was like I was a kid again, running for my life.

"You're the guy with the microphone?"

"Yeah," he said. "But I'm gonna forget about it. You don't owe me nothing."

"You're damn right I don't owe you nothing," I said. "You owe *me* something. I was a kid and you scared the hell out of me. For no reason. Over a fucking microphone! Let me ask you something, did that make you a better man?"

"Look, I'm not here for that, so cut the shit. That was my property, but I'm willing to forget about it."

"It seems like you're here threatening me," I said.

"I'm not threatening you," he said. "I need two tickets."

"What?"

"I need two tickets."

"To this show?"

"Yeah, to this show."

"Well," I said, "I have no authority. You'll have to go see Sandler and Young."

I knew we were sold out anyway, and thank God for that. I might have dropped the microphone on this guy's head.

"You're not going to get me tickets?"

"No," I said. "I'm not gonna do it. *I can't.*"

"That's bullshit," he said. "You go talk to the boss." He pushed his way in the door a step, and I shouted.

"Security! Security! We have a problem over here!"

The guy from security looked like Bruno Sammartino the wrestler. His chest was like the grillwork of a Mack truck, and his neck was like a fire hydrant.

"What's the problem here?" the security guy said.

"This guy is threatening me for tickets to the show," I said. "I can't do it, and he won't take no for a fucking answer."

"Listen," the security guy said to Mr. Microphone, "you got two minutes to get out of this building or I'll bend you in fucking half. Do you understand me?"

This wiseguy turned around and walked down the hall, and the guy from security followed. I didn't know if the wiseguy was thrown out through the front door or the back. I kind of hoped they pushed him out the bathroom window.

9

No Patsy

When you're a stand-up comic, you pay all sorts of dues. When you see a stand-up comic do a good five minutes, he's paid for it with five bad years. But eventually you've paid enough dues so that you can do more or less what you want to do on stage. Then maybe you can make the leap to television and pay dues all over again.

When I was booked on *The Ed Sullivan Show* in 1969, Sullivan had a reputation as a czar. He looked more like an insurance salesman than the host of a popular variety show. My main experience on national television to that point was four episodes of *The Jackie Gleason Show,* where Jackie made you feel comfortable. Ed Sullivan looked like he forgot to take the cardboard out of his shirt and made you feel even less comfortable than he looked. It didn't matter that he kept calling me "my paisano" or referring to me as "Pat Henry," I wanted to be invited back.

Ed Sullivan was uptight about any word uttered on his show that didn't fit in with his world. It was well known that when the Rolling Stones appeared on the show, he had them change "Let's Spend the Night Together" to "Let's Spend Some *Time* Together." Realizing for the first time in my life that "night" was a dirty word, I wondered what the hell Sullivan would pull from my act.

After rehearsals I got my answer. He walked up to me and said, "My paisano, you can't say 'pregnant.'"

"Mr. Sullivan," I said, playing dumb, "is that a curse word?"

"My paisano, the word 'pregnant' implies a sexual act."

"What am I supposed to say?"

"Well," Sullivan said, "why don't you say 'expecting'?"

"Mr. Sullivan, no disrespect, but 'expecting' is not a funny word."

"Mr. Henry, do you want to do a second show?"

"Well, yeah," I said. "I expect to."

"Then you'll avoid using the word 'pregnant.' That's why we have rehearsals, my paisano. To eliminate the garbage."

So I went along with it. I didn't want to lose the next show for my friend, Pat Henry.

You went along with everything in television in those days. It wasn't like stand-up. In stand-up, a red light goes on, and if you're nobody, you have a minute to get off the stage. If you're somebody, you have two. In television, when they give you the cut signal with the finger, it means "cut." When you get the finger, it doesn't matter if you're in the middle of a routine or getting a standing ovation. It's bye-bye, arrivederci, au revoir, sayonara, shalom, or you'll be doing the rest of the bit during an Alka-Seltzer commercial—and you won't be back for another one.

When I did *The Dean Martin Comedy Hour* in late 1967, I was thrilled. I thought Dean was a tremendous talent from the first time I saw him on stage at the Loews State Theater in New York over twenty years earlier. When I saw him later with Jerry Lewis, I knew they were both gold. When I flew out to the NBC studios in Burbank, California, to do Dean's show, my understanding was that I would get to be in a skit as well as do stand-up comedy.

Dean Martin came from the streets like I did, so I felt there was an automatic relationship there. We chatted and got ready to do a skit where Dean was in the barber's chair and I was his barber. The show was taped, and one of the first things I noticed were the cue cards that were all over the place.

Dean was a member of the freewheeling Rat Pack, but on his show, he didn't ad-lib. Sometimes when you watched the show on television, you could actually see his eyes or even his whole head moving back and forth while he read from the cards. He didn't care. It was almost a joke, like they were having a good time doing a parody of a variety show and the audience was in on the joke.

I felt like I was in on the joke, too. So as the skit began, with Dean under the barber cloth and me pretending to cut his hair, I said my first line, which was some small talk about something that happened the day before. There was a pause. Dean Martin didn't answer me. So I said, "Dean, are you awake?"

Then he turned around, looked right at me, and said, "Why do you think we have these cue cards?"

"To read," I said.

"Then why did you leave out two words?"

"Dean, I'm sorry. I didn't know you wanted me to read every word."

"Why do you think these guys get paid?" he said.

As much as I hoped this was a gag, it wasn't. The whole incident was over a "this" and a "these." I had no idea how sensitive a guy like that could be. So we went back to the skit and I did the thing word for word.

I was glad to get to my stand-up routine, which was four minutes on the nose. I was comfortable. This was my territory. I wasn't holding a scissor to someone else and no one was holding one to me. The last thing in the world I wanted to do was look like I was reading something, so I told the director, Greg Garrison, no cue cards.

I heard the announcer say, "Ladies and gentlemen, Pat Cooper!" I walked out on stage, hit my mark, and for some strange reason I couldn't remember my first line. It might as well have been the first line of *Moby Dick*. I recalled zilch. My mind was a blank canvas. So I jumped to the second line, and I couldn't remember that one either. Or the third. It was as quiet as a funeral home without the funeral. The silence lasted a minute or two but felt like an hour. So I broke the ice like Jerry Lewis.

"Dean! Dean! Where's the cue cards? I forgot my act!"

There was some laughter, and then Greg Garrison calmed me down. They set up a few cue cards for me, and I did the four minutes. Maybe needing cards was contagious. I hoped I would shake it before my next engagement. But I understood television a little better having made a few appearances, and it would be a while before I ad-libbed again on camera.

In 1973 I got my chance. My manager at the time was a wonderful man named Bernie Brillstein. Bernie was a New Yorker from my era. He worked with the William Morris Agency when I was with them, but in 1969 he opened the Brillstein Company. The Brillstein Company produced *Hee Haw* and *Muppet* specials and was busy developing new shows.

I was thrilled when Bernie got me an engagement with Sergio Franchi at the Coconut Grove. I wasn't thinking too much about television, but Bernie Brillstein was. He brought some people from NBC down to the Coconut Grove and they liked me and the idea that Bernie had pitched them. And that's how the TV show *Patsy* was born.

The tagline for *Patsy* was "The manager of a small Italian restaurant must deal with his oddball relatives." For years, Bernie heard me tell audiences about things from my culture, like how sauce talks to you and how if you slice onions thin enough they melt in the pan. And all about my hardheaded mother and my wonderful big-hearted Uncle Viduche. In a business where an actor is rightly thrilled just to get a job, I was getting more than that. I was getting a vehicle.

The writers Duke Vincent and Bruce Johnson sat down with me to get my input. I really liked the basic plot. I was Patsy, of course, and Patsy's dream was to extend the restaurant to create a banquet room. I get the permit to push the rear wall twelve feet into the rear yard, but there is one problem. The rear yard is my Uncle Viduche's zucchini garden, and he lives for his zucchini. I don't have the heart to tell him.

I thought the main scene between my uncle and me was beautifully written because it captured the clash between progress and tradition. My uncle was painted as eccentric, but more because of his big heart than being out of touch.

The back story was another classic Italian dilemma. My girlfriend is a non-Italian, and my Mama won't have it. We didn't want Mama's reaction to be too cliché, so we gave her a real edge. She loads up my girlfriend's antipasto with garlic and serves her thirty-year-old wine gone sour. She waits for her forty-year-old son's return home from a date, and gets a case of *agita* over the time he gets in—two-thirty-six-and-a-half in the morning. From that moment on, Mama refers to my girlfriend as Miss Two-Thirty-Six-and-a-Half. I know that Mama's first meeting with my girlfriend is headed for disaster when I tell my bartender, "The last time there was a WASP in the house, Mama killed it."

Then we went a little further with the repartee. I have trouble explaining to Mama exactly how Shirley, my girlfriend, wound up with a pan of lasagna on her chest the night before. I call it an accident, and Mama calls her "a freak." She explains that she gets her information from *As the World Turns*. Mama never steps out of her classic character, but she comes dangerously close, and that's what I thought gave the script a little extra something.

And speaking of a little extra something, we wrote a funny scene where Mama teaches me how to make sauce the right way. She shows me the "rhythm" of stirring and warns about always doing what the tomatoes expect you to do. By the time the sauce is bubbling, I'm singing "Bada-bing" and "Bada-boom." I was excited, because I thought the script had the right ingredients. It was genuinely Italian, but also a bit ahead of its time.

The actor they hired to play Uncle Viduche was Joe DeSantis, who had the perfect face for the part and had done probably a hundred similar roles. Penny Stanton played Mama. She was small, feisty, old country, and full of garlic—and you wouldn't know that she actually sounded nothing like her character a second after they yelled cut. Our director was Garry Marshall, who was already well known for *The Odd Couple.*

We were on the set in the NBC studios in Burbank, California, at six in the morning. The plan was to shoot the episode like a movie, piece by piece, shot by shot, and go all day until we got it right. Bernie Brillstein and his co-producer, Irv Wilson, really wanted to nail it before showing it to the network. I was wired and nervous. I couldn't believe this was really happening. I was up the night before looking over my lines, but I didn't *memorize* them. I didn't want this to be *The Dean Martin Comedy Hour.* I wanted this to be a spin-off of stand-up, where things were funny because they were in the moment. I did make notes and go over the notes, but then I threw the notes away. The more I read them back, the less funny they sounded. So I decided to trust my balls.

My balls got put in a vise-grip by nine AM. Penny told me what I was doing was wonderful, but she couldn't follow it. She needed her cue line or else she would be left standing there, which is what she did the first part of the morning. So I did what I had to do. I continued improvising here and there, but I made sure I finished with the cue line. This worked, in so far as we started getting work done. But I could feel the flow stiffening up a little.

Then the vise-grip got a little tighter. To begin with, I couldn't say "damn." A minute later, we tried using the phrase "breaking your balls," but that wasn't going to fly on the network. We had to put something else in there. It could have been a butt or a back or a belly, but we settled on brains. Yes, Mama was breaking my brains. Brains are broken by mortar shells and algebra exams, but not by Mamas. Mamas break balls. Then during the big tomato sauce scene, we had to stop and take out "marinara," because someone thought it sounded too much like "marijuana." As someone who got high on marinara all his life, I told them to stop breaking my brains.

It was a long day. We did certain pieces of certain scenes over and over again. Part of me knew that each take ran the risk of getting flatter. Another part of me wanted to stop when I screwed up a word, but half the time they told me not to worry about it. We would do pickups later. We didn't start those till about ten at night, and it went on till two in the morning, when we finally wrapped. They told us we got everything, and after twenty hours on the set, who was going to argue?

Patti and I got to watch the final cut. It was decent, but I thought they threw away a lot of laughs. It wasn't supposed to be a hundred percent laughs in the first place, but seventy-five percent would have been nice. It was really a mixture of laughs and pleasantness, and not a bad mix. There were scenes where music was used and probably shouldn't have been, because the music worked against the gags.

There was a minute here and a minute there where there was rhythm, but the rhythm wasn't all the way through. That was a lot to ask of a dozen actors thrown onto a set for a day and a night. There was no doubt in my mind that four, six, eight episodes down the road, we could have found that rhythm, but the nature of the business is that you hardly ever get that chance.

When it was over, I turned to Patti and told her I felt in my heart that the network wasn't going to pick up *Patsy*. It wasn't because of the rhythm or the cue lines or the censored words. That didn't help, but it was more about the content. There was no such thing as an Italian-American sit-com in the history of television to that point. At least nothing genuine or even close to genuine. And I didn't feel we were going to be the first. Maybe we were ahead of our time by ten years, but in 1973, *Patsy* would have to be more than a sit-com with a thirteen-week deal. It would have to be a cultural revolution.

When they brought me in to the NBC executive offices to tell me they weren't going to pick up *Patsy,* I was disappointed but not shocked. I already knew they showed it to a test audience who gave it a lukewarm reaction. Of course, a few years on a successful show could make or remake a career, and I wanted that for the other actors as much as I wanted it for myself. But I was already successful, so I asked myself if I really wanted to work that hard every week. The pressure to come up with that much material twenty-six times a year and maintain the quality was something I could probably do without.

I could have gotten up out of that big leather chair at that very moment and walked away satisfied and grateful that at least I had my shot and took it. But then the executive from NBC looked me in the eye and told me not to feel bad because they were going to develop an animated version of the show. I thought that would work about as well as a cartoon version of *The Godfather.* Maybe at the end, the Corleones could all get up and sing a song about what they learned. I could take being cancelled, but not being bullshitted. I was no patsy. But I backed off and held my tongue. It was a great experience and that's how I wanted to remember it.

The show, however, wasn't completely dead. It came back for a little while to haunt me. They aired the pilot episode of *Patsy* exactly once, and the biggest reaction came from a small but loud audience who claimed the show was presenting Italian-Americans in a negative light. NBC was flooded with calls, and I was flooded with memories of the Italian Anti-Defamation League filing a suit over the "Italian Wedding" routine. I couldn't believe anyone could take this kind of offense over an endearing look at Italians, and that I had to take shit for a show that wasn't even picked up. If anybody deserved the cartoon version, it was these people.

I made a point of thanking Bernie Brillstein for sticking his neck out on my behalf from beginning to end. "Bernie, I love you," I said. And I went back to doing stand-up.

There was plenty of television to do without developing a sit-com, and I did all of it. If I got called, I went. For years, hardly a month went by without being called to do a major talk or variety show. But in 1976, something came along that I thought was really special. Willie Weber called me to say *The Don Ho Show* wanted to book me. I said of course. Then a bell went off in my head, and the second I got off the phone, I told Patti we were going on a trip down memory lane.

Almost twenty years earlier, I was a bricklayer, laying bricks at the new NBC studios in Midwood, Brooklyn. Those were some of the most crooked bricks ever laid by mankind. It was a joke, a sad joke. And when we finished that job, I thought they'd try to turn the building around to put my sloppy joints in the back where they belonged. I thought they'd rename the studio Nasty Brickwork by Caputo.

But the studio survived and was the home to wonderful shows by folks like Perry Como and Mitch Miller. My understanding was that *The Don Ho Show* was shot there as well, so I told Patti to get ready to cross the East River and see why I chose comedy as a profession. At the same time, it would be a triumph to return to the scene of the crime without my back against a brick wall. But before we could hop on the Number 2 train, I found out *The Don Ho Show* was being filmed that week at the Don Ho Theater in Hawaii.

Fourteen hours was a long way to fly to hear three bars of "Tiny Bubbles." The flight from New York to San Francisco was five hours. There was a layover (or in this case, a lei-over) of a couple hours, and then another seven hours to Honolulu. A limousine was waiting for me at the Honolulu airport, and I arrived at the Don Ho Theater twenty minutes later. There was Don Ho and his tiny bubbles. Don said aloha, and there were palm trees and coconuts everywhere. There were cameras all over the place, and for every camera, there were ten beautiful girls with hula skirts.

Like me, Don Ho was a little tired, having just flown in from somewhere. It didn't matter, because there was no audience. The Don Ho Theater was so empty you could hear a pineapple drop. As long as a weary performer could go out there and get it right—on take one or take five—they could dub in the audience later.

After I got off the stage, one of the producers told me they had a nice cabin waiting for me so I could get some rest and see the islands the next day. I said thanks, but told him to give the cabin to the hula girls. There was a plane leaving for New York in four hours and I was going to be on it. For me, work was work. And when it was over, I didn't hang out very long, whether it was Brooklyn or Hawaii. I took my vacations at home.

When I showed up at our apartment door in New York, Patti looked like she had seen a ghost.

"What happened? I don't believe it."

"Believe it, darling."

"We just said goodbye," she said. "What about sleep?"

"I slept on the plane. Don't be so upset. I'm a good husband. I'm home in time for dinner. I could have been dining with hula girls."

Patti started laughing. She got me. She always did. A few hours later, I got a phone call from Willie Weber. He was in deeper shock than my wife.

"Patti told me. Thirty-six hours to do six minutes. What the fuck is wrong with you? You were in Hawaii. Why didn't you go in the ocean?"

"I'm not a swimmer, Willie. The fish don't come to my fucking house, and I don't go in the fucking ocean."

The truth was, I would have preferred to visit the studio in Brooklyn to flying halfway around the world, so I treated both the same. For me, it was all about working. I laid bricks back then and was paid in gold bricks today, but I still had a job to do. I wasn't a lingerer. I wasn't a tourist. I wasn't into hanging around. The sooner I got home, the sooner I could work again. It was always soon.

In television, the more you did, the more you could do. Whenever I was in the Los Angeles area, I would visit a nice couple I knew. They had a lovely daughter named Elaine Joyce, who was an actress and did guest roles on what seemed like every popular television show from *Love American Style* to *Green Acres* to *Kojak*. Before long, she was appearing on every popular game show from *Match Game* to *What's My Line* to *I've Got a Secret*.

Elaine's husband was actor Bobby Van, who was probably best known for starring in the movie *The Affairs of Dobie Gillis*. He was also a song-and-dance man and had roles in MGM musicals of the '50s like *Because You're Mine* and *Kiss Me Kate*. Bobby originally had a nose like Ray Bolger—the Scarecrow in *The Wizard of Oz*. But he had that nose fixed, which I thought was a mistake. It was never broken in the first place.

In 1979, Bobby Van was the host of a syndicated game show called *Make Me Laugh*. Three professional comedians each had a minute to make a contestant from the audience laugh. The contestant got a dollar for each second he didn't laugh, and if he survived all three comedians, the $180 doubled to $360. When I got a call to do the show, I knew it was because I was in the mix in California. That was fine. When someone said "Make me laugh," I always did.

But not this time. It turns out that when people are paid sixty bucks a minute not to laugh, they're pretty good at it. When the first contestant came out, a sweet girl in her twenties who looked like she came straight off the plains of Nebraska, I figured she'd go back to the Midwest with about eight dollars in her pocket.

"Hello, Rebecca. I saw your movie *Rebecca of Sunnybrook Farm*.

You were marvelous. I got a daughter who looks just like you. Peculiar, but she looks just like you. She says to me, 'Could we go on a vacation?' I never had a vacation. I said to my father, 'Pa, could I go on a vacation?' He says, '*Yes. You gonna go on a the fire escape.*' One afternoon I'm sitting on the fire escape, it starts to rain. I bang on the window. I say, 'Pa, it's raining.' He says, '*I cannot a hear you. You on a vacation.*' Then my mother got mad at me because I didn't write. Rebecca, this is it. This is the big time. If I do good here, next year—Albany!"

This was classic material that had made audiences laugh for two decades. The studio audience was no exception. But they got in for free. As for Rebecca of Sunnybrook Farm, she was like the Scarecrow, though not exactly. The problem on this game show was there were no half-points or half-dollars. When it came to scoring a laugh, they didn't count lip-biting, lip-quivering, or swallowing your own gas. It was a lot like diving into deep water for a minute then coming up for air. It was a tough show. It was like trying to make Hitler laugh in a Jewish neighborhood.

The highlight of the show was having Howie Mandel follow me. Howie was a young comedian from Canada who made a splash at The Comedy Store in Los Angeles. He was a good guy and fun on the set, not like a lot of game show stars who were always looking for perks. Howie came out looking like a cross between Groucho and Chico, and did a routine about how his toupee looked so real people thought his face was fake. By the end of his minute, he had transformed his act into a revival led by a Southern Baptist preacher. He won the audience over, but he couldn't crack Rebecca of Sunnybrook Farm.

That made me feel better, and not so much because I wasn't alone. I knew I was watching the birth of something special. There's nothing more wonderful than watching a guy grow like that before your very eyes. Howie had the kind of energy that you couldn't buy. There were always a few special comedians who had you laughing *before* they said something. You knew what was coming next was funny, so you laughed in advance. Howie Mandel had that quality. When he put that rubber glove over his head and blew it up, I blew up, too. I didn't know exactly what was coming next for Howie, but I knew it would be good, and I knew it would go on for a long, long time.

Unfortunately, Bobby Van was diagnosed with a brain tumor and left the planet the next year. When these terrible things happened to people you knew and liked, you never had an explanation. You only hoped they were in a better place . . . with a better time slot.

F. Scott Fitzgerald said there were no second acts in America. This was funny because he came to Hollywood and had a second act. In America there are third, fourth, and fifth acts if you live long enough. I wasn't really looking for it, but at the end of 1979, Bernie Brillstein had another NBC pilot for me called *The Son-in-Law.* I was going to be in more of a supporting role, and that was fine with me. In fact, it was better than fine. In a supporting role with less pressure on you, sometimes you could be more creative and funnier.

The star was Johnny Yune, a young man who was just getting known at that time as a Korean comedian trying to make it in America. I didn't know much about him, except that his stock line was greeting people with a big "Herrrr-o!" The premise of the show was straightforward—a struggling Korean comedian marries a young lady and they move in with her parents. The father is less than supportive. The mother tries to make it all work.

I had the role of the father, and for my TV wife, they got Rue McClanahan. I would have done the pilot for that reason alone. Rue was a professional's professional and near the top of the A-list for any project like this one. Basically, there was Betty White and Rue. Millions of people knew Rue McClanahan from *Maude* with Bea Arthur, but her resumé was among the longest in the business. Any woman who looked like that, acted like that, and worked so hard had my complete respect.

The similarity between *The Son-in-Law* and *All in the Family* was not lost on me. Just about everything good is stolen anyway. *All in the Family* itself was based on a British television series. Who knows what that show was based on? Copying, borrowing, whatever you want to call it, can go back fifty or sixty years, easy. I had no problem, in particular because *All in the Family* was one of my favorite shows. I loved Carroll O'Connor's comedic anger as Archie Bunker. If I could develop a little of that in the role, it would be wonderful.

The truth was, I didn't care. I would have taken anything. I would have played the Korean comic if they asked me. As it was, my character, Manny Sugarman, was Jewish, and most people already thought I was a Jewish comic who did Italian routines.

Filming was in Los Angeles, and we got off to a good start. Rue was giddy and wonderful. She would turn around and give you a hug out of the blue. She was flirtatious, but I didn't take it seriously. And if you forgot a line, there was no one better to be around. Rue would say, "Don't worry about it. Anyone on this set who knows all the lines perfectly, I have news for you—we don't like you."

The script was decent, and the director let me go off a little. When my character tried to offer Johnny a loan so he and my daughter could get their own apartment, Johnny said, "I have my pride." I said, "What have you got to be proud of?" I pushed the loan on him and explained, "I've always considered a Korean comedian a good credit risk." To which Johnny replied, "My father doesn't."

Rue had her share of good lines too, like when she explained to our daughter, "It's very difficult for two men from different cultures to live together, especially if they have to use the same bathroom."

But we had problems, too. Judith-Marie Bergan, who played my daughter, was a doll and wanted the pilot to succeed as much as a human being could. But there was no chemistry between her and

Johnny Yune. They had a kissing scene near the beginning of the episode, and shooting it went on longer than the Korean War. Johnny was insecure. He came into the project expecting to become a star. People on the set tried to calm him down, but nobody could handle him. He wasn't a bad guy, but he slowly became unbearable.

At one point, he insisted they allow him to do some of his stand-up act in the middle of the show. So they did: "In the Orient, women walk five feet behind the men. In America, women walk all over men. And where I come from, we pay big money for that." Not bad, but where they put it in the show was pure device, and you could feel it being shoehorned. Johnny's sense of delivery as a stand-up comedian was passable. As an actor, though, it just wasn't there.

I thought the biggest mistake was casting Johnny Yune as an aspiring comedian. With his delivery, the show would have been better off casting him as an aspiring waiter, chef, or storeowner, all of which would have been less complicated and more believable. I didn't think Johnny or the producers understood, or wanted to understand, something very basic about a comedy—that if you fight for laughs, everybody loses. The laughs were always going to be there if you knew how to deliver. Just the same, when we wrapped, everyone, including me, was hopeful we had a series.

A few weeks later I was in Chicago doing an engagement, and I got a call from Bernie Brillstein. When the pilot was screened before a test audience, they liked it overall, but they were giving Pat Cooper screaming laughs. So we had a problem. The problem was Johnny Yune's manager convinced Martin Sturger, the executive producer, that Johnny was being shortchanged.

"What the fuck do you want *me* to do about it?" I asked.

Bernie told me that they wanted me to fly back to California to re-shoot the second half. They were working on a rewrite that featured more of Johnny Yune and his stand-up. Bernie apologized like he had just run over my foot. "Don't worry, Pat," he said. "It's still your pilot." I told Bernie he didn't owe me an apology any more than I had to apologize for getting laughs. I wasn't trying to upstage this man. I was just doing my job. The producer was the boss, and he was just trying to do his job.

And as it turned out, together, we did a real job on *The Son-in-Law*. A real hatchet job. We shot about twelve minutes with as much of Johnny Yune's stand-up act as possible. Anyone who wanted that could have gone to see him at The Improv. The worst part about it was that the original pilot had a real plot, with a real beginning, middle, and end. The Sugarman family was losing their apartment because it was going condo and management wouldn't sell them the apartment. The family was convinced it was a case of discrimination over Johnny's being Korean, but the real problem was Manny Sugarman's big mouth. For a pilot episode, it was tight. And then we re-shot it, and it all unraveled.

I was performing on the East Coast when I found out that the show wasn't being picked up by NBC. I was already a pro at this shit. Patti was more upset than I was. She kept saying if they had left it the way it was I would have had a series. She was probably right. But it wasn't me to fight to be top banana. I didn't care if I was third banana. As a performer, I was doing better than ever, so it seemed silly to analyze the fate of the pilot again and again and feel sorry for myself. Just the idea that someone like Bernie Brillstein was out there trying for me was plenty.

Whether it was game show stars looking for crazy perks or wannabe sit-com stars blowing the wheels off their own vehicle, I had been around the block enough to know about egos. Sometimes it's not even a star pulling crap. Sometimes it's a guy with no resumé who has one word in the script. The problem is he's looking for two words. And sometimes it's not a small-time insecure actor being a pain in the ass on the set. Sometimes it's an angel.

In 1981, I got a call from the producer of the ABC television show *Charlie's Angels*. The show's heyday ended when Farah Fawcett left a few years earlier, but the show still drew a decent audience. The producer explained to me that the storm they were having in California prevented a few of the actors from flying in from the East Coast. So they wanted to know, because I was in Vegas and only an hour's flight away, if I could be a replacement on short notice. I said of course.

I flew in the next morning and went over the script with the director, Dennis Donnelly. I was playing Jonathan Tobias, an arrogant movie producer whose studio employees were being victimized by a psychotic archer who hid up in the catwalks. By that afternoon, I was shooting my first scene with the Angels. In it, I was discussing my case in Charlie's office. While doing that, I was also supposed to be telling Cheryl Ladd how to mix my drink, the Jonathan Tobias Special.

Dennis Donnelly had explained to me that he wanted me to be rude to Cheryl Ladd's character. To show the audience what my character was all about, I had to order her around like I was a king and she was my barmaid. So that's what I did, because, in reality, the director was the king and I was his bartender.

I barked at Cheryl, "First the ice! Then the bitters! What's your problem, honey?"

Then I got the bitters.

"I don't like the way you're talking to me," she said. "I don't like your tone." She was off script, speaking out of character. She was the great Cheryl Ladd, and she was no angel.

"Listen," I said. "This is the way Dennis asked me to do it. I don't mean anything by it. I'm just doing my job."

But the director wasn't doing his job. He didn't back me up. He just stood there and asked me to temper it a bit. So I swallowed a bitter and softened it up. We shot the scene again and Cheryl Ladd made it a double.

"He's doing it again. Don't tell me how to stir a drink."

"I'm being paid to tell you how to stir a drink!" I said. "Hey, where are you going?

She walked off the set. I was not hoping for another sip of that poison, but Dennis ran off to her trailer and coaxed her into coming back. We did the scene again. I softened it up some more—but it wasn't like the third time was the charm. Cheryl Ladd was scowling on camera, and there was no acting involved. We got through it. Her last line in the scene upon swallowing the drink was, "Hey this really works. I think maybe we'll be able to work for you, Jonathan."

I was tired of acting, too. I knew the next scene I had to shoot was a couple of days off, so I told everybody I would stay away till then and save them the aggravation. If I wasn't around, I wouldn't have to take this abuse and I wouldn't have to give it back.

"She can shove it up her angel ass," I said. But a few people from the crew grabbed me.

"Pat, calm down. Things will cool off. You don't have to do this."

"I'm a gentleman. I came here to work. I came here to cooperate. How dare she disrespect me!"

For the rest of my time on the set, neither Cheryl Ladd nor Jaclyn Smith said two words to me. My one guardian angel was Tanya Roberts, a lovely woman from the Bronx who seemed to understand my Brooklyn work ethic. And at least the rest of the cast laughed at my remarks when Cheryl Ladd wasn't around. They knew a pain in the ass when they felt one. The one who really hit the target was the guy who played the mad archer. He said, "Man, you have balls. You're a professional, and she's not."

"Hey," I said, "you don't happen to have an extra arrow, do you?"

There weren't many slings and arrows out there that could hurt me. That's the way it always is until one of them does. Only this one didn't come from someone else. It came from me.

In 1982, I got hoarse and stayed that way. At one week you think it's a cold. At two weeks you think it's laryngitis. At three you aren't sure. At four you think it's cancer. I could barely talk. I was scared. As a comedian you live through your voice. Without it you're like an archer without a bow or an angel without wings. I called one of the few people I could really depend on in a case like this, my friend and agent Bernie Brillstein. Bernie sent me to a guy he said was the best throat specialist in the country.

The doctor's office was huge and loaded with electronic gadgets. He took me in the back and put a mirror down my throat. An image appeared on a big screen, and I said, just barely, "Did I come here to get a checkup or make a movie? What is this *Deep Throat?*"

"I don't like what I see down there," the doctor said.

"What do mean you don't like what you see down there?"

"I just don't like it."

"What are you trying to tell me?" I said. "Do I have cancer?"

"I want to do further tests."

"Not on me. If I'm going to fucking die, I'm going to die on my terms. Don't you throw the thing on the side like that and scare the shit out of me."

Bernie called me the next day and wanted to know what the hell I did to his throat specialist.

"I don't like the fucking guy," I said in my gravelly voice. "He's got the bedside manner of a fucking mortician."

"He's the best. What else can I do?"

"You can stay home and not leave the fucking country!"

Bernie was headed to Italy for a couple of months. In my mind, for him to go away like that when I was facing the end of my career and maybe the end of my life was proof that he didn't care. I told him as much. He left anyway. I told him when he came back that he wasn't my manager anymore.

I called up my accountant, who sent me to a Japanese throat specialist. He was one of the nicest human beings you could ever meet. He also had a heavy Japanese accent, and looked a little like Keye Luke, the actor who played Charlie Chan's son. I hoped he could solve the mystery of Pat Cooper's throat.

"I gonna look at you throat," he said. "And we see what happen to you. No get afraid."

"Oh, we're gonna shoot another fucking movie?"

"I put this all down and you gonna see ona squeen. You gonna see ona squeen what we got there ina you throat. Okay? You gonna gag. No worry. You try, just don't worry. I take care everything."

He put his fingers down my throat and there was my movie again up on the big screen. And now the doctor looked excited.

"You see what happen?! This no cancer. You got a node."

"What's a node?"

"Like a little pimple," he said.

"Well," I said, "the other doctor . . ."

"Forget other doctor," he said. "Other doctor full of shit. Other doctor scare you. No good. What you do, go back to Vegas, get a throat specialist. He take node out."

I thanked him and arranged to see a Dr. Belich, a throat specialist who removed nodes. When I sat down in his office, he said, "Mr. Cooper, how are you? I enjoy your work."

"Well," I said, "I hope I enjoy *your* work."

I did. Belich took out the node. The follow-up the next week showed everything to be clear. He told me the best thing I could do for myself was to see a throat specialist once a year.

I was relieved, and the way I expressed relief was to go back to work as soon as possible. I had just missed a show with Mac Davis, and it bothered me. I was like the Lou Gehrig of comedy. I never missed a show.

As my voice improved and I got into the rhythm of performing again, something else was bothering me. I knew I had jumped the gun with Bernie. I loved and respected the man. A person can love and respect you just the same but not show it the way you want. That was where I blew it. It was an Italian thing. I got angry. I pointed a finger in the wrong direction.

I apologized to Bernie some time after he returned. We had dinner and stayed in touch. But it was never the same and I felt terrible. The most hurtful arrows are the ones you shoot yourself. And the most painful lines are the ones you can't take back.

10

Gourmet Sucks

Do you realize that the Jewish people consume more Italian food than any nationality on the face of this Earth? That's the truth. And the Jewish people consume more Chinese food than any nationality on the face of this Earth. If they stop eating, they close down two countries.

A lot of Jewish people have been asking me why, when they go to an Italian restaurant, do they get the business. If there are any Jewish people in the audience, I'm going to explain why. You don't know how to order Italian food. Because Italian people bring in from Rome, Italy, special waiters to annoy you. I'll give you an example. You walk in and say, "Can we have an auntie-paaasto?" The Italian waiter wants you to say, "We want an antipasto." Then he'll jump. Then hit 'em in the navel. He'll kiss you, he'll hug you. I'm telling you that now.

Then you say, "Can we have a dish of la-zag-anah?" Let him know you want "lasagna." Then let 'em have it in the face. I'm telling you, he'll love you.

And we have a pastry that's known all over the world. It's called a cannoli. With cream inside. Here's where you make the mistake. You say, "Can we have a few ganoolies?" Do you know what ganoolie means in Italian? Up your doogie, that's what it means. And can you imagine some guy saying, "We want six up-your-doogies, please"?

Mamas have certain habits you can never change. I go to see my mother. I knock on the door. She opens the door, she has a meatball on a fork. We have forty-five statues in my mother's house. Every time I sit down to eat, I have ninety eyes looking at me.

Every Sunday all over the world, all Italians say the same thing: "Put the water on!" My mother to this day says, "When you go out, watch out." So I got a piece of pepper in my pocket. She says, "Put garlic around your neck. It keeps away the evil spirits." I ain't got no friends, what spirits?

And let's be honest. The kids today go to school, they want eight dollars for lunch, ten dollars for lunch. My mother gave me artichoke sandwiches. I'd sit in the schoolyard [sounds like munching on sandpaper]. They'd say, "Look at that kid! He's eating flowers!" I'd get peppers and eggs. Spinach and eggs. My mother made sure the oil dripped out of the bag. Then she followed the oil to make sure I went to school.

My mother got one gift when she got married—the wooden spoon. Her mother gave it to her, and she said, "You make the sauce. And your kids, you break their legs if they get out of order!" And everybody makes the sauce different. Every Sunday, my mother puts a Gallavotti record on. And Carlo sings, "La-da-di-da!" And the sauce goes, "Baddabum!" And it tastes so nice.

Twenty years ago, we had a tragedy in my house. There was a mouse. We couldn't catch the mouse. Three o'clock in the morning, my mother gets a hot pepper. She puts it in the corner. Three-fifteen, the mouse comes out. All of a sudden he yells, "Madonne!" Did a flip-flop, had a heart attack. Right out the door.

For a performer, there may be a greater honor in this world than playing Carnegie Hall, but I don't know what it is. The list of legends who have had the opportunity reads like an international artist's hall of fame—Richard Strauss, George Gershwin, Sergei Rachmaninoff, Benny Goodman, Duke Ellington, Igor Stravinsky, Leonard

Bernstein, Pasquale Caputo. *Pasquale Caputo?* Who put his name in there?

In 1967, when I, Pat Cooper, was asked to perform at Carnegie Hall, I wanted to live up to the glorious history of that world-famous venue built by Andrew Carnegie in 1891. I also wanted to make my audiences laugh their asses off. I figured the way to do both was to talk about Italian food. As I've said more times than you can probably stand, I'm as proud of my culture as can be. And what shines more brightly in Italian culture than our food? Even if I'm not worthy of Carnegie Hall, *our food is,* without a doubt. I could have served two thousand people a little bruschetta that night and not one of them would have complained. That is, until they got the check.

That's the problem with everything today, especially Italian food. The whole point of Italian food was that anybody who knew what they were doing could make a great dish with the right ingredients. Period. There was no such thing as gourmet cooking. There was no gourmet pasta. There was no gourmet anything. My mother never made pasta. My mother made macaroni. If you would have said "pasta" to my father, he would have said you're in the wrong house. *"We eatta macaroni here!"* All of a sudden you put a knife in macaroni, it's called pasta. There's a difference between pasta and macaroni. Pasta is seventeen dollars a dish. Macaroni is a buck and a quarter.

When I was a kid, my father would send me down to the railroad tracks to pick up flowers. Not flowers to look at and smell. Flowers to eat. My father would say, *"Patsy, a tonight we having a company. You have to getta the salad. You know where to go."* And I did know where to go—the IRT line at Flatbush Avenue, right through a hole in the fence. But I didn't pick flowers. I picked dandelion leaves and wild celery and something called *cardoons.*

Anything green, we used to call a salad. Because we had to have a little red in there, we picked tomatoes. And tomatoes weren't just good for the salad. They were for healing. My mother figured the only way to cure something was to put tomatoes on it, because that acid would burn anything.

It wasn't like we had gourmet dishes one day and regular dishes the next. A chicken cutlet was a chicken cutlet. All chicken cutlets sound alike when you pound them. Years ago, you couldn't give a chicken away. Today a chicken's ass is a delicacy. My plumber told me it was the best part. Another problem with chickens today is no one has seen a whole chicken in twenty years. In my family, when we had chicken, there was a whole bird on the table. Today everything is parts. If you asked ten college kids to draw you a chicken, they would draw a cow.

This is why, if I ever wrote a cookbook, I would call it *Pat Cooper's "Gourmet Sucks."* No gimmicks. Because when it comes to gourmet, you're paying for the word "gourmet," not for the food.

Not long ago, I was in a restaurant with a buddy of mine. We got the check. My friend looked at it and said, "Jeez." I took a look and saw it was for two hundred and eighty dollars. I said, "Okay, I'll get it." What am I gonna do?

But I wondered how it all started. What did we have—a bottle of wine and a few hors d'oeuvres? Then I remembered. A nice-looking Italian man came out of the kitchen with a tiny plate. On the plate were two tiny clams and a couple of little shrimp. He bent down, put the plate in front of my nose and said, "Here, just taste it."

"What?" I said.

"The chef wants you to taste it."

So I tasted it. An hour and a half later I was analyzing the check, and I saw eighty dollars for an appetizer. I asked the waiter, "What's this?"

"That was the appetizer," he said.

"Wait a second," I said. "I thought you said you just wanted me to taste it."

"You did."

But I didn't get angry. I considered the situation and I realized it was fair. What I was doing for two hundred and eighty dollars was dining. When I was finished dining, I went home and ate. For two hundred and eighty dollars I can stock my house for two weeks. And that's exactly what I do.

When I stock up, I buy only the best ingredients—and they are the same exact ones I've eaten all my life. Wild greens make anything better. Kale will help you live to a hundred. Same thing goes for red peppers. Years ago, when my mother and father sat at the table, we always had artichokes. My sisters and I thought our parents were going broke because it was a disgrace to eat artichokes. Today it's a delicacy. It's eight dollars a dish in a restaurant. My father ate basil. My father ate parsley. My father ate calamari raw, and they called him a pig. Today it's called sushi.

When my father ate garlic, people said he smelled. What did they expect? My father had bad breath, but he kept breathing. Garlic is good for you. Today, it's medicine. Today you pay twenty-five dollars for a jar of garlic vitamins. But my father made us eat garlic for nothing. He said, "Eat and shut up." We ate and we shut up. And we went to school when it was ten below zero without a coat. We died, but you can't have everything.

When we were little, my mother put garlic around our necks before we went to bed in case we had nightmares. That's the truth. Because of that, my father never came in the room to kiss us, because then he might have nightmares of his own.

Our parents were oil paintings, but they were ahead of their time. Now the medical community is turning around and studying exactly what those oil paintings did all those years. They hold symposiums and pay millions just to figure out that broccoli has a lot of vitamins and opening up a can of anchovies once in a while won't hurt you.

But when it comes to the tomato, you're looking at the first and last ingredient on the list. The Italian national flower is the tomato. If we don't eat tomatoes twice a week, we can't function. We gotta see red. You don't need a cookbook to tell you how to take a tomato off the vine, put it in a pot, and make sauce out of it. My mother didn't do a thing to the tomato. She just said, "Do the right thing." Maybe if the sauce began to boil she'd drop in a little oregano. Maybe when I wasn't looking, she smoked some of it. But here's an ancient family secret. If the sauce is not right and you throw it on some macaroni, look closely, because the macaroni will let you know. It'll give you a little *Ayyy* and a little *Ahhh*, like an angry Italian.

But a quick word on lentils. Watch out when someone tells you they're going to give you a delicacy with lentils in it. Lentils go right through you. You won't be able to walk. You won't be able to run. Lentils are peasant food. Trust what I tell you. I know a lot of peasants.

Which is not to say you can't throw some lentils in a soup. Soup is the best thing for you. My father was in shape like a forty-year-old at seventy, and the reason he always gave was soup. And the reason soup is so good is that you get all your vitamins *and* the water. People today are brainwashed. They're trying to drink eight gallons of water a week just by drinking it from bottles! Go down into the subway in New York on a cold winter day. Everyone's freezing their asses off drinking bottles of water. They're like babies nursing, and at a dollar a bottle, they're going broke, filling up landfills, and peeing forty times a day till they wind up with prostate problems at age thirty-two.

Why not mix it up a little? Get some of that water from a nice bowl of soup. Throw in the chicken, the beef, the broccoli, the kale, the tomatoes. Don't worry, there is plenty of water in the food. My father always said, *"When you eat a something, eat a something wet."* Be like me. Eat soup ten times a week. Stay healthy. And stop the drinking and peeing, the peeing and drinking, the drinking and peeing.

If you need to drink, consider a little bit of wine. Wine makes you cook better in Italian. Wine speaks Italian. Add some wine to whatever you're cooking. I always thought my mother put a little wine in my milk. Now the medical community is reporting that wine is good for your heart and makes you live longer. But don't forget what Italians have always known—that wine makes you live *better*. Another thing I always do is sauté garlic. I chop it up really thin so it dissolves in the pan. The next time you do that, try stopping for a moment and really breathe it in. Then tell me if you've ever smelled anything so healthy.

Don't worry too much about cholesterol. Instead, worry about if you're eating food that's good for you. Take *bracciole,* for instance. First of all, there is no such thing as gourmet bracciole. Bracciole is a flattened piece of rolled-up meat that's filled with ingredients— Parmesan cheese, onions, eggs, bread crumbs, and black pepper, to name just a few. The roll is made from an inexpensive cut of steak. That's what they used in the old days, so if anyone is using a prime cut, it's not a bracciole anymore. In case you're worried about your breath with all the onions, eat some sweet peas afterwards or get a chunk of parsley and chew on it. Then you can kiss me.

As for the cholesterol, I've been eating bracciole and cervellata— which is a cheese sausage—for eighty years. My cholesterol level is around eight hundred, but I don't worry about it. When it hits a thousand, I'm selling.

If you want to worry about something, I'll give you something to worry about. Crossbreeding food is dangerous. For instance, I'm Italian. My intestines are Italian. My intestines don't like egg foo young. My intestines don't want chop suey. My intestines are waiting for some cavatelli or a little linguine with clam sauce.

We're eating things outside of our culture constantly, and it's getting us sick. You would never give a horse a steak sandwich. Don't give an Italian pork fried rice. Once a month is fine, but don't make a habit of it or your intestines will go *Bacalaba-bacalaba!* And please, stop with the hamburgers already. I didn't have a hamburger until I was sixty-three. Today we're eating billions and billions. That's why people are getting so fat. There's nowhere left to put them.

Yes, my mother drove me insane, but she knew what she was doing in the kitchen. My mother didn't have all these utilities. All these fancy tools! My mother had no blender, but she blended. My mother had no thermometer to put in the turkey's ass. My mother said to the turkey, "Get in. I'll tell you when to come out!" My mother cooked on Christmas morning for thirty people by herself, and it was no problem. She had a dishwasher named Mrs. Caputo. She scrubbed the pots herself one by one with no complaints.

When have you ever seen a television chef scrub a pot? I would pay to see that. There's a chef on television named Emeril Lagasse who says, "Bam!" If we heard that in my house, we would duck, because when my mother went "Bam!" my father went "Boom!"

When it came to all things in the kitchen, my parents had it down to a science. We didn't have a telephone until I was sixteen, but when my father wanted me home for dinner, he whistled. He whistled so loud and clear I could be on Avenue X and hear him from Avenue S. If the dog got home first, the dog got my dinner. Today that's called child abuse. Years ago it was called raising a family. My father never got the credit he deserved for inventing bungee jumping. If I was late for dinner, he told my mother to throw me out the window.

Of course, some things my parents did were great mysteries to me, and maybe that's the way it should be. One of my sisters married a very milquetoast guy who was a piano player. At least he said he was a piano player. I never knew for sure, because he never finished a song. His hands would get tired. My mother and father and sisters would stand around him holding him up. He would get so pale we would wonder if he would make it to the end of "O Sole Mio" alive.

To solve this problem, my mother would buy a steak, drain the blood, and give it to my brother-in-law to drink. She would give me the shank or whatever was left and tell me, *"It's a the best a part."* So every time my brother-in-law fainted during "O Sole Mio," I got stomach cramps. And every time I got stomach cramps, my brother-in-law became a vampire.

When I had a cramp, my mother said, *"The doctor says you should a rub it."* If that didn't work, she had another treatment. She'd say, *"Patsy, you gotta infection in a you stomach. You gotta getta rid a that little thing in a there."* I could have a fever of 130 and her solution was always the same—she'd make me throw up. *"You gotta getta rid a the poison. You gotta putta you finger down a you throat."* If I didn't do it, she would. You should have seen the fingernails on her. She could pull out your fucking tonsils.

Maybe it's because of all those years under my mother and father's roof that when I go out to eat, I don't want any mysteries. I don't want any blood. And I don't want anybody's finger down my throat.

No matter how good food is, I can't really enjoy it if I'm getting ripped off. A few years ago, I was at a restaurant called Nanni's with a bunch of close friends. One of them was Vic Damone, a singer who Frank Sinatra once said had "the best set of pipes in the business." Damone sprang on the scene as a kid in 1947 with a song called, "I Have But One Heart." Though he may have had only one heart, he had more than one song. In fact, he recorded over two thousand songs over the next half century or so.

With us that night was Charlie Cumalla, a dear friend of Vic's. Charlie was Vic's best man when he married Diahann Caroll. Also with us was the Senator from New York, Alphonse D'Amato. Altogether we had about eight people at a big round table. Within ten minutes, there were a couple of bottles of wine on the table and for each person, a small dish with a single shrimp, a tiny bit of lettuce, and a toothpick. Nanni himself was helping serve us, and I said, "Nanni, no disrespect, but who ordered this?"

"You mean this?"

"I mean these little shrimp things? Who ordered them?"

"Well," he said, "that's to get you started."

"Yeah, it got me started, but who ordered it?"

"Well," he said, "it's to give you something to chew on . . ."

"Take it back," I said.

"What am I going to do if I take it back?"

"Take it back. I didn't order it. This is all my check. I'm buying the dinners. Don't put anything in front of me that I didn't fucking order. That's all I ask."

Everybody at the table looked at me like I stepped over the line, but that was a line I gladly leaped over. Nanni looked like he swallowed a sword.

"Now we have another problem," he said. "I have a striped bass for eight people already in the oven. It's almost ready. What am I going to do with that?"

"I'll tell you what," I said. "Take the shrimp back, take the striped bass back, feed the shrimp to the striped bass, and shove the whole thing up your ass."

Everyone at the table was falling down laughing. By this point, they knew that I was just joking with Nanni. Nanni knew it, too, but he did his best not to show it. I felt I could still get a smile out of him, so I went on.

"Nanni, why on earth would I ever order a striped bass from you? Last time I ordered a striped bass, you brought it out without the stripes. I'm still looking for the fucking stripes."

Vic Damone was crying from laughing, but Charlie Cumalla, who was a delightful human being, had had enough. "Pat," Charlie said, "what are you doing? Why are you starting a fucking war?"

"There's no war," I said. "Everybody, order off the menu and we'll have peace."

But they knew me and the fact that sometimes I couldn't leave it alone. Another thing I never ordered that night was the huge wedge of Parmesan cheese for the table. As was customary, everyone at the table would cut off a little cheese from the wedge with their own knife to have with the wine. This was a huge piece of cheese, probably big enough to reuse at every table the whole night. When Nanni came to take it back, it was still ninety percent uneaten, sitting there like a birthday cake. So I said, "Put it in a bag."

"Put what in the bag?" Nanni said.

"Put the fucking cheese in the bag. I'm paying for it. That's a twenty-pound piece of fucking cheese. You could feed the Sicilian army with that. You're going to reuse it, so please do me a favor and put it in a bag for me."

"You know something," Nanni said, "I don't want you to come here no more."

"Doesn't matter. I'm coming anyway."

Nanni's wasn't the first restaurant I was banned from for life and it wouldn't be the last. A couple of months later, I was out with Patti, dining at Emilio's. We started by ordering a seventy-dollar bottle of wine. Then I ordered some pasta, which came out soon after. A minute or two later, Patti wanted to share the pasta, so I told the waiter, "Could you please bring out an extra dish? My wife and I are going to share."

"Two-and-a-half dollars for the extra dish," the waiter said.

"What?! She just wants a dish. Nothing on it. Just a dish and some air."

"Two-fifty for the dish."

"Okay," I said, "forget it. My wife don't want it."

The waiter walked away, and at that point I slid the dish of pasta over to Patti after taking a portion for myself. My portion went right on the tablecloth, directly in front of me. Now we had our extra dish, and the price was fair.

"Waiter," I said, calling him back, "could I have a little grated cheese on my pasta?" The waiter walked over, looked at the pile of pasta on the tablecloth, and looked like he had seen a man from Mars.

"So," he said, "you want the dish?"

"No, I don't want the fucking dish. Bring me the cheese!"

The waiter went back to get some cheese, and I poured some sauce over my pasta. With my napkin on my lap, I started eating. This wasn't just to make a point. I was hungry. Patti was embarrassed and tongue-tied. She said, "Pat, you're a celebrity. You're not supposed to do this."

"The question is, how can people do this to *me*? How can they do it to *anybody*?" I felt bad for my wife. She was in a restaurant with me one time when I was offered a three-colored salad for fifteen dollars. I asked if I could get two colors for ten.

Now people in the restaurant were looking at this spectacle. I couldn't blame them. I would have been looking, too. A well-known judge happened to be there and came over to us. "Pat," he said, "I just want to tell you that was the funniest thing I ever saw."

"Your honor," I said, "I think I'm in the right, here. I just paid seventy dollars for a bottle of wine, and he wants two-fifty for a dish? I'm a customer!"

"What a pair of balls," he said. "I could use a pair like that sometimes."

"Don't you think enough is enough though?" Patti asked the judge.

"Well," he said, "the man is right in this case."

A minute later, the waiter sprinkled grated cheese over my pasta and sauce, and it felt like the whole world was watching. A little later, after I paid the check and my wife and I got up, the owner said to us, *"You come here no more!"*

"Fuck you and fuck your pasta!" I said.

The incident made the Page 6 of the *New York Post,* which claimed I was thrown out of Emilio's. I wasn't thrown out. I walked out gracefully on my own terms. If they had tried to throw me out, it would have made the front page. The *Post* didn't report that I left a big tip.

Why did I tip big? First of all, what happened wasn't the waiter's fault, it was the restaurant's. This guy still has to make a living, and believe me, he earned it. Second of all, it's an Italian thing. We're always sending two bottles of wine over here and nine bottles of wine over there. And we're always giving a guy ten dollars to walk from the kitchen to the table and walk back again. If we don't do that, we're bums. Over the years, it's gotten out of hand. It's become a joke, but it's better than being cheap, and I guess it makes us feel good. It's like, *"Ay, I just took care of him, uh!"* Just make sure you take care of us, too.

In case I appear too sure of myself, here's one more story about Pat Cooper and food. A while ago I was in Genoa, Italy. I figured, here I am, an Italian in Genoa. What can I do here that I can't do back home? Get some Genoa salami. It's about the best-tasting thing in the world, and it's practically illegal to ship it back to the States. So I walked into a delicatessen and the man behind the counter said, "Yes sir, what can I do for you?"

"Could I have a pound of Genoa salami?"

He looked at me like I was crazy.

"Listen to me," he said. "We're in Genoa. What do you *think* we sell here? If you want salami, you get salami. If you want bologna, go to Bologna!"

"You're absolutely right," I said.

Which just goes to show you that sure, I know all sorts of things about great food—how to prepare it, how to stay healthy, and how to live long. I even made it to Carnegie Hall. But I can be just as stupid as anyone else. I'll still send a bottle of wine to your table, and hopefully you'll still send one back.

11

The Yankee Franchi

Sometimes the world is a valley of heartaches and tears
And in the hustle and bustle, no sunshine appears,
But you and I have our love always there to remind us
There is a way we can leave all the shadows behind us
Volare, oh, oh! Cantare, oh, oh, oh, oh!
Let's fly way up in the clouds
Away from the maddening crowds

"Volare," or "Nel Blu Di Pinto Di Blu" as it was known in Italy, was the first Italian song to reach number one on Billboard's Top 100 in the United States. The year was 1958, and the artist was Domenico Modugno. The song won a Grammy and in the following years, all sorts of artists recorded their own versions of "Volare," including Dean Martin, Bobby Rydell, The McGuire Sisters, and a gentleman named Sergio Franchi.

Sergio Franchi was born in Italy in 1926. His father's dream for him was to be an electrical engineer, but he always sang on the side. After the family moved to South Africa, Sergio worked as a draftsman in the early '50s and toured the country singing the great operas, like

Carmen, La Traviata, and *Rigoletto.* But Franchi's big break didn't arrive until 1962. He had been singing popular music in concerts throughout Europe and was asked to appear on the British television show *Sunday Night at the Palladium.* That led to a recording contract in the United States with RCA Victor.

When Sergio Franchi did *The Ed Sullivan Show* for the first time in 1962, women's hearts melted all over America. He was a handsome, rugged-looking Italian with personal grace and a tenor voice that could put you on a gondola and make you fall in love all over again. He worked all over and recorded a string of successful albums covering classic songs such as "Funiculi, Funicula," "Mamma Mia," "Speak Softly, Love," and of course "Volare," which means "to fly." Sergio Franchi flew, and for a while, we flew together.

We had worked together on and off, and in 1969 we were booked to do the Flamingo in Las Vegas. I was the opening act and was getting the same as the headliner—twenty-five thousand dollars a week. At that time, I was usually getting around five thousand a week, which was great money. So twenty-five was a thrill. It was even more of a thrill working with Sergio Franchi. He could do everything on stage including tap dance. He was also a wonderful human being and, unlike certain great singers, he had a fabulous sense of humor.

One night I finished up my act and went backstage to change. As an opening act, I never tried to make a quick exit after I performed. My feeling was that I never knew what would happen to the star. It was almost always an adventure, and I wanted to be part of it as much as anyone in the audience. That night, I left my dressing room wearing only my robe—I hadn't put my pants on yet. I was standing just offstage watching Sergio sing one classic after another. All of a sudden he stopped singing, scratched his throat, and said, *"Ahhhhh, I think I'm a losing my voice. Pat, where are you?"*

I walked out on stage in my robe without any pants underneath, which was funny enough. But I wanted to go one better than that. I had developed quite a nice Sergio Franchi imitation. His speaking voice was lower than his singing voice. It was a little reserved and stuck in his throat, and very, very Italian. With the star beginning to lose his voice right on stage, now was the perfect time to debut my own Sergio Franchi voice.

"Sergio, what a seems to be the problem?"

"Pat, I'm a losing my voice."

"It's a no problem, Sergio. I gotta you voice right a here. And it's a doin' a fine."

"Please, Pat, don a screw with a me. Go getta me a glass of a water!"

"Whad a you crazy? Do I look a like a you water boy? I'm a the star! The people, they get a water for me!"

The audience was laughing, then screaming. They got it right away. We did a few minutes of back and forth, and by the time I got offstage, Sergio had his singing voice back and finished the show.

The next night before the show, Sergio came up to me and said, *"Pat, do me a favor and stay close. I'm afraid I might lose a my voice again. Then I lose a this engagement and twenty-five thousand dollars a week. I kill a myself."*

So I finished my act, stayed in my tuxedo, and waited around like a relief pitcher in the bullpen. Sure enough, Sergio was in the middle of singing a medley from *West Side Story* and it happened again. *"Maria! I just met a girl named Maria! And suddenly . . . Excusa me, ladies an a gentlemen. I think I'm a losing my voice. I need a water. Pat, wheres a my water?"* I came out in my tuxedo with a tray and a glass of water and went into my best Sergio Franchi.

"Here you go, Sergio. Drink a you fucking water."

"Wait a second. What are you a doing? Why you a sound like a me?"

"That's a funny," I said. *"I gotta the same a question for you. Why you sound a like me, the great Sergio Franchi?"*

"Only one a man can sound like Sergio!"

"But a Sergio," I said. *"You tell a me backstage this is a what you want. You want a me to sound just a like you in a case you lose a you voice. Make up a you fucking mind."*

The audience—a different one from the night before—was hysterical seeing and hearing two Sergios up on the stage. The real Sergio loved every minute of it, and so did the fake one. And then came the *coup de grace.* I said, *"You know, Sergio, if a we keep a this up, we're going to be maybe another Dean a Martin and a Jerry Lewis."*

Then he looked at me and said with an absolutely straight face, *"And of course, I'm a Dean Martin!"* Hearing this, the audience howled. As a comedian, you tend to hear a lot of laughter and even some screaming now and again, but this one soared off the charts. Sergio's expression was deadpan. He really and truly didn't get the obviousness and, therefore, the humor of his statement. And the more puzzled he looked, the more the audience laughed their asses off.

"Sergio," I said, *"are you a really sure you're a Dean a Martin?"*

"Just a remember," he said, *"who's a handsome and who's a not."*

As the engagement went on, the Flamingo got more and more packed each night. It was standing room only. Management told us to do our thing as often as possible, and we did. Every night, even if Sergio's voice was feeling great, he would get through two or three songs and give me my cue. We took what we did and built on it. I would not only sound like Sergio Franchi, I would dress like him and walk like him. His walk on stage was like the strut of a bullfighter, chest out, chin out, back and legs straight with a bit of a tiptoe. I got it down fast. I knew my cue perfectly, and the laughs started even before I opened my mouth.

"Pasquale Caputo," Sergio said, *"you talk like a me and sing like a me. Now you walk like a me and breathe like a me? Whad a you doing to me?"*

"Shut up an sing a you song!"

Our act got tighter and tighter, and it was getting to the point where we were going to be a pair. The people at the Flamingo thought we already were. But there was one person who didn't like it—his manager. She was crazy about Sergio Franchi, just like millions of women. But as his manager, she felt especially close to him. Close enough to ruin a good thing. One night before the show, she got a hold of me backstage and decided to speak her mind.

"You know, Pat, you're not going to be Sergio's partner. There's just no way."

"And why are you telling me this, darling?" I asked.

"Just so you know. Just so you get that through your skull."

"First of all, I didn't expect to become Sergio Franchi's partner. I didn't expect that. You're the one talking about it."

"Yeah, well . . ."

"Second of all," I said, "there is magic on that stage. Why do you think management says keep doing it? So we're going to keep doing it, whether you think we're fucking partners or not."

And we did. We worked together a lot, on and off all over the country—not because his manager did or didn't want it to happen, but because audiences did. Like a good friendship, the act grew. As good as he was, Sergio was never too good for comedy. In Rhode Island, he had a young lady working with him who was a beauty queen. In fact, I think she was Miss Rhode Island. As small as the state is, she was gorgeous enough to be Miss Texas. Between songs, Sergio would announce, *"I'm a very thirsty now!"* So this lovely girl who couldn't have been more than eighteen or nineteen would come walking out with a tray, a bottle of wine, and a glass for the star.

"Oh, Denise, a very good. You bring a the wine!"

One night, Sergio took a sip of the wine and looked like he was going to gag. *"I cannot drink a this crap,"* he said. The poor girl just stood there as the star went on. *"It's a gotta be from Italy. This is a Merlot. I cannot a drink a Merlot. Please, a no disrespect."* He put down the glass, launched into something from *La Traviata,* and the poor girl walked away with her head down. I saw this and asked myself, *Now what can I do to break his balls?*

The next day, I rented a deep-sea diving suit with flippers and a snorkel. That night, when Sergio announced he was thirsty, instead of Miss Rhode Island walking out, it was me, dripping wet and holding a bottle of red wine. He looked at me and his surprise was genuine.

"Is that a you, Pasquale Caputo?"

"It's a me!"

"Whatta you doing in a that thing? Are you a crazy or something?"

"I'm a not a crazy, Sergio. You say thatta you cannot a have a Merlot. You can only have a wine straight from Italy. So I swam straight from Italy, and here I am. Salud!"

The audience was on the floor, pounding, and Sergio was down there with them. He was no more ready for this than they were. But his selfish broad manager stopped us from doing it a second night. "You're upstaging him!" she said.

"Don't you understand,?" I said. "He's just happy to be part of all this, just like I am and the audience is."

At times, I could have strangled her for strangling the show. She couldn't, however, strangle the rest of his life. In 1970, Patti and I bought a house in Las Vegas next door to Sergio and his lovely wife, Eva. We moved in with our daughter, Patti Jo. The next year, he became a United States citizen and began calling himself a "Yankee Franchi." He was always adding on to his huge home, building garages all over the property for all his cars. He had around a dozen Rolls Royces and was busy collecting more. I drove a Dodge Dart.

But when an acre of land adjoining our properties went up for sale, I thought it was a good investment and bought it for $12,500. Sergio turned to me and said, *"Why do you buy that a piece of a shit? You ought to be ashamed of a youself."*

One afternoon, I was driving around the neighborhood and saw a

Rolls Royce pulled over on the side of the road. I pulled my Dodge Dart alongside it, and saw that it was Sergio looking under the hood.

"*Oh, the great Sergio Franchi!*" I said. "*What a happened to you genius fucking car? Its a no wanna drive?*"

"*Pat,*" he said, "*don a fuck with a me. This motherfucking car cost a me twenty-two thousand dollars, an a now it won a start.*"

"Okay," I said, "you want me to call a tow truck?"

"*No, no. That's embarrassing for me. Can a you give a me a push with a you car?*"

"*Let a me get a this straight,*" I said. "*You wanna me to push the great Sergio Franchi with a my '73 Dodge Dart, a car you make a fun of?*"

"*Yes,*" he said. "*You son of a bitch.*"

And that's exactly what we did. I pulled my Dart behind his Rolls Royce, pushed him to the next gas station, and never let him forget about it for years.

Meanwhile, our show went on one way or another, no matter who was pushing or who was pulling. One time, we were performing up in Buffalo, right near Niagara Falls. The place was packed with about three thousand people, and Sergio came out in a tuxedo and sang "The Impossible Dream" from the musical *Man of La Mancha*. After the show, I asked him, "When are you gonna take that fucking thing out of the show? Everyone on the planet sings this fucking thing. 'To dream the impossible dream! To scream the impossible scream!'"

"*But it's a wonderful for me,*" he said.

"It's the same shit over and over again. Take it the fuck out!"

"*I'm a never take it out!*"

This went on day in and day out. So the afternoon before closing night I decided to do something about "The Impossible Nightmare" once and for all. I rented a horse from a local stable. Then I rented a suit of armor and a lance from a costume store.

That night, I did my act as if it was any old closing night. But once

Sergio got on stage, the woman from the stable led the horse backstage and I got into my knight's outfit. She let me know she'd be nearby the whole time, because who knew what this horse might do when he saw three thousand people.

When I heard the opening chords "To dream . . ." that was the cue. As Sergio sang the words, "To live," he knew something was wrong. The audience was laughing, and you could hear the clop-clop-clop of hooves on the stage.

"I know Mr. Cooper is a someplace around a here!"

I certainly was. There I was, Don Pasquale Caputo Quixote, in a bad costume, high atop a horse, saddling up next to the great Sergio Sancho Franchi. The audience was howling so loud, they were spilling out into the aisles.

"Cooper, you're a crazy. You're a crazy!"

"Am I?" I said. "Am I?" I dismounted and stood there with my lance at my side. I looked at Sergio and said, "Now will you stop singing that fucking song?" It brought the house down.

After the show, his manager gave me a hard time as usual. "You know," she said, "you have no respect for that man."

"I have tremendous respect," I said. *"Tremendous* respect. I just also happen to have balls, madam. These are moments you can't fucking buy!"

Sergio himself had a different problem. *"Cooper,"* he said, *"I don know if I can a do that song a no more, you cocksucker. Because the next a time I do the song, I'm a thinking, Cooper, he's a coming down with a horse. Where did you find a that horse?"*

"Never mind where I found him," I said. "Just be glad he didn't shit on the fucking floor."

Of course, the horse was worth every penny I paid for it. Sergio Franchi never sang "The Impossible Dream" again.

The year 1976 was a big one for Sergio. He had big dreams, and some of them were not impossible. In 1965, he had starred in the Rodgers and Sondheim Broadway musical *Do I Hear a Waltz?* In 1969, he co-starred with Anthony Quinn and Anna Magnani in the movie *The Secret of Santa Vittoria* about a small Italian town that hides its wine from the Nazis. Over the years, he appeared in dozens of television dramas and sit-coms and performed on *The Ed Sullivan Show* an incredible twenty times. But in 1976, Sergio Franchi was given the highest honor an American performer could possibly be given—a car commercial.

The car was the Chrysler Volare. Sergio was a natural. He was closely identified with the song of the same name, sang the new lyrics like he was falling in love, and looked better than anyone on the planet in a tux. Whereas before, millions of fans enjoyed his music, now hundreds of millions knew him as the Volare guy. He *was* the Chrysler Volare.

There was one problem, though. Sergio Franchi wouldn't drive a Volare. Not in a thousand fucking years. Not a two-door, a four-door, or a fifty-eight door. Sergio drove to the set in a Rolls and left the set in a Rolls. The strange thing was that the predecessor of the Volare was the Dodge Dart, and that was driven by yours truly.

That same year, Sergio Franchi was asked to co-host *The Mike Douglas Show,* which went on in the afternoon on NBC-TV. There was never a finer Irish gentleman than Mike Douglas. Sergio and I had both done the show before separately, but this time, I was waiting in the wings as a special guest. The show that day was about Italian culture. To his credit, Mike Douglas forced Sergio to introduce his dear friend and neighbor, Pat Cooper, without the use of his hands. Sergio called that unfair, explaining, *"If a you see an Italian with a his hands in a his pockets, he has a nothing to say."* But with Mike Douglas physically pinning down his hands, the great romantic singer gave it a shot:

"The first time I shared a the bill with the gentleman I'm about to introduce, was in 1964 at a the Palmer House in Chicago. Since a that engagement, I have a not had a moment of a peace. To make itta worse, a few years ago, he moved to Las Vegas and became a my neighbor. I taught him how to dress a well, walk a well, and speak a well, but I was very unsuccessful with a the last two. My very good friend, Pasquale Caputo . . . Pat Cooper."

Mike Douglas cut to the chase by asking me what kind of neighbor I was.

"One of the finest neighbors you'll ever find," I said. "This guy, however, is a definite madman. Complete madman. My property is devalued now forty-seven percent. He had what they call a one-room house twelve years ago, now it's an eighty-seven room house. But it's ninety-percent garages. And he's got a used car lot that says 'No Hanky-Panky with Franchi.'"

The audience loved it. Whether it was a room in Kenosha, Wisconsin, or the studio audience for a nationally syndicated television show, we always seemed to pick up where we last left off.

MIKE: He loves cars, doesn't he?

PAT: Yes, because he loves to suck on exhausts.

MIKE: How many cars have you, Serge?

SERGIO: Ahhh . . .

PAT: Ahhh . . .

SERGIO: I don't know.

PAT: I'll tell you how many you got. You got about a dozen. That's in the front. Then he's got a few in the back and about nine in the desert with Big Al over there [making a "wiseguy" nose]. He's got a lot of cars.

MIKE: What is it, a hobby with him?

PAT: No, it's a junkyard.

SERGIO: It's a hobby. A hobby.

PAT: It's a junkyard, a junkyard. Mary Hartman, Mary Hartman. He turns around and comes to my house. The nerve of this man. My beautiful estate! And he pulls up with this '36 Cadillac. Opens the hood. He says, *'Look a what I bought.'* Yeah, more junk. He's standing there saying, *'When I finish this, Pat, it's a gonna be so beautiful.'* All the oil's coming out of the crank shaft on my driveway, and he says, *'Oh, this is a very expensive a car.'* I say, 'Get it off my driveway.' Then it went, *Bubajiyt, Bubajiyt, Bubajiyt.* And I got a spot on my driveway. It's called the Sergio Franchi spot. And I haven't seen him since."

Mike Douglas asked us if we liked all the automatic features on new cars, and my answer was automatic, "I'm not into that. I don't have time for that. I want the key to go in, I want the thing to move. See, this guy loves it. He takes the engine apart, then what do you think he does? He puts a Ford engine in a Rolls Royce. He don't know what he's doing. He had a car one day going sideways."

Then I told a true story about the portrait Sergio hired an artist to do of him in oil, not the motor kind. The first time I saw it hanging in his house, I really thought there had been some kind of mistake.

"That day Sergio must have had chapped lips or something," I said. "And you put the Vaseline on it, you know. He's sitting there with the Italian pose, which it's supposed to be, and the idiot who painted the picture put in the chapped lips. On the oil painting! Sergio here wouldn't let me take it down, because he knows I would have brought it on national television. He had a painting that actually had the chapped lips in it! So he's sitting like this here [neatly posed with hands to the side] and there's a crack here, a crack here, a crack here. So I grab the picture, and I put Vaseline over the lips. They're still cracked."

Naturally we got to talking about the car commercial that every last person in the country watching a football game, soap opera, or news show had seen at least a hundred and forty times. But Sergio was also doing a coffee commercial, and I couldn't possibly let that one go. *"How are you?"* I said in my best Sergio voice. *"This is Sergio Franchi.* No, you're Glen Campbell. Of course you're Sergio Franchi. *I want to soothe myself sometimes, so I have a café mocha. When you laying in a the bed tantalizing about the mecca de mocha de mecca, you have some mocha de mecca.* So now, people all think he's selling a mocha automobile. It's a Calabrian coffee. They don't know what the hell he's selling."

Mike Douglas asked me to do my version of Sergio Franchi walking. I was only too happy to oblige. I took a few steps like a matador and struck a pose somewhere between Enrico Caruso and Napoleon. I turned up my palms and shouted, *"What do you mean you don a like a the show? Well, I singa my HEART out!"*

The audience flipped, but Mike Douglas gave Sergio his ups in the bottom of the ninth. Sergio Franchi stood and did his best Pat Cooper walk. It was three quick steps—a comic waddle, Groucho Marx meets Charlie Chaplin. The band played the "Tarantella." I had no idea I looked anything like that, but when the audience goes berserk, you know the performer is on to something. It was a home run. I had barely let the great Sergio Franchi get a word in edgewise, but now he had stolen the show with the last laugh—and rightfully so.

Not long after that, Sergio's wife wanted a tennis court. But with all the garages her husband had built, there was no land left. What *was* left was the lot I had bought for $12,500 five years earlier and still hadn't built on. I knew it would be valuable some day. And sure enough, the great Sergio Franchi made me an offer. *"Pat,"* he said, *"I wanna take a that piece of a shit away from you."*

"What piece of a shit?" I said, doing Sergio to Sergio.

"*That thing that a you bought,*" he said. "*I feel a so bad, I want to give you back a your $12,500.*"

"*How about a forty a thousand?*"

"*Are you fucking a crazy?*" he said. "*What are you trying to do? Rob a you best a friend?*"

"*All a sudden you a my best a friend, Sergio?*"

"*Stop a talking like a me!*" he said

"*You fuck a with me, Sergio. And now I fuck a with you. I give a that land back to the Indians. We took a that fucking land. It's a no mine, it's a no yours. I give it a back. Soon, you a have a tent on a you property.*"

But the tent never came to pass. His wife got a tennis court, and I got the forty thousand.

Our act never got old because I never lost the will to one-up him, and somehow he never really minded being one-upped. We were at the Westbury Music Fair in Long Island one evening in 1983, and for his encore, Sergio sang "I Am What I Am," from *La Cage aux Folles*. Now, whether you knew Sergio Franchi from a car commercial or you were his next door neighbor for a dozen years, you knew there was never a straighter guy in the history of the world to sing "I Am What I Am." This was a number sung by a drag queen to his boyfriend, who owned a gay club. So with the audience standing and applauding, I came out in a wig and a long evening gown. The people screamed. No one was sure which one of us was the lead. But they knew the same thing we knew—we were a pair.

In 1990, my friend Sergio Franchi succumbed to brain cancer. My wife loved him, my daughter loved him, and most of all, I loved him. We had a running joke going for a quarter century, but near the end we hugged each other.

He had always been a supporter of kids who suffered abuse. His favorite charity was Boy's Town—an organization in Italy that gave him the Michelangelo Award for a lifetime of service. Sergio was always very charitable with his money, and that didn't stop when he passed on. In 1993, his widow founded the Sergio Franchi Music Foundation, which provides scholarships for aspiring young singers.

As incredibly premature and sad as my friend Sergio Franchi's passing was, I could never be sad when I thought about him. We flew. And somewhere, he's still flying.

With the great Tony Martin in Sparks, Nevada, 1966.

The legendary George Burns, 1966.

At the Flamingo Hotel with Bobby Darin, 1963.

With Peggy Lee and Tony Bennett at the Latin Casino, 1969.

Jerry Vale at the Riviera Hotel in Las Vegas, 1969.

On the Mike Douglas Show with Van Johnson, 1970.

Patti and I at the Copa with Steve Lawrence and Eydie Gorme, 1969.

Patti and I with friends, including some of the hottest Vegas headliners. Can you spot Sergio Franchi, Jerry Vale, Tony Sandler, Ralph Young, Dick Roman, and Fred Travalena?

At a 1980's Friars Roast with the great Anthony "Zorba the Greek" Quinn.

Patti and I with Robert De Niro on the set of *Analyze This*, 1999.

12

Better Pissed Off Than Pissed On

If you ask ten people who Pat Cooper is, five will tell you, "He's that comedian who's always pissed off." That's what you get for telling the truth. And the truth is, I can think of only one time in my entire life that I was genuinely, literally pissed off.

The year was 1973. Patti and I were living in Manhattan on West End Avenue. One night we went downtown to have dinner at Jilly's on West 52nd Street. There were always celebrities in there, but that night there was an extra buzz because Johnny Carson and Ed McMahon were in the place. *The Tonight Show* had been moved the previous year from the NBC Studios in Rockefeller Center to Burbank, California. I was a guest on the show a bunch of times—four times in 1972 alone—and when you were a guest, Johnny was God.

He earned it. Jack Paar and Steve Allen, who hosted the show before him, were both very good. But Johnny Carson was a dynamo, and his timing was perfect. Not only behind the desk—but in life. When he took over in 1962, the late-night talk-show format was really just starting to catch on, and Johnny took it to the next level. Carson was truly a great interviewer. He engaged his guests, and the humor came naturally out of the conversation. Ed McMahon was along for the ride, and so was the rest of the country. If you were old enough to stay up past 11:30 on a weeknight, there was a good chance you were watching *The Tonight Show.*

But off the set, Johnny Carson wasn't a nice guy, to the point where you thought there had to be something wrong with him. Ed McMahon, on the other hand, was friendly. He was a standup guy and an ex-Marine. He was also a big drinker. That was a running joke on the show, and in those days it was almost a badge of honor. But what very few people knew was that of the two, Johnny Carson was the bigger drinker. And the further he got from being sober, the nastier he got.

On this particular night, I walked into the men's room at Jilly's. When you're a guy standing at a urinal, there are only two rules, and one of them is to look straight ahead. But that was getting harder for me to do every second. First, I heard a gentle brrrrrrrrrr sound that wasn't normal. Then I felt a trickle on my left leg. The trickle was getting bigger and warmer. So I broke the one rule and turned to my left to find that the guy peeing in the urinal next to me was breaking the other rule—never pee on the guy standing next to you.

The guy standing next to me and peeing on my leg was Johnny Carson. There was a metal divider between us, but that didn't matter. He was bombed out of his mind, staggering back and forth, and peeing all over the place like a fountain in a fucking amusement park.

"Hey!" I said. "What the fuck are you doing?"

He was so blitzed, all he could do was mumble and pee.

"Listen," I said, "you may be a dog, but I am no fucking fire hydrant!"

Then he started slurring that he was Johnny Carson.

"I don't care if you're *Kit* Carson! You don't pee on my fucking leg! Do you let anybody pee on your fucking leg? You don't even let Ed pee on your fucking leg! If you can't hold your liquor, at least learn to hold your fucking dick!"

Jilly Rizzo came running into the bathroom, which was amazing because Jilly didn't run anywhere. He wanted to know what all the noise was about.

"Jilly," I said, "this fucking guy pissed on my leg. All right? Here's Johnny! And here's Johnny's pee all over my nice pants!"

Once Jilly saw who the pee-er was, his expression changed from upset to accommodating. There were house rules and there were Johnny rules.

"Well, okay," Jilly said. "I'm sorry, but don't make a big thing out of it."

"Oh," I said. "I see. So he's your buddy. So fuck me."

I looked down and Johnny's pee was all the way down my pants, soaking through my shoe and my sock. Jilly dragged Johnny out of the men's room, and I cleaned up the best I could. It wasn't good enough. *Now I gotta go all the way back to my apartment, take a shower, and change.*

During the cab ride, I started to calm down. I asked Patti if I did the right thing by blowing up. She said absolutely, and that was coming from someone who was always telling me not to blow up. She said you have to be able to look at yourself in the mirror. That, I could have done no matter what. But if I had said nothing, it was Patti I wouldn't have been able to look at anymore.

I wasn't exactly sure why we went back to Jilly's later that night. Maybe to get the other leg peed on. And just like I rehearsed in my mind exactly what I was going to say before walking onto the set of *The Tonight Show,* as we pulled up to Jilly's, I thought about what I would say to Johnny if I ran into him again. But it didn't matter. When we got there, the maitre d' told us Johnny and Ed were both so ripped, the staff had to cart them out of there. That was a relief, but at the same time, I wondered if I blew *The Tonight Show.*

About a year later, I was in the NBC studios in Burbank doing a game show right down the hall from Johnny and Ed. The guys knew

I was there because on the way in I said hello to some of the crew. I found out a few minutes later that the producers of *The Tonight Show* were stuck because a guest had cancelled at the last minute. I let them know by word of mouth that I could do the show, no problem.

But by the time the credits were rolling on the game show and they were giving out free Turtle Wax, I found out it was not going to happen. My name came up, and Johnny said no. And I was never asked again. That was okay. I didn't take any shit, and I didn't take any pee. And I didn't let a wet leg here and there keep me from going back to Jilly's.

In the movie *The Manchurian Candidate,* when Frank Sinatra's character walks out of a bar, if you freeze the frame, you can see the bar is Jilly's. It wasn't the real Jilly's, just a Hollywood movie set. But the tribute was real. Jilly's was Frank's home away from home. It was his. They should have had Jilly in a movie walking out of a bar named "Frank's."

The Sinatra association is what made Jilly's. When Frank walked in there, it was chaos. Nobody was supposed to know he was coming in, but the staff would let out the word and the place started filling up wall to wall. You knew the "Chairman of the Board" was going to stroll in any minute when you spotted a string of big-name celebrities walk in within about a half hour of each other—names like Tony Bennett, Sammy Davis Jr., Al Martino, Jerry Vale, Robert Wagner, and his wife, the beautiful Natalie Wood.

In any other famous club, that alone would have been the event, but at Jilly's, it was like the trombone section at the head of a parade. It was like John the Baptist before the Messiah. The way management saw it, Frank Sinatra couldn't walk into a half-empty place. The whole thing had to be a coronation.

Sinatra had his own table. There were many times I was near the table and many more times I sat at the table. This was something you never saw before and may never see again. Here was someone larger than life sitting three feet from you. It was a big deal, and it wasn't a big deal—somewhere right in between. And that was part of the magic.

Everybody wanted to get near Frank, to touch Frank. "How ya' doing, Frank?" "Wonderful to see you, Frank." He was shaking hands and his arm was pumping all night long like he was milking a cow. And he was—a cow named Jilly's. The waiters would get a hundred dollars a pop to let someone walk past Frank. These people paying that kind of money had no balls. They could have done it for free.

It took an old soldier like Don Rickles to turn that around for just an instant. As legend has it and Rickles himself has confirmed, one night at Jilly's he asked Sinatra to do him a favor. "Frank," he said, "could you walk past my table a little later and say, "Don, how are you doing?" A half hour later, Sinatra walked by Rickles' table, which was packed with a bunch of his friends, and said, "Don, how are you doing?"

"Excuse me," Rickles replied. "Who the fuck are you?"

There were just a few people on the planet who could get away with something like that. You either could or you couldn't.

The management got away with something else, over and over again. If the place was a little slow, they would start spreading rumors that Sinatra was coming in. In reality, Sinatra could have been in California somewhere or in Turkey for all they cared. It didn't matter. People would start showing up out of nowhere awaiting the Chairman. If you understood about the trombones and the parade, you could tell the difference between the real thing and this sort of bullshit. But most people wanted to be caught up in the bullshit. In fact, the next day people would say, "Yeah, I was at Jilly's last night, and I saw Frank Sinatra sitting there in the corner."

In truth, Jilly's still had a lot to offer with or without Frank Sinatra. The establishment was part of the great tradition of New York clubs, which included the Copacabana, Jimmy Weston's, and the Latin Quarter. It had an atmosphere of being someplace special, at the center of the world. At Jilly's, the food was also exceptional. It wasn't Italian food that everyone raved about. It was Chinese food. People would kill for a Jilly's eggroll and massacre for Jilly's egg foo young. Jilly was capable of eating these dishes, but he didn't know the first thing about making them. That was the job of Howie, the Chinese head cook, who worked like a madman in the kitchen down in the basement for literally decades.

Jilly's had great bands coming in and out constantly, and the house band was something special. The house singer for many years was Frankie Randall, who was almost as good at being Sinatra on stage as Sinatra himself. The piano player was a fine gentleman named Bobby Cole, who before Jilly's had worked with Judy Garland and was a favorite of Sinatra. Bobby Cole ranked up there with any jazz musician you could find.

Every wiseguy in the world was at Jilly's at one time or another, there were just more of them when Sinatra was in. Celebrities came in, and generally they were approachable. You could have a conversation with Jake LaMotta or Rocky Graziano. One celebrity who wasn't approachable was Joe DiMaggio. He'd walk in and tell the maitre d' that he didn't want anybody near him. And he didn't want to sign any autographs. So they put him off in a distant corner somewhere, watched his back, and the great Joe D sat there and ate alone like a poor bastard.

Of course, the man was one of the best athletes ever to put on a uniform, but once he hung up his spikes and walked out of the stadium, he was not much of a human being. I had dinner with him many times, and he had a personality like a mop. He never picked up a check. Not even once. That streak was a lot longer than the fifty-six consecutive games he hit in. He never even got the tip. He never went for a dime. When he made an appearance at a wedding, you had to pay him fifty grand an hour, and he didn't give a fuck. He would still sit in the corner.

But it would take a lot more than one sour ex-ballplayer to kill the majestic atmosphere at Jilly's, and the person to thank for that was not Jilly. It was his wife, Honey. Honey was really the backbone of that place. Jilly was like a host. He walked around and acted like somebody. Honey took the place from being a hole in the wall saloon to a celebrity mecca. She had connections, and those connections were a matter of lots of speculation.

Earlier in her life, Honey was an abortionist, long before it was legal. But not just an abortionist—an abortionist to the stars. Frank Sinatra's mother, back in the day, was in the same profession. According to one version of the story, Sinatra had knocked up a starlet and needed help. His mother referred him to Honey, and that was the beginning of a long relationship. Ultimately, Jilly met Sinatra through Honey, and the rest was history.

Honey was a real piece of work. She wore her hair green. She cursed like a sailor and operated like a pimp. She and Jilly lived in style—her style. They had a houseboat outside the Fontainebleau Hotel in Florida that was so palatial no one knew how it stayed afloat. It looked like a wiseguy's version of the Queen Elizabeth II.

Up in New York, Jilly's couldn't float either, but it didn't have to. From the outside, it was just another small four-story building with an alleyway. Inside, it was either a dream or a nightmare, depending on the eye of the beholder. Jilly and Honey's apartment was on the second and third floors, connected by a spiral staircase. Like the menu downstairs, the décor was Chinese. There were bone carvings in the doors and walls. There was plush carpet, a steam room, and a huge bathroom with wall-to-wall marble. The third floor was one large bedroom, with a huge circular bed that was like a theater in the round.

I don't know exactly how much performing Jilly and Honey did there, and I don't want to know, but Frank Sinatra was the main event there many times. Jilly and Honey had another apartment in New York, so the apartment at Jilly's was Frank's whenever he was in town. According to Jilly, over the years, Frank banged half of Hollywood and half of Broadway in that bed.

The entertainment downstairs at Jilly's was a little less racy but still over the top. Sinatra had an entourage beyond the Rat Pack that few people knew about. Pat Henry was a comedian who opened for him going all the way back to The 500 Club in 1958. From that time on, if you went to see Sinatra, there was a good chance that first you would see Pat Henry dishing out funny stories and one-liners for twenty or thirty minutes.

Pat Henry and I had something in common aside from our first name. He was Italian, born Patrick Henry Scanarto. Like me, he found out that getting booked with a name like Scanarto or Caputo in the 1950s was next to impossible. For a long time, he didn't know I was Italian, and I didn't know he was Italian. It took Ed Sullivan, who was completely out of it, to make the connection by accident. When I did *The Ed Sullivan Show,* he kept calling me "My paisano, Pat Henry." I figured as long as my check said "Pat Cooper," who gave a fuck? When Pat Henry did the show, during rehearsal Sullivan kept addressing him as Pat Cooper. The crew tried to explain the difference, but Ed Sullivan was in his own world.

There was, in fact, a big difference between Pat Henry and Pat Cooper, and it had nothing to do with names or heritage. I noticed the difference the first time I performed on the same bill with Frank Sinatra. Pat Henry and some of the other members of Frank's entourage acted like they wanted me to bomb. Actually, I don't think they were acting. I was sipping from their gravy train. I didn't want a gravy train. I just wanted to make a living being funny.

The price Pat Henry paid over the years for being Frank Sinatra's lap dog was enormous. He lived in fear that Frank would dump him, and if you feared something like that, Frank might just make your nightmare come true. Meanwhile, Jilly got a piece of whatever Pat Henry made—an agent's fee. But Jilly Rizzo didn't book anybody, least of all Pat Henry. Booking Pat Henry to open for Frank Sinatra was like ordering lighting before the thunder.

But Pat Henry was his own worst enemy. He was always walking around half broke, even though he should have been a multimillionaire. He made as much as fifteen thousand dollars a week, but he gambled away everything he made and sometimes more. Sometimes on stage he would tell jokes at Sinatra's expense. He might have imagined for a moment that he had Sinatra by the balls, but Sinatra had *him* by the balls.

Then there was Morty Storm, who was missing a pair of balls. It wasn't always that way. He was an army medic in World War II and served on Guam or one of the bloody islands in the Pacific. When he came back, he decided he was going to hit the stage and make people laugh, but he got bloodied all over again.

Morty Storm was an unfunny comic. He stood on stage and garbled a bunch of jokes that no one could understand. His act started with, "Hello, I'm Morty Storm the Thoid" and it went downhill from there. He growled a lot, and it sounded like *Badabadabadabada. . . .* He wore big, thick-rimmed glasses. He had a hairpiece that sat on his head like a dead raccoon. He looked like Detective Columbo if you threw him in the washing machine and put it on spin cycle. Someone should have. Morty would wear the same suit for a week and never bathe. When he performed in the Catskills, there were certain maids who would not do his room. You always knew Morty was coming half a minute before he arrived.

When Morty finally caught up with his odor, you were treated to a series of jokes and one-liners that had been discarded backstage during the days of vaudeville—around the time George Burns was in diapers:

"I could have gone to college. One thing stopped me—high school."

"Actually, I went to college. I took medicine for four years. I feel much better now."

"I come from a broken home. A tree fell on it."

Morty's big routine, his "Who's On First," was a bit about his dog named Sex.

"I went to city hall to renew his dog license. I told the clerk I would like a license for Sex. He said, 'I'd like one, too!' . . . My wife and I took the dog on our honeymoon. I told the clerk I wanted a room for my wife and me, and a special room for Sex. He said, 'You don't need a special room. As long as you pay your bill we don't care what you do.'"

Somewhere along the line, Frank Sinatra caught a whiff of Morty Storm and never exhaled. Frank took him in, and Morty never realized he was being laughed at rather than with. Morty Storm was a constant fixture at Jilly's. He was the mascot. He was like a trained pup that did tricks and was then thrown a bone. I tried to explain this to Morty—that not only were they throwing him a bone, it wasn't even a bone he could suck on. They were hitting him over the head with it.

The guys at Jilly's used to do things like put cupcakes in his suit pockets and then pat him down so they got smashed. They would throw firecrackers between his legs to see him jump. One time, Sinatra was throwing a bachelor party for a friend of his and he hired Morty. Morty probably prepared ten minutes of material, but that wasn't this gig. He was hired to pop out of a cake. The guys who were there later said it was the funniest thing they had ever seen in their entire lives, expecting to see a gorgeous young lady pop out and instead seeing an old Jewish comic dressed like a hobo and reeking like a sewer.

But I liked Morty, and told him on several occasions that if he wanted to break out on his own and make a million dollars, have some balls. Bill yourself as the worst fucking comic God ever put on this earth. Now that was something people would pay top dollar to see. "Listen to me, Morty," I said. "You could become an icon. Who the fuck is worse than you?"

"What are you talking about, Pat?" he said. "I just worked with Frank."

He worked with Frank like the sole of Sinatra's left shoe. I had the displeasure of watching Morty Storm open up for Sinatra once at Caesar's Palace in Las Vegas. He walked out in a suit that looked like someone left it at the airport in 1948. The audience got a whiff of him and he started going *Badabadabadabada:*

"I seen a miracle. I read the obituary column. Everybody died in alphabetical order. . . . I got hit by a truck. I flew fifty feet in the air. Would you believe I got a ticket for leaving the scene of an accident? . . . Last week I made $3,500 as a parking attendant. I sold two cars."

Three minutes into the act, Pat Henry came running out to grab Morty like a lifeguard. "Excuse me, son," Pat Henry said. "You must be in the wrong place. This is a stage. This is for entertainment. Frank Sinatra's gonna be here soon." The place went wild. They were screaming and, in the process, taking away what little dignity Morty Storm had left. Then Pat Henry stayed on and did twenty minutes until Sinatra got there. When it came to getting pissed on, nobody took more hits than Morty Storm.

Jilly's was magic for many years, but by the mid 1970s, Jilly and Honey were divorced, and Jilly was getting older. He didn't have the energy anymore. So with Frank's consent, he closed the place down. Jilly's may be long gone, but fortunately, it will live forever in my heart.

13

Raging Bullshit

If we had to pick the single greatest filmmaker of the last generation or two, there might be an argument, but the winner would have to be Martin Scorsese. The bigger problem would be picking out your favorite Scorsese film. *Taxi Driver, Raging Bull, Goodfellas*—the man makes classics. Scorsese can show you the darkest parts of the human psyche and still keep you entertained every second.

In 1994, I had the pleasure of entertaining Martin Scorsese and a bunch of his friends at his party in New York. I got up and did a few minutes, and Hollywood's A-list laughed. I shook hands with Martin, and that was that.

A couple of weeks later, I got a call from Martin Scorsese's secretary. Apparently, his mother was a fan of mine and wanted to meet me. The bonus was that we were going to be meeting on the set of his next movie, *Casino.* I was being asked to read for a scene opposite Mrs. Scorsese, so we would be killing two birds with one deck. I would have flown halfway around the world to be in a Scorsese movie, but since the picture was being shot on location in Las Vegas, I only had to drive a couple of miles up US Interstate 15.

They sent over the script, and I looked for the part. It was harder to find than snow on a summer day in Vegas. When I finally found it, I thought there was a mistake. I told Patti there had to be more. The part was three lines. It was barely enough to get a SAG card. I had a lot more lines at Scorsese's party. The part was a nothing. A zero. The great director was throwing me a bone with no meat on it. Not even his mother would remember me after the credits rolled. "This," I said to Patti, "is a fucking insult."

"Pat," she said, "this is a Martin Scorsese movie."

"I don't care," I said. "It's still a fucking insult. I've been doing roles for thirty years. I'm a name performer. A name performer!"

I settled down later that night and read the whole script through. It was a great script, but that was no surprise. De Niro's Sam Rothstein was a professional sports handicapper sent out to Vegas to run a casino and make money for the mob back East. Joe Pesci's Nicky Santoro was De Niro's childhood friend and a gangster half out of his mind looking for a piece of the action—actually, all of it—in Sin City. Sharon Stone's Ginger McKenna was a hustler who De Niro tries to tame and make into a wife. The scenes were jumping off the page onto the big screen in my mind. And so was the perfect part for me.

The part of Billy Sherbert was written as Sam Rothstein's right-hand man. He wasn't supposed to be a bodyguard or a heavy, but more like Rothstein's shadow. He was a casino manager, always there with a quick move or a few choice words. He knew the score even when De Niro's character didn't want to see it. I knew I could eat that part up. Patti said, "Well, you can't tell them that."

"What the hell do you mean I can't tell them that?" I said. "All I have to do is pick up the phone and call Scorsese's office." And that's what I did.

As it turned out, I could tell them whatever I wanted to. They just didn't have to listen. When I got to the studio, I was introduced to Scorsese's mother, Catherine, a lovely woman. "Senora," I said, "it is an absolute pleasure to meet you." I asked a few assistants about the

Billy Sherbert part, but as far as anybody knew, I wasn't reading for anything except the part I'd been offered originally.

This wasn't your average audition. Aside from Martin Scorsese, Robert De Niro, Joe Pesci, and Sharon Stone were all sitting there. But there was no pressure. Three lines wasn't even enough to fuck up if I wanted to. I did the lines, Catherine Scorsese did hers, and that was it. Martin wanted us to try it again, but I put an end to that.

"I can't do this fucking thing," I said. "I'm a name performer. I'm a name performer, and you're throwing me a fucking bone."

Robert De Niro, Joe Pesci, and Sharon Stone all stopped and looked like they were about to die, even though that didn't come till the end of the script. No one walked away from a Martin Scorsese film—even the chance to play an ashtray—but there was a first time for everything.

"I'm sorry, Martin," I said. "It's not for me. I gotta do what's in my brain. I gotta have something I can do something with."

"Well," he said, "I don't know what else there is at this point . . ."

"See what you can do," I said. "I'd appreciate it."

The one person I didn't want to offend was sitting right next to me.

"Senora," I said, "please don't take this as any disrespect whatsoever. This is nothing personal. I loved working with you."

"I understand, Pat," she said. "You need something more." Then she told me that she would talk to Martin, and that he could probably add a few more lines.

"Do me a favor, Senora. Please don't do that for me. Please don't. Your son is a great talent. I respect him. I just want him to respect me."

"Are you sure?"

"Listen," I said. "God bless your son. But I don't care if I ever make a movie."

As proud as I was, I was still hoping to get a call over the next few days to read for another part—a real part. But the only call I got was from the actor who got the role. When you throw away a throwaway part, someone will pick it up. This gentleman was basically a walk-on who walked off with a part in a Martin Scorsese movie. He thanked me for turning it down. He thanked me like I was a surgeon who had just given him a heart transplant using my own heart. I told him not to mention it and that I hoped it worked out great for him.

It worked out great for Don Rickles. He got the part of De Niro's sidekick. Rickles is one of the funniest comedians who ever lived. The problem was that this part was not for him. He was out of his element. He had no presence. Instead of a shadow, he was more like a fly on the wall. He barely said a thing, and that was not Don Rickles. When he did say something, it barely made it out of his mouth, which is especially not Don Rickles. The bottom line is that if you were watching the movie, you didn't understand why De Niro's character, a very savvy guy, had the Don Rickles' character around.

It wasn't as if I was rooting for the movie to be bad. All the wishing in the world couldn't make a Martin Scorsese movie bad, and this one was no exception. *Casino* was up there with any movie he ever made. It was an epic with all the elements. De Niro, who could play the toughest of the tough, wasn't a tough guy here. He was someone using his wits to make it through one more day with the mob breathing down his neck, his best friend completely out of control, and his wife always a half-step away from going off the deep end. And the best thing about the movie was that there was no happy ending. Scorsese wouldn't stoop to that. The ending was bloody and tragic.

For me, this wasn't an ending but a beginning. I stayed friends with Scorsese's mother, and Patti and I had dinner with her in New York. I was glad I stood my ground on *Casino*. I remembered what happened to Jilly Rizzo years before. Jilly, who had a face on him like Edward G. Robinson meets Boris Karloff, had a reputation, deserved or otherwise, as a tough guy and had fans all over the world. One of those fans was the actor Mickey Rourke, who got Jilly a small part in his upcoming movie *Year of the Dragon*. To the surprise of absolutely nobody,

Jilly would be playing a Mafioso. He had about five lines. The twist was that Jilly's character, Schiro, had his vocal cords removed and spoke through an electronic voice box.

One afternoon in the fall of 1984, I was having lunch at the Doral Hotel in New York with Jilly and our friends the Delvecchios. Tony Delvecchio had run Jilly's in the late '70s and early '80s. He was the ultimate tough guy who was a sweetheart of a man inside and never settled anything with force unless there was no other option. His wife, Cathy, was his match—a woman who could march to hell and back without blinking. We sat there at the Doral and had Jilly for lunch.

The shoot for Jilly's scene in *Year of the Dragon* was about a week away. He had been rehearsing for months, but apparently that still wasn't enough. So he was going over his lines at the table. The man couldn't remember two of the lines, much less five. Tony said, "Jilly, you mean to fucking tell me you've been at this shit for six months and you don't know the fucking lines?" But that wasn't Jilly's main problem. He was trying to sound like he had an electronic voice box in real life.

"Jilly," I said, "first of all, you sound like you have a voice box already. Don't disguise your voice. You don't gotta try. You always sound like you just got out of fucking bed with a smoker's cough. What the fuck are you disguising it for and trying to make it something it already is?"

"I'm tryin' to get it just right, Pat."

"Well then leave it the fuck alone," I said. "You sound like a voice box talking through a voice box. One fucking voice box is enough. Besides, if they don't like the voice box you got, they'll put it through their own voice box."

The movie was shot mostly in North Carolina. When Jilly got back to New York, he told us he really nailed it. Six months of going over five lines really paid off. So when the movie premiered in August 1985, Jilly, Tony, and I went to see it.

Rourke, who goes after the Chinese gangs and starts a war. It was not Scorsese, but it was a decent movie. Of course, the whole time we were sitting there in the theater waiting for Jilly's big moment on the silver screen. Finally it came. Jilly was sitting at a table like a big capo. He said exactly one word. And then it was over. Six months, one word. We couldn't even tell if it was Jilly's voice or a special effect.

So I didn't second-guess myself on *Casino*. After what Jilly went through, I knew my three lines could have been cut to no lines, and the bone I was thrown could have become a shaving. I could have gone from being embarrassed to being humiliated.

Not long after *Casino* came out, my phone rang in our Greenwich Village apartment, and the woman on the other end told me she was calling on behalf of the producers of *Seinfeld*. She said, "Mr. Cooper, we would like you to do an episode of *Seinfeld*." I said, "Sure, I would love to." And I hung up.

Ten seconds later the phone rang again. It was the same woman and she was laughing. "You know," she said, "they told me you were a little sick."

"A little?"

"Everybody in the cast loves you on *Howard Stern*," she said. "And your reputation at the Friars Club is marvelous. We're doing an episode called 'The Friars Club,' and we'd like you to appear."

"This isn't bullshit?"

"This isn't bullshit."

"Then my apologies," I said. "No one warned me. I thought this was a prank phone call."

It was no prank. There was a ticket waiting for me at JFK the next day. There was a rental car waiting for me at LAX in California. They had a hotel room reserved for me for that night, but shooting was that day, so I drove right to the studio. I would have appreciated having a script to read on the plane, but as I walked into the studio, all I knew was that the plot had something to do with the Friars Club. It didn't bother me, though. *Seinfeld* was the funniest show around, hands down, and I was happy to get on.

Jerry Seinfeld and Jason Alexander were in the room along with the executive producer and co-creator, Larry David. The set looked a little like the Friars Club with the paneling and all the framed pictures on the wall. I walked over and said hello to Jerry, who said, "Hi, Pat." Then Jason said, "Pat, you are the fucking greatest on *Stern*. You're so fast. Howard doesn't have a chance against your mind."

"Howard's biggest problem is Howard," I said.

Larry walked over carrying a sheaf of paper. I asked him if that was my script. He shook his head no and told me there was no script for this part.

"Excuse me?" I said. "No script? Now I'm thinking there's no actors, no director, and no fucking pay."

What I was really thinking was how strange this was after going through what I went through on *The Dean Martin Show* about thirty years earlier. Because of Dean and his cue cards, it was etched in my brain that TV sketch comedy was strictly by the book.

Not anymore. Larry told me I could do whatever I felt was right for the scene. He then proceeded to explain the entire plot of the episode. George was losing his mind thinking about his upcoming wedding to Susan, who bored him to death. The only way George thought he could survive was to double date with Jerry as much as possible. So Jerry suggests they all go to the Friars Club, where his friend Pat Cooper had recommended him for membership.

The maitre d' at the Friars Club won't let Jerry in without a jacket and lends him one with the official Friars Club logo. Jerry forgets to give back the jacket on his way out. Then the two couples go to see the Flying Karamazov Brothers, who jump up to the balcony and toss Jerry's Friars Club jacket into the orchestra. Now Jerry has to go back to the Friars Club and explain to Pat Cooper that the gypsies took the jacket. Jerry is scared to talk to Pat Cooper, and who could blame him? I would be scared, too.

We started the scene, and the first thing I noticed was that George was with Jerry. It wasn't George's jacket, but he was there backing up his friend.

JERRY: Hey, Pat.

PAT: Hey, Jerry. What the hell went wrong? What's the matter with you? Are you a kleptomaniac, or what?

JERRY: I forgot to take it off.

PAT: You forgot to take it off? Oh, you go into a department store, you put a suit on, and you walk right out. What are you, some sort of an idiot?

JERRY: I'm sorry.

PAT: Where's the jacket?

JERRY: One of the gypsies took it.

PAT: Oh, the gypsies took it! Of course. New York has a lot of gypsies. Oh, on every corner there's a gypsy!

GEORGE: Well, it's true. I saw it.

Here was the opportunity I waiting for. The words barely made it out of Jason's mouth, which was perfect.

PAT: Excuse me, are you an entertainer? Are you in show business?

GEORGE: No, I, uh . . .

PAT: Then what am I talking to you for? Jerry, bring back the jacket tomorrow.

JERRY: All right.

With that, I walked off. Jerry and Jason had a few more lines, the maitre d' kicked them out, and the scene was over. Right away, Larry, Jason, and Jerry told me what I did was great, and I thanked them for going along with it. At least in my opinion, no scripted line in the world could top a well-placed ad-lib or two. The reality of a nicely ad-libbed scene comes through when you watch it back. When I crushed George, Jason looked crushed, too. In a way he really was, and that came through immediately. Jason Alexander is a tremendous comedic actor. But for a moment, he wasn't exactly acting. I was grateful I had the opportunity to do what I did best on the best show on television.

Considering that I had done *The Don Ho Show* in Hawaii many years before and turned around and flew all the way back home the same day with no sleep, it was at least even money that I would do the same from Hollywood, which was a lot closer to New York. But I decided to check into the hotel, which the show had arranged, and stay the night. The truth was, I was a fan of the show and wanted to meet Julia Louis-Dreyfus and Michael Richards the next day.

But when I got up in the morning, I changed my mind and decided to skip the studio and take the next plane home. I called Patti and told her I would see her that night. She asked me why, after staying overnight, I would change my mind like that. I told her I was done with my part, and if I showed up at the studio again it would look like I was just hanging around to meet people and maybe look for another scene. That was not me. So I Don-Hoed it across three time zones and arrived back in New York.

Back at the real Friars Club, there was trouble, and it wasn't over a jacket. At the real Friars Club there was no "keeper of the jackets." What there was, however, was a dean of the club, and that was Freddie Roman. Freddie is a terrific veteran comic and a friend of mine. But I heard through the grapevine he was a little upset that the gig on *Seinfeld* went to me and not him. I heard it from comic after comic until I got bent out of shape myself. "You want to know why they picked me?" I finally said. "One word. *Talent!*"

On the inside, I understood why Freddie was upset. He had the right to be a little hurt. He was, after all, the official face of the club, not Pat Cooper, no matter how many roasts I closed. So one day I walked over to him and said, "Jesus, Freddie, what the fuck do you want me to do? The show's in the can."

"Pat," he said, "I'm not mad at you." Which was a gracious thing to say whether he meant it or not.

All sorts of friends were sincere when they saw the "Friars Club" episode and called me. The opinion was almost unanimous. It wasn't one of the funniest *Seinfeld* episodes ever, but my two-minute scene near the end made the show. "Pat," one friend said, "that was so fucking real! That was natural. That was *you.*" Unlike George Costanza, this friend was in show business, and he was sure they were going to call me back for another episode.

Seinfeld shot its final episode before that happened. But my consolation prize was that people called me up every time the "Friars Club" episode was rerun, which seemed like every few weeks.

But still no movie. Not unless you counted a movie called *My Boy*. We shot the film in Florida, and I did my part in seven days. I was excited to finally do a movie, and I thought I really nailed the part. But months went by and I didn't hear anything. I called the producer to try to get a print, and he told me there was a problem. The director was bent out of shape about not being paid, so he went back to his homeland, the former Yugoslavia. Of course, with my luck, he took the only prints with him. And that was that. No one ever heard from him again. For all I know, I may be an A-list movie star in Serbia. In Croatia, Pat Cooper may be rumored to be the father of Angelina Jolie's next baby!

One night in 1997, I was at a benefit where Anthony Quinn was auctioning off one of his sculptures. It fetched seventy-five thousand dollars. It wasn't a sentimental purchase. Quinn was that good. Before he was an actor, he studied architecture under Frank Lloyd Wright. Quinn's paintings and sculptures were hot items for many years. So was Quinn himself. He kept making movies and kids into his eighties.

I got up at this benefit and did about twenty-five minutes. Afterwards, Anthony Quinn walked up to me and shook my hand.

"How the hell did you do that?"

"Do what?" I said.

"I'd give anything to do what you just did," he said. "Not even a piece of paper for you. You just go up there and let it fly. Me, I gotta read a script. I gotta work it out."

"Well, Tony," I said, "do you know of any good scripts?"

A few months later I was closing a roast at the Friars Club and Anthony Quinn was there. Afterwards he asked me to talk to him in his car. There I was in the back of his limousine, sitting between him and another gentleman who was quite a few years younger.

"Hi, Tony," I said. "Who's this?"

"This is my lawyer."

"I'm not in trouble here, am I?" I said.

"No, no," Quinn said. "I'm going through a divorce. We decided to take a break."

"Because I know you're looking to play Paul Castellano, but this is fucking ridiculous."

"Pat!" Quinn said. "You did it again!" He put his arm around me. "How do you do that, Pat? Do you know what that means, to do that? I'm an artist. I need brushes. I need clay. You just walk up there and tell them to fuck themselves."

"That's pretty much it."

"But it's brilliant!"

"I do what I can."

We became friends, Zorba the Greek and I. To this day, a lot of people think he actually was Greek. He was Mexican-American, but the truth is, he could have done anything he put his mind to. He could have played my father in a movie, straight from Mola di Bari. He would have eaten it up. But in his heart, he wanted to be a comedian like I wanted to be a movie actor. We coached each other and both got absolutely fucking nowhere.

Until one day I got a call from a producer. The movie was *Analyze This,* about a mob boss who's having anxiety attacks and goes to see a psychiatrist. Just the idea of a mob boss visiting a shrink was funny. But the mob boss was going to be played by Robert De Niro, and the shrink was going to be played by Billy Crystal. I didn't hang up. I was being offered the part of Salvatore Masiello, the consigliere. I would have a couple of scenes with Paul Vitti, De Niro's character. They sent the script over, and in my mind I started painting a picture.

When it came time to shoot my first scene, I was ready. We were at a table in the crew's headquarters, which from the outside was supposed to look like a hole in the wall that was reminiscent of the Bergin Hunt and Fish Club from the John Gotti days in Queens. I was sipping cappuccino with Paul Vitti, Jelly, and another soldier in the family. In the scene before, one of the other families had just tried to whack Vitti, and now he was having trouble breathing and speaking. One thing I knew from years of performing was that a big part of acting is reacting. So the moment Vitti has classic symptoms of an anxiety attack, my character has to notice something is wrong.

Speaking of method acting, Robert De Niro was having a real anxiety attack during the next scene we shot. Okay, a small one. This was my big scene, the one in which Masiello tells Vitti he has to whack his shrink because the shrink knows too much. We were sitting at the bar inside the club. De Niro was having a little trouble remembering his lines, so he wanted cue cards put over my shoulder.

"No fucking way, Bobby," I said. "No special treatment. When this picture comes out, I'm gonna go into the theater and tell everybody the great Robert De Niro is reading over my fucking shoulder."

This got a big laugh from everyone on the set, including Harold Ramis, who co-wrote the screenplay. "Pat," he said, "we've gotta keep you around. Otherwise it's going to get boring around here." He was right about that. Making movies wasn't like shooting *Seinfeld*. We shot scenes again and again, and there was a lot of down time. Days were long, and if you didn't have people around to crack you up, you could wind up a basket case.

Once, after we had wrapped for the day, I asked De Niro if I could have a couple pictures of him with Patti, who was a tremendous fan. He was happy to do it. Then Patti pulled me aside and said, "Why are you doing that?"

"What do you mean why?" I said. "So you can have a picture with one of the greatest actors who ever lived, that's why."

"You're making him nervous," Patti said. "You'll upset him."

"I'll upset him?" I said. "He's a fucking human being. He's taking a picture with you. Is that so fucking hard?"

"Well, he had trouble with the lines before."

"He did that on his own, darling," I said. "I had nothing to do with that. We all have trouble with lines on occasion. Besides, I might as well get you a picture, because I'm never going to work with him again."

"What makes you say that?" Patti asked.

"He doesn't like what I'm doing. As an actor. I can feel it."

I was dead wrong. That's only happened about a million times in my life. Now it was a million and one. *Analyze This* was a big hit and even inspired a TV show that was centered around a mob boss who goes to a shrink—*The Sopranos*. You might have heard of it. In 2001, I was asked to play Masiello again in *Analyze That*—the sequel to *Analyze This*.

My first scene with De Niro was in a local Italian bar. Paul Vitti had just been sprung from jail and was trying to stay out of the war between families. As in the first movie, my character's job was to convince Vitti to be a boss and not the pussy patient of a headshrinker. But when the cameras weren't rolling, I had another role—agent. The bartender in the scene was an unknown actor who had come far enough to be in a scene that millions upon millions of people would see, but not far enough to be heard by any one of them. He needed just one line to be heard and to join the union.

"Come on, Bobby," I said. "Someone throw this nice young man a fucking line. He's got six starving kids at home crawling around. Give the man a fucking line. How about, 'You shot me'?"

Harold Ramis said, "Okay, just say, Mr. Vitti, would you like a drink!"

"Brilliant!" I said. "That's why *you* write for *us!*"

The producers said they were going to keep the line in the movie. The actor was so happy he gave me a hug.

"See, Bob," I said. "They love us. Let's give everybody words. Words. Everybody take a word!"

After we wrapped, I was talking with Billy Crystal, who turned to my wife and said, "How do you live with this guy?"

"It's not easy living with a genius," she said. She didn't miss a beat. She was really taking notes all those years.

"Billy," I said, "don't look so shocked. It's called *up yours!*"

Billy laughed hard, and that's when I knew I would be part of *Analyze the Other Fucking Thing* if they ever made it.

A couple years later, we were honoring Billy Crystal at the Friars Club by opening the Billy Crystal Lounge. This was a big deal. Frank Sinatra had a room. Milton Berle had a room. Lucille Ball had a room. The rest of us were lucky to get a spot on the carpet. There was a big crowd there and every one of us, me included, talked about what a giant of a talent Billy Crystal was. Afterwards, I walked over and congratulated him. Then I dropped the bomb.

"You know, Billy," I said, "I don't want to upset you, but I turned it down."

"What?!"

"Shhh, shhh . . . don't say anything. It's all right. To be honest, I didn't really want a Cooper Lounge. Then I have to be here all the time. I'm glad you got it."

With that I walked away. Billy actually looked a little stunned. Jean Pierre, the maitre d', who loved me, told him, "What are you listening to him for? You know he's nuts."

As time went on, Patti wondered whether Billy Crystal was mad at me.

"What the fuck is wrong with America?" I said. "Why the fuck should he be mad at me? It was a joke. If Don Rickles did it, everybody would be laughing. If Milton Berle did it, it would be a legend. But when Pat Cooper does it, it's in poor taste. I mean, give me a fucking break already."

On June 9, 2006 we roasted Jerry Lewis at the Friars Club. Richard Belzer was the roast master. When I got up, I had plenty to say about Jerry Lewis. But suddenly I found myself playing the part I wanted so badly for so many years—the part of an angry comedian getting back at a great director. The part of the great director would be played by Martin Scorsese, who was sitting on the dais behind me.

"Marty Scorsese's here, ladies and gentlemen. Marty offered me my first big break in the movies. It was a scene in *Casino*. In fact, it was a scene with the director's mother, who he also gave her first big break. And here was the scene. 'Hello, Ma. Goodbye, Ma. *Cut!*'"

"Marty, you told me you were a fan. Is this what you do to a fan? What if you weren't a fan? Then things wouldn't have turned out so good. Then I would have played a deck of cards. Then I would have played Don Rickles' scalp. You're the greatest director who ever lived. Martin Scorsese! And you threw me a bone! Look at me. Do I look like a dog? Do I look like I eat fucking Alpo? I do your party and you give me three words. Well I got three words for you, Martin—Leo Kiddy DiCaprio. You put this kid in every fucking scene. Marty, please, whatever you do, please don't make me Leo's dog in your next epic."

People in the audience were screaming. Lisa Lampanelli looked like she was going to cough up her tits. It was a command performance.

Since June 9, 2006, Martin Scorsese hasn't called me for another audition. Neither has Serbia or Croatia. But I'm waiting patiently by the phone. Meanwhile, I'm putting the finishing touches on my life story and working on the movie rights. I heard they're getting DiCaprio.

14

Private Darts

In 1986 I was doing a benefit and a nice guy named Gary Dell'Abate walked up to me and said, "Howard Stern would like to put you on his show."

"Who's Howard Stern?" I asked.

Gary looked shocked. Maybe he thought I was putting him on, but I wasn't. I really didn't know. Apparently I was the only one.

He explained that Howard Stern had the most popular radio show in New York and Los Angeles, and I told him I'd do the show. I would have done it even if it was two guys talking to each other with Dixie cups and a string.

Before my appearance, I learned a little about Howard Stern and how big he was getting. He was opinionated, over-the-top, and on occasion told everybody to go fuck themselves. As far as I was concerned, he was stealing my act.

When I got to the K-Rock radio studio in New York, the first thing I noticed was how everyone was groveling at Howard's feet. He was a tall, skinny, gawky guy, and they worshipped him. It wasn't what you'd call a regular radio show in there. It was a madhouse. The producers, the writers, the interns—they all just wanted to touch him.

They told me, "We're going to introduce you to Howard." I asked, "Do I get a fucking autograph, too?"

I looked at Howard, looked around, and said to myself, he's crazy, and I'm crazy to do the show. But we hit it off. And it wasn't like we were two guys stroking each other's egos. I let Howard know I was an individual. I wasn't going to do or say the things he wanted me to do and say. And he liked that—not that I gave a shit if he liked it or not, but I thought he really did. We went back and forth on the air, and it felt honest. When I talked about celebrities that were hypocrites, I wasn't doing it to get Howard Stern ratings. I was doing it because that was what I did. On one of my first shows, I talked about a run-in I had with Steve Lawrence and Eydie Gorme.

"Morty Gunty passes away, God love his soul. I go to his funeral, and Steve and Eydie are there. Eydie comes over and says how we lost a good friend. I said, 'Eydie, what are you talking about, a good friend? How dare you? Now that he's dead he's your friend? If a person was your friend, you wouldn't give him just a ten-percent billing. What happened to asking someone to be an equal? What would it have cost you? Nothing.' She was shaking. These people, they don't understand. They walk on water, but they don't understand that it takes six people to hold them up."

Howard said, "You're not playing the game."

Of course I knew the game he was talking about. It was the same game played by headliners to control their opening acts. The same game that Tony Bennett and Walter Kane once played on me. I don't like games. I don't play them.

Then I started talking with Howard about some of the promoters I dealt with throughout my career—more hypocrites. How they promised one thing and delivered another.

"People say to me, 'Why don't you back off, get the money, and run?' That's no fun. You know what the worst thing to do is, Howard? Give the money back. They get crazy."

Howard said, "I never tried that myself." And I believed him.

"You give the money back," I said, "you become King Kong. They hate you. If you don't give it back, they call you a dog. If you do give it back, you're still a bigger dog for trying to embarrass them. But they don't give *you* the money back. They figure if they got the money, keep it."

It seemed like we could talk about anything. That was Howard's business, and it was my business back when he was still in diapers. Robin, his sidekick, was a wonderful person. She kept the ball rolling for Howard, and as a smart man, he knew it.

And I was fast. Someone mentioned the singer, Helen Reddy, and I said, "They should arrest her for loitering in front of a band."

We were off and running. I did a couple of shows, and all of a sudden Howard was getting calls to put that guy on again—the funny guy who yells. Young kids were stopping me on the street. I knew these kids were not going to come see my shows, but maybe their parents would. It didn't matter. We were all having a good time.

A comfort level developed between us over the next few years. Not the kind of comfort where you don't have to think on your feet anymore because everyone's throwing everyone else softballs. It was the kind of comfort where you knew you could go further, and you knew the people around you would appreciate it. You knew you could hit fastballs. And on the *Stern* show, they threw them. One morning, Robin just started hurling names at me to see what I would say.

"Dean Martin."

"Could have been the greatest entertainer of all time."

"Malcolm X."

"Could have been the greatest entertainer of all time."

"David Letterman."

"Indiana. Without corn, he'd be off the air. In other words, he's got the right face, the right everything. He's like America. Mooooo . . ."

"Sonny Bono."

"How dare he become a congressman!"

"Chevy Chase."

"Goodbye. It's over. The luckiest man that God put on the planet."

"Whoopi Goldberg."

"Probably one of the greatest American actresses we have."

This threw Howard, Robin, Jackie, Fred, and the whole crew for a loop. They were expecting insults. But I was not there to insult people. I was there to tell the truth. I was there to entertain. On occasion, the truth is easy to swallow because it's just an old veteran comic in his pajamas looking out at the world. Whenever they asked me about myself, I told them the truth, like what I watch on television.

"My favorite show is anything on the Discovery Channel. I love anything with animals. I gotta buy all the films—all the films with prey. I order them. I pick up the phone and say, 'Send me the thing with the animals eating other animals.' It's marvelous. I love animals. I am an animal. But I didn't love all animals. I said it before. I want the dinosaurs dead, the ugly bastards! If the dinosaurs were alive they'd be dumping all over the highway!"

We also did the news on the show, which Howard and Robin had been doing since they started working together in Washington, DC. I'm not Ted Koppel, but I do read the newspapers. Half the time, that's not even necessary. You just have to be quick and have lived a while. I had both qualifications. So when Robin read a headline that New York's Off-Track Betting establishment was losing a lot of money, I was there by a nose.

"How can a bookmaker be broke? No way. I'll show you how to make money. You buy a horse. If the horse doesn't win, you can't write the horse off. So you know what Italians do? They eat the goddamned horse. We make the best *bracciole*. Horse meat. During the war, everybody ate horse meat."

When a name in the news came up, I was there, even if it meant being banned from another show. Robin mentioned Regis Philbin.

I said, "Regis Philbin was on the radio and he said, 'You hear about Diane Sawyer making seven million? That should happen to us.' Here's a man making nothing but money, and he's counting Diane Sawyer's money! Now he's in the hospital, and what's on his mind? *How can I make money from almost dying?* He put out an exercise video—how to walk. He should walk into a wall. How dare he? He would sell you air. Kathie Lee, now she's got her husband in the commercials on the boat. Next the kid'll be dancing on the boat."

True, there were still a few shows I wasn't banned from, but all in good time. When more serious news items came up, I was like Howard for the most part. Not much was off limits. My point was not to make fun of victims or people who couldn't defend themselves. But something tragic and sick, like the Unabomber, was clearly on the menu.

ROBIN: Montana is a hotbed.

HOWARD: I was thinking of moving there.

PAT: You would be a big hit over there.

ROBIN: Here, if someone lives in a tarpaper shack down by the East River, they call him homeless. This guy's not being called homeless. He had no water. No facilities!

PAT: That's why they call him the Unabomber. You should have nothing but bombs. How did this guy get a bomb? I can't get a pistol locally. I can't buy a bullet. This guy gets a bomb to blow up Utah.

ROBIN: This guy's a genius.

PAT: With no water?

ROBIN: He went to Harvard.

PAT: You know what happens? You become such a genius that you collapse. Doesn't he get thirsty?

HOWARD: He wanted to go back to nature.

PAT: To blow up everybody in the world? Let me tell you something
          I was in a delicatessen. I stole an olive and an alarm went off.
          This guy's got bombs, bombs . . . nothing's going off.

HOWARD: I understand the Unabomber gets along with his mother
          though.

My family was fair game, because everything was fair game.
Almost everything. And as everyone eventually learns, it's the "almost" in life that gets you into trouble. Neither Howard nor anyone
else in the world could hit my "almost," because I was usually
there first. When we were discussing *People's* 50 Most Beautiful People in the World, Howard told me I looked like Paul Newman. I told
him I looked like Alfred E. Newman.

There were people who thought I was mad for going on *Stern,* and
not the kind of mad usually associated with Pat Cooper. They thought
Howard's humor was not my kind of humor and the audience wasn't
my audience. They heard about naked pole dancers in the studio and
lesbian love acts. On occasion, my own wife complained. One time she
told me—begged me—not to go on the show. She had relatives back
in Ohio who said this was beneath me. I told her they should stop listening to the show.

I told her I didn't give a fuck what those people or any other people were saying. This was like telling me not to take the subway. The
subway is me, and sometimes the low route is the best one. Sure, I was
putting my foot in my mouth plenty of times, but that's the fun of it.
Millions listen to you put it in, and millions listen to you pull it out. It
was controversy. It was good for me.

I had celebrity friends who didn't want me on the show either.
When I went to see my good friend, singer Rosemary Clooney, perform at Rockefeller Center, she said, "Pat, do me a favor, don't go on
that asshole's show anymore."

"I'm going on next Thursday, Rosemary. The controversy is good for him, it's good for me, and it's good for the people out there."

"Pat," she said, "come on. You're too smart for that."

"The truth is, I'm too smart *not* to do it."

Howard was smart, too. Some days he bordered on genius. He was a ballsy guy. He broke barriers. Sometimes he broke a few at the same time. There were moments when I really thought they were going to lock him up, and I was going to be locked up with him. Now *that* would be a radio show.

But one morning we did better than a show from a prison cell. When you go to prison, you don't want to go, but at least you have warning. On some level you're ready. On this particular morning, I had no warning. Gary Dell'Abate walked over to Howard while we were on the air and said they had Mike, Pat's son from his first marriage, on the line. Howard asked me if I was okay with putting him on the air, and from the look on his face, he expected a no. I said three words, "Put him on."

Mike was thirty-four at the time. We had spoken on and off over the years. There was a lot of history there and, unfortunately, Mike knew almost none of it. He didn't know that I never left, that his mother threw me out—even though I was driving a cab twelve hours a day. He didn't know that when he and his sister were little, I tried to spend time with them, but their mother wouldn't allow me to take them out to lunch or to the playground, as if I was some kind of monster. He didn't know that I paid every cent the court ever asked me to, and that when I tried to pay more, his mother made it impossible.

He didn't know that in order to support them, I was working three jobs and living a half step from the street. He didn't know that during that time, no one from the family reached out to me even once to see if I was dead or alive. He didn't know that once I became successful, these same people—my ex-wife, her sisters, and my mother—came after me time and time again for one reason and one reason only. Money.

He didn't know that in spite of it all, I set up a two-million-dollar tax-free trust fund for him and his sister, but that his mother destroyed it by demanding it all be put in her name. He didn't know that I gave money to strangers all the time, and would have given anything to him and his sister.

He didn't know these things because he heard only one side of the story. He didn't know, because he never bothered to ask me. Mike had become a lot like the rest of them. But when he started to speak on the air, I could tell he was not going to be a raving lunatic. He was leaving the door open a crack. Before he started talking to Howard, I told him to be honest—that I respected his right to say what he had to say. After a few minutes of conversation, Robin asked him if he loved his father.

MIKE: I do love my father, but I don't know my father.

PAT: Your mother said your father's a bum, and you never defended your father.

MIKE: How do you know what I said?

PAT: I know, Mike. Mike, I got people coming over to me when I'm working. I hear stories. I want to throw up.

MIKE: People talking. They don't live in my house. They don't know what I said.

The conversation started getting heated and Howard and Robin were trying to smooth things over, but Mike continued.

HOWARD: How 'bout dinner on me?

MIKE: I tried to get to his apartment one time and he had all these people tell me not to come by.

I had to stop him right there. What he said just wasn't true. If this was a trial, Mike was misleading the jury, all ten million of them.

When the apartment incident he was referring to occurred, some people that I knew started it by going down to Mike's flower store and telling him where I lived. When I found out, I told these people to stay out of my business. Then these people happened to see Mike outside my apartment one day, and they told him his father wasn't home. I had nothing to do with the beginning, middle, or end of the episode.

Mike knew he could call me anytime. The airwaves were not the place to make that call, but if he made it, I was answering, on or off the air. I explained what really happened. Howard suggested we let bygones be bygones. When Mike got off, it wasn't exactly the Geneva Convention, but we made a loose arrangement to continue the dialogue off the air. Then Gary told Howard that my daughter Lou-Ann was on the line. Howard told me, and I told him to put her on, let's go.

Round two was nothing like round one. Round one was a few bottle rockets. Round two was a series of Scud missiles. Lou-Ann came out swinging like Mike Tyson, only she couldn't wait for the bell and tried to bite off a lot more than my ear.

LOU-ANN: I'd like to know what he has to say to me after twelve years.

PAT: I don't have anything to say to you after twelve years.

LOU-ANN: Well, I think I have a lot to say after twelve years.

PAT: You can say anything you want, and I respect your right to say it.

LOU-ANN: Okay. Very good. Well, I resent the fact that in your act you make demeaning statements toward my profession.

Lou-Ann was a schoolteacher. There is hardly a comedian around who doesn't make observations about teachers, priests, politicians, and family members for that matter. If you take away that sort of material, you're left with a couple of kitchen utensils. She was being ridiculous, but more than that, she was yelling and screaming right out of the box. Exactly what kind of pain had I caused her by breathing, eating, and sleeping the last dozen years? I wasn't going to let her have her way.

PAT: I don't make demeaning statements toward your profession because, number one, when I do comedy I'm not doing you. I'm not doing my mother. I'm not doing my father. I'm doing comedy. And if you take it personally, you have a problem.

LOU-ANN: No, I don't have a problem, personally. I feel that it's a disgrace that you use your family to make your money.

PAT: In other words, Bill Cosby is a disgrace that he talks about his kids.

LOU-ANN: Bill Cosby did a little bit more for his children than you did for your children.

PAT: I did everything I was supposed to do, and I did it with a smile, and I did it well, and I got nothing but proudness in my brain. And I am not guilty of doing anything wrong. And I will tell you one thing. I just feel bad, because you blew a hell of a father.

LOU-ANN: I blew a hell of a father? You were never there for me. . . . I paid for my whole college education!

Now I understood the rage. She was telling half the story—her half. I could have leveled her right there, but I took the high road:

PAT: That's what you're supposed to do.

LOU-ANN: Did your stepdaughter pay for her college education?

PAT: I don't have a stepdaughter.

LOU-ANN: As far as I'm concerned, you don't have a daughter.

PAT: I don't want a daughter

HOWARD: You can cut the love in here with a machete.

Then I asked her what she had in mind when she left pineapples at my door. So she told me and everyone else. "I wanted to let you know I could find you whenever I wanted to find you."

And now we knew. It was like the Unabomber all over again.

Howard told Robin that suddenly her family looked like a love nest. I had a parting shot for my ex-wife's daughter. "You see the way your mouth is? That's the reason I wasn't there."

Then Gary whispered in Howard's ear, and that was the bell for the next round. My mother was on line one. She didn't miss a beat from the last time I spoke to her. It was like someone hit the pause button, left it there for four years, then took it off.

She started right in, "Can you believe a man talks about his family so much and makes millions of dollars on them, and then he quits? He don't want to bother. He hates them. They're all after his money."

Yes, my mother picked up right where she left off. Money was the first word and the last word. The last time we spoke, it was because she wanted five thousand dollars for back rent. What I hadn't known was that for many years, when my ex-wife was living in my mother's brownstone, she wasn't paying rent. That was between the two of them. I paid the alimony I was supposed to pay. But my mother saw an opportunity and she took it. She probably thought I would write her a check for five thousand dollars just so I wouldn't have to hear it anymore. And she was right.

PAT: Can I tell you something, Howard? Now she wants to be the mother. I never asked you to give me a loan, Ma. I never said, 'Ma, help me.' Look at this, God have mercy on them. I don't want anything from them. [But] I want to know one thing. You see, they feel they gotta get paid because you mentioned the word mother or father or sister or daughter. 'Look, we made you successful!' They didn't help me in my career. They didn't care about my career. And I didn't care. That's okay. I made something of myself. And I speak well about my mother and father on the stage. I put words in my father's mouth . . .

MOM: Because you make money on it.

PAT: Did you hear what she just said? Because I make money on them! On her life I make money! You never turned a saint upside down, so don't con me.

MOM: I wish you would tell the truth once in a while.

PAT: I have never lied. And I will not lie. And Mother dear, I wish you well. And may I say something? It's a shame, because I'm an only son. And what did I do? Did I kill you? Did I shoot you? Did I rob you? I know people who killed people, and their mothers want to sit in the electric chair for their sons. I never asked you to do that.

MOM: Forgive and forget.

PAT: Oh, now you want me to forgive and forget. Did you get your five thousand dollars? Did you get your rent money? That's what was on your mind. Not where's my son. Not let me help my son. Where's my back rent?

MOM: Five thousand dollars for ten years of my life.

PAT: Oh, now I owe you for being born. How much do I owe you for food? How much do I owe you for clothes?

When it was all over, I felt fabulous. Howard, Robin, Gary, Fred, Jackie, and the entire crew looked stunned. They thought I was going to fold up like an envelope. No chance. It took a lot of courage to stay on the air. Ninety-nine guys out of a hundred with a bad divorce wouldn't have stepped up to the plate, but I was number one hundred. And I looked at Howard and said, "This is the greatest thing that ever happened to me. I thank them."

I felt like people finally got to see my point of view. Whatever came out of my mouth over the last hour wasn't the point. I held my own. But these people made my case for me. Millions of ears heard their attitude. Anyone who had a legitimate complaint against their father would never have gone on the air to make it. But this wasn't legitimate. It was meanness and pettiness and greed from people who needed to get a life. Everyone heard it. I wasn't making it up. Who on earth could?

Every epic has an epilogue. I did take Mike out to lunch. He told me his car was breaking down and he needed money to get it repaired. I gave him two thousand dollars right there. The waitress caught wind of what was going on and said to Mike, "You're a lucky guy. Where did you find a father like that?"

Every great epic also has a prologue. In this prologue, twelve years before Lou-Ann called in to *The Howard Stern Show,* I got a call from my ex-wife's lawyer. He wanted to talk about paying for my daughter's college education and asked me to come out to Brooklyn. When I got there, the lawyer thanked me for coming and explained that Lou-Ann would be walking in shortly. So I waited.

When she walked into the office, she looked pissed off. She didn't say hello to me. She just looked at me and said, "Are you going to pay for my college education or not?"

"Yes," I said. "I'm going to pay for your college."

Then she walked out without saying thank you or even good-bye. It was a disgraceful display. Maybe she had a bad day. Maybe she had a bad year. Maybe she had problems I didn't know about. But if there was one simple rule in life, one thing to know about dealing with another human being—whether he was your father or a guy pressing your shirts—when you asked for a favor and got it, you said thank you. At that moment, I felt the loss of not being her father. Whatever else I might have fucked up, I would have taught her that one thing.

"I ain't paying for her college," I said. The lawyer was not surprised.

"I apologize," he said. "She was very rude, Pat. You were nice enough to come all the way out to Brooklyn to try to do the right thing. The problem is, she didn't do the right thing."

I took a hundred dollars out of my pocket and paid the lawyer for his time.

Time after time—once on the airwaves, the rest of the time in private—we had a chance to make a little progress, but it didn't happen. All my kids had to do was sit down and talk to me and treat me with basic respect. Instead, they treated me like garbage. So they learned that I would never fold. They learned that they would have to kill me before I folded. And the whole thing was a waste. I wasn't asking for much. If they had common sense, they would be my children today.

It's a terrible thing to tell your children, "I'm not your father." I have feelings. But if I listened to my feelings, I'd crumple up, crawl into the corner, and cry. I wasn't going to let them put me through that. I wasn't going to let anyone put me through that.

Some people go to therapy. My therapy is to tell the truth in front of one person or a whole country. Some of that raging hour on the FM dial made it to Howard Stern's anthology *Crucified by the FCC*. For years, that hour made waves. It was like the gold standard for shock radio. It was the *Family Feud* meets Hiroshima. But all families feud, and my on-air relationship with Howard Stern was no exception.

We all knew and liked Sam Kinison, the wild preacher turned wilder comedian. How could I not like a funny guy who raged like that? But I thought Sam was on the edge in his life, not just his comedy. I thought he was going to swallow himself at some point. And I thought cocaine played a big role in the tragedy I saw coming. I talked about this on the radio with Howard, but he thought it was no big deal.

I told Howard to tell his daughter that he worships a guy who uses cocaine all the time. Howard responded that the cocaine had nothing to do with anything. So I told him that I hoped his daughter married Sam Kinison.

Howard Stern didn't like that. His crew looked at me like I was going to the doghouse, but there was no doghouse that could hold me. I proved something. You could take my most private family moments, put them on the air, and put them on an album, and I was fine with that. But if I so much as mentioned Howard's daughter—not even in a personal way, but simply to make a very important point—I was suddenly over the line. It was crystal clear. This man who made an unbelievable living abusing people couldn't take the smallest degree of abuse himself. Like a billion bullies and egos before him, he could give it, but he couldn't take it.

I was banished from the show for a while. It wasn't anything official, but I knew what it was about. And it could have been about a number of other things, too. Although Howard's making a charade out of his wife's miscarriage was old news, it was so infamous that it came up on the show now and again. When it did, I didn't have anything reassuring to say to the host. Instead, I told him he was lucky, because he was way out of order and that it could easily have cost him his career. Even a schmuck like me knew nothing was more sacred to a woman than the baby she carried, and nothing more devastating than losing it. And I made the observation that maybe, just maybe, his marriage was never the same after that.

When I came back to the show, it was business as usual. There was always someone else to abuse. One morning, Howard called Chevy Chase out of the blue. Chevy was asleep on the West Coast and woke up to find he was clearing his throat for millions of listeners on the

East Coast. Chevy yelled and screamed at Howard. He told Howard he hated him and even threatened to kill him.

It was none of my business, of course. The show was built on pranks and controversy, and when you took those out of the equation there wasn't much left. The thing that bothered me, strangely, was that Howard would later make "friends" with Chevy and other celebrities he was feuding with. On one level it seemed wonderful. On another, it made me wonder if all of it—both the good and the bad—was insincere.

But as I said, this was Howard's show and he called the shots. That included who to take shots at. As a popular guest, I was entitled to a few free shots myself, and I decided to take one at Joan Rivers. Joan Rivers took shots at everybody—even the defenseless—and no one ever took a shot at her. Whether it was Elizabeth Taylor's weight problem, Karen Carpenter's weight problem of a different kind, Princess Grace plunging to her death, or some stewardess Joan didn't like, no one returned the fire.

What I saw when I looked at Joan was someone who didn't like herself. I saw someone who didn't like the ugliness in her own heart, no matter how much talent she started out with or money she wound up with. So she began to change her face.

She thought surgery on her face would change her heart, but it didn't. She thought a cut here and a tuck there might make her a better person, but it didn't. When it was all done, it was still Joan Rivers under that mask. It didn't matter if they put fifty pounds of cement on her head, she was not a better person. She couldn't run away from Joan Rivers. When you're born a dog, you can't die a cat. In fact, the surgically altered Joan Rivers went after defenseless people harder and longer than ever. So I decided to go after her.

For a few thousand bucks and a little help from my friend comedian Morty Storm, I put out a one-time collector's item comic book entitled *Justice for All.* The cover featured yours truly in a boxing ring delivering a hard right to a dazed Joan Rivers. The illustrations were first-rate and the captions were hard jabs: "Joan Rivers is the only woman with scar tissue on her tongue." "Congratulations, Mrs. Rivers, you just gave birth to an 8-pound mouth." "Joan has a new sponsor . . . rat poison." As it said inside the title page, it was written to balance the books. But it was just a gag. It was something to talk about. It was my wake-up call to Joan Rivers.

Howard Stern read it, or at least parts of it, on the air. But he really brushed it aside. If Sam Kinison had come into the studio with a bombshell like that, Howard would have called Joan at three in the morning. He would have made it into an epic spanning across three or four shows and running on and off for months. But this was Pat Cooper, who got under his skin with his opinions and sometimes challenged him directly.

At the other end was Joan Rivers, a friend of Howard's. You never knew how these people were friends or even if they were friends. But if they said they were friends, the rules of engagement changed. In any case, I sent Joan a basket of fruit—not to make friends, but just to let her know we were all just human beings with problems.

When Howard's movie, *Private Parts,* came out, he asked me to MC on opening night. I was honored. First of all, the movie was great. It really showed the kind of obstacles you face in entertainment—or anyplace for that matter—if you try to be different. And Howard was wonderful as Howard. He played himself as a young, gawky nebbish with no embarrassment.

Second, I wasn't being thrown a bone. If I thought I was, I would have told Howard to shove it up his ass. I was the right guy for the MC job. It was as simple as that. I was one of his best guests, and I was always one-hundred percent comfortable getting out there and greeting the people.

The theater was jammed and there were television cameras everywhere. I had a tuxedo on and was interviewing people from the A-list, the B-list, and the Z-list. And these people were interviewing me, too. One thing about Howard Stern's audience—they have a memory like a steel trap. They remember more about what you said than you yourself do. That was a wonderful thing to experience and a credit to Howard.

The biggest credit to Howard Stern were his parents. Not that he had anything to do with it. They were on the planet first. They were very nice people, and they were proud of their son. But I got the feeling that with their old world values, this night was not the most comfortable night for them. Even less so when Howard came out in a dress. But what could I say? I was doing that when I was five.

Back on the airwaves, when Howard mentioned his parents, I made my observation. I told Howard to face it. His parents wanted their nice Jewish boy to be a doctor or a lawyer, not a lunatic in a dress waking up celebrities at three in the morning. But what were they going to say? That they hated the millions of dollars he was making? That his millions of delirious fans were wrong? That they just wanted him in an office in Syosset removing nasal warts? That he was a schmuck? No, they just had to grin and bear it, and they did a damn good job of it.

Howard didn't want to hear it. That could have been a very funny and honest conversation, but once again, Howard couldn't take it. It really wasn't much to take. Compare that to a guy's son, daughter, and mother coming on the air to perform character assassination. But this was *The Howard Stern Show,* and I was less and less welcome. The things I said got under his skin more and more. I told him I was his friend, not the people who kissed his ass or whose asses he kissed. But he saw it differently, and when I wasn't there, he would go nuts on the air about some of the things I said.

It was strange—the federal government fined him half to death and it never fazed him. But Pat Cooper rattled his cage. So I drifted away quietly. That was okay. We had a nice run. I was around a lot longer than Howard Stern, and I knew one fundamental thing—nothing lasts. Music changes. Comedy changes. You had to know when to get off the stage.

When it came to exiting, money was never a factor with me, and this was no exception. For one thing, I was blessed with a great living for many years, and as much as I gave away, I rarely pissed it away. Second, Howard Stern didn't pay me a thing. It was nothing personal—he didn't pay anyone. And I kept showing up bright and early, so I can't blame Howard. But I would have done it differently if I was in his shoes. I would have hired me or someone like me as a regular, maybe once or twice a week. But that wasn't his mentality. If he could get you for free, he did.

Where it hurt me to watch was with his interns. I called them his slaves. He paid them nothing, and they had nothing to fall back on. They ran around the studio practically putting grapes in the mouth of the King of All Media. They pissed their pants when the King grumbled. They believed he was going to help their careers, because what else could they believe? A few hundred dollars a week would have flown well below the radar of Howard Stern's wallet and would have gone a long way for those kids. But they were proud. They said, "I'm an intern!" I told them, "No, you're an *out*-tern."

As far as the permanent staff went, they were all good people, but they were also there to service the King of All Media. With that length of service, the King should have taken care of his most loyal subjects in a big way. The King should have given them all a profit-sharing plan. Instead, they got a salary that kept them hungry. And Howard gave Robin a car. Wonderful. What the fuck are you going to do with a car in New York City?

As history records it, in 2006, Howard left the free airwaves after landing a hundred-million-dollar deal with Sirius satellite radio. I became an occasional unpaid guest, which was fine. My final appearance on the show took place a week before my October 2007 roast at the Friars Club. My stated purpose was to promote the roast, which raised money for charity.

But when I got into the studio with a lady friend of mine, there were three so-called comedians lying in wait for me. Howard explained that he was doing me a favor by getting me ready for the roast. He wanted to prepare me to take verbal abuse. More to the point, he wanted to see if I could stand there and take it. I had a strange feeling in the pit of my stomach. This was payback. But with Pat Cooper, payback on the payback is a bitch.

The first comedian was a guy named Bob Levy. Bob had a paper in his hand. Without a doubt, he was up all night scribbling notes down to make it through. So I sent Bob to comedy school. I got up out of my chair, walked over, and told Bob to get rid of the paper. Be a man. *Be an entertainer.* Ad-lib! Then Howard told me I was already cracking and that I couldn't make up the rules of the roast. So I sat down and gave Bob a chance to cook me. He hung on to the paper and read.

"I'm not saying Pat's a bad parent, but he couldn't pick his kids out of a police lineup. Pat's always yelling and screaming. I don't scream that loud when I get my cock caught in a zipper."

The kid would never make it as a professional roaster. Maybe he could be one of Howard Stern's interns. I explained to him a good roast grew out of a purpose and a relationship. It wasn't about reading notes. Then Howard told me I'd never make it through the real roast, and I told him he should eat something. "Ninety million dollars and you can't get a fucking sandwich."

The second comedian was about as good as the first and clung to his paper even harder. But when he ran out of notes, he threw his paper aside. I was impressed. We were going to see what he was made of. And then, unfortunately, we did.

"Who's that ugly cunt you brought?"

"Where's the paper?" I said. "Get the paper."

Howard was pissed off and embarrassed. "That's not funny," he said. "What kind of thing is that?" Then Howard proceeded to throw the guy out of the studio.

And that's why Howard Stern is not on my shit list. I really like Howard. I always have. But Howard went to the Hamptons. Howard remarried and went A-list. It wasn't because of the satellite radio deal. That was just a part of it. Howard's real audience is riding around in cars and trucks and cabs listening to AM/FM for what Howard pays his interns. They're not subscribing to a satellite company to get a hundred and twenty channels. Howard left his real audience in traffic.

But in reality, Howard Stern left his audience very gradually. The deal meant a lot of money quickly, but money is nothing in the end. The crown worn by the King of All Media—like the crown that is lost when families fall apart—came off one jewel at a time.

15

Deaf Comedy

They say as you get older you get wiser. Actually, as you get older, you make the same stupid mistakes one day and forget about them the next. I'm not so lucky. I remember most of mine. In my eighth decade going into my ninth, having been ripped off by agents, managers, wiseguys, investors, and especially my own people, you would think I was scam-proof. Think again.

A few years back, I got a call from an Italian-American guy I'll call Silva. He lived in Fort Lauderdale and was looking to open a restaurant down there. I told him I wasn't interested in going into the restaurant business. He told me that it wasn't your average opportunity. The lot he wanted to build on was right next to a Hooters. "Pat," he said, "it's a fucking gold mine."

So I flew down to Fort Lauderdale and Silva took me to the site. There was Hooters, and there was the empty lot right next to it. A tremendous amount of traffic was going in and out of the Hooters. Another restaurant next door, maybe one with a little more refinement, would do well. "When you're right, you're right," I said to Silva. I pulled out my checkbook and wrote him a check for thirty thousand dollars.

About a month later, I got a call from Silva. Once you go in on a real estate deal, there are only two reasons they call you again. One is to tell you they may need more money. The other is to tell you they *definitely* need more money. Silva was looking for at least another quarter million dollars. A quarter of a million dollars was too much money for someone who didn't want to go into the restaurant business in the first place, even if it *was* next to Hooters. But I had a feeling that if I couldn't come up with the quarter million, I would lose my thirty thousand.

"Who are you all of a sudden?" I asked. "Bugsy fucking Siegel?"

"Pat, we have something special down here."

"Well, I know a couple of investors who might be interested," I said.

"Bring 'em down," Silva said.

I called not a couple, but rather three Jewish guys from Philadelphia. They were smart, educated, and usually interested in getting in on the ground floor of a good deal. I told them they couldn't get any more ground floor than this. There was Hooters and the traffic and plenty of room for parking. They told me it sounded interesting.

"I'll tell you what," I said. "I'll take you guys down there. I'll pay your way down and we'll take a look together."

"Pat, you don't need to . . ."

"No, don't mention it. You'll be my guests."

So the four of us took a plane down to Fort Lauderdale. Our first stop was Silva's house to have a meeting. I had on a nice business suit and so did my three friends. We sat down in the living room around the coffee table and Silva pulled out a folder.

"Now this here is a rendering. The architect sent this over. It's just to get an idea. He's still working on the final plan."

"Is this going to be more of an upscale place?" one of my friends asked.

"Absolutely," Silva said. "We're shooting for the moon. Lauderdale is a growing economy, economically speaking."

About ten minutes into the meeting, I started hearing pounding on the wall. Then more pounding. Then a woman's voice.

"Yes! Give it to me, baby! Give it to me, baby!"

Then a man's voice.

"How's this? You like it like this, baby?"

"Keep going! Keep going!"

And more pounding. My friends and I looked at each other. We knew what it had to be, but we couldn't believe it.

"Silva," I said. "What the hell is all that?"

"My nephew. He's screwing a broad."

"Oh, that's wonderful," I said. "We're out here talking business, and your nephew's in the next room screwing a broad."

"He ain't bothering nobody," Silva said.

"He's bothering the shit out of me!" I said. "It's twelve-thirty in the afternoon. Doesn't this guy have a fucking job or something?"

"Just ignore it," Silva said.

"Ignore it? Next thing you're gonna tell me your nephew's gonna be the maitre d'. Or the head fucking chef."

My three guys stood up and walked out. And that was the end of that. I knew that if I stayed there any longer I was going to lose my head, so I got up and followed them out the door. Outside by the car my three friends apologized to me. But I told them I was the one who needed to apologize to them for bringing them all the way down to Florida to hear a guy banging a broad. I didn't think this guy and his nephew were such sick human beings.

I got on a plane with my friends and headed back north. Enough was enough. I figured it was better to just forget about it and lose my thirty thousand than listen to any more humping.

About three months later, I got a call from Silva. He said they got the rest of the money and they were about to start building.

"That's great," I said. "I know you had an architect. Who's the builder?"

"Don't worry," he said. "I got a guy."

When an Italian says, "I got a guy," that is precisely when you *should* start worrying. But I didn't. Instead, I figured I made back the thirty thousand I thought I lost.

About five months later I got another call from Silva. He said the place was ready and I should come down. I was in shock. Here was the exception to the rule. So I got on a plane and left my checkbook at home.

We walked toward the new restaurant. It looked nice, but there was something funny about it. Silva explained that they were hoping to open for business in a few weeks and took me around to the back. We walked in, and the place was well appointed. The bar was mahogany, the floor was marble, and the walls were stone that could have been straight off the boat from Sicily. Still, I had to ask my friend a question.

"Silva, how come we came in through the back?"

"That's not the back. That's the front."

"What do you mean that's the front?" I said. "That was the back."

"Yeah, but the front is in the back."

"Then where the fuck is the back?"

"In the front."

I tried to ignore it. I walked around and tried to imagine the place filled with customers—paying customers, each one wining, dining, and making sure my thirty thousand was paid back. But my daydream was rudely interrupted by a knock on the back door, which was in the front. Silva walked to the back, which was in the front, and opened the narrow service-entrance door. A guy walked in wearing a blue collared shirt and holding a clipboard.

"I got a delivery for you," he said. "Sixteen cases of soda. Where should I come in?"

"You're good," Silva said.

"I went around to the back," the delivery guy said. "But it looked like the front. So I came back around to the front."

"This is the back," Silva said.

"So where do you want these?"

"Just put 'em in the back," Silva said.

"Where's that?"

"Make a left."

"Wait a second," I said to Silva. "If this guy's a delivery guy and he don't know, how the hell are the customers gonna know?"

"They'll figure it out."

"Wrong!" I said. "They won't figure out shit! The only thing they'll figure out is how to go next door to Hooters!"

"Pat, why are you getting all upset?"

"Because we're in deep shit here," I said.

"How can we be in deep shit, Pat? We're not even open."

"Maybe we *are* open and we don't even know it," I said. "Where's the architect?"

"The architect's out of town this week," Silva said. "Anyway, it was not the architect. It was the builder."

"What kind of fucking builder is that?" I asked. "Now I'm afraid to go to the men's room because it might be the ladies' room."

"He made a little mistake," Silva said. "He's okay. He's one of us."

"One of us? He ain't one of me. And I ain't one of him. He may be one of you, and you may be one of him, but he ain't one of me!"

"What are you getting all bent out of shape for?"

"Can we switch the signs?" I asked.

"Like how?"

"Put the front sign in the back and the back sign in the front."

"That's not gonna work," Silva said. "Because then you're telling people that the front is the front and the back is the back, when the front is the back and the back is the front."

I flew home to New York really pissed off. I called my lawyer to see if there was anything I could do to get my money back, and he told me the best thing I could do was nothing. If I went forward, my lawyer told me that he would only be taking more of my money so that he could file some papers, and then another lawyer could file more papers in return. I needed to just write the whole thing off. But my lawyer did have one suggestion for me. He said we should open the place as a Ripley's Believe It or Not museum.

I was back down in Florida about a year later doing some shows and decided just out of curiosity to take a look at Ripley's. When I got there, the place was closed. It didn't look like it ever opened. Chances are, the sixteen cases of soda were still inside. The front was still in the back, the back was still in the front, and more people than ever were going into the Hooters next door.

"Is something wrong with me?" I asked my wife. "Is there something wrong with me?"

"Where do you find these people?" she said.

"What's that?" I said.

"I said, where do you find these people?!"

"The question is where do they find me?"

When you're getting older but not wiser, you start to believe that maybe you're not getting older either. But you are. In my case, the first real sign was hearing loss. It wasn't deafness, but a word dropping out here and there. More and more often, I was asking people to repeat themselves. This is death for a comedian. As a comedian, your job is to come back at people—not with answers to the questions they ask, but to the questions they are afraid to ask. But you can't know what they're afraid to ask when you can't hear what they actually do ask. My favorite answer was quickly becoming, "Huh?"

I figured the hearing loss might have been caused by years of being on stage in front of a large band. But then I realized that it probably started a lot earlier than that. When I was growing up, everybody yelled. Not screamed. Yelled. It was a way of life. I talked about that on one of my albums, *You're Always Yelling*. My big sister didn't say, "Pass the macaroni." She yelled, "PASS THE MACARONI!" My mother didn't say calmly, "Why can't you come home at a decent hour?" She yelled, "The next time you come home so late, DON'T COME HOME!"

Patti convinced me to go to an ear doctor. As we drove to the doctor's office, she told me, "When you finally muffmaffmmuff, then you'll miffmaffmuff." And who could argue with that? We waited in the office for about fifteen minutes, and the receptionist said, "Dr. Cooper will see you, Mr. Cooper."

The doctor was a very nice guy. I shook his hand and sat down.

"Is your name Dr. Cooper?" I asked.

"Yes it is."

"Good," I said. "I wasn't sure I heard right."

"You're having trouble hearing, then?"

"Doctor, I think I'm going deaf."

"You've heard what I've said so far, is that right?"

"Well, doctor, I can hear, but I can't hear the way I want to hear. I'm missing words. I'm getting better and better at guessing the words that I can't hear, but I'd rather just hear them."

"Of course," the doctor said. "What we're going to do is give you a test."

He put me in a booth and put headphones on me. Sometimes I heard a voice in my left ear telling me to raise my left hand. Sometimes it was a voice in my right ear telling me to raise my right hand. And sometimes it was a voice in my left ear telling me to raise my right hand. Sometimes it was loud, sometimes it was soft, and sometimes I just sat there with my hands down.

Dr. Cooper had me come back a week later. He pulled two hearing aids from a box and showed me how to put them in my ears. He told me to go back into the booth and put on the headphones, which I did. Then I heard him ask me a question.

"What is your birthday?"

"July 31," I said.

"What is your wife's birthday?"

"September 29," I said. "How am I doing?"

"You're doing great."

"Thank you, Dr. Cooper. My God, I can really hear with these things. Can I ask you something, Dr. Cooper?"

"Absolutely," he said.

"How much are these going to cost?"

"Five thousand dollars."

"What's that?" I said. "I can't hear you."

"Five thousand dollars!" the doctor said. "What are you doing?"

"I'm raising both my left hand and my right hand."

"Why?"

"Because," I said, "this is a stick-up."

I paid the five thousand right off the bat at the front desk and wore my hearing aids out the door. Patti and I got into our car and as we pulled away she said, "Muffmaffmmuff, miffmaffmuff."

"What the fuck did you just say?" I asked.

"Muffmaffmmuff, miffmaffmuff." I pulled over and stopped the car. I looked directly at my wife so I could read her lips.

"I couldn't hear a word of what you just said."

"But I thought you said it worked."

"In the booth it worked. In the office it worked. Here it sounds like a canary going through a carwash."

Patti convinced me to go back to the doctor's office a few days later. I told Dr. Cooper that Mr. Cooper could hear Dr. Cooper in his office, but that Mr. Cooper couldn't hear Mrs. Cooper in the car, in the kitchen, or in the shower. Dr. Cooper said he would try adjusting it. At least that's what Mr. Cooper heard. With my hearing, for all I knew, he might have said he would make it worse.

He did. For the rest of the week I heard one word clearly and the next word like I was scuba diving. So Mr. Cooper went back to Dr. Cooper a fourth time, but the fourth time wasn't the charm. Dr. Cooper played psychologist, and Mr. Cooper couldn't believe what he was hearing.

"The problem is," the doctor said, "you're fighting it."

"Fighting it? What the hell am I fighting? I can't fucking hear!"

"This is not the first time this sort of thing has happened," he said. "It's kind of a shock to hear so clearly all of a sudden after so many years."

"The only shock was the price tag."

He told me to give it ten days, and if it didn't work I could return the hearing aids and he would only charge me for the visits. I took the hearing aids home again and after two days I threw them in a drawer. I preferred my own crappy hearing to a machine's crappy hearing. So I kept on living and kept on performing, and if I didn't hear laughter from an audience, it didn't mean they weren't laughing.

Then about a year later, a lovely lady in her forties told me about her experience with a very well-known hearing aid company. She was practically in tears as she explained that when she put on this hearing aid, it was the first time in her life that she could really hear.

The company was located in a small Midwestern town. It was world famous and got a big boost when one of our presidents went there to get fitted for a hearing aid. I didn't want to make such a fuss, so I told the Secret Service they could stay home, and I took a cab from the airport. The place was impressive. It had a large factory next to the office. A technician ran some tests on me and twenty minutes later he presented me with two small devices that fit snuggly in my ear canal. It was like ordering hearing aids to go.

I heard the technician as clearly as I heard Dr. Cooper in New

York. Unfortunately, when I got in the cab to go back to the airport, I heard the cab driver about as well as I heard my wife, and cab drivers are hard to understand as it is.

"Turn this fucking cab around!" I said. "Do you fucking hear me?"

"Where we gibbagabba?"

"Don't give me any of that shit!" I said. "Take me back to the hearing place!"

When I got back to the place, I made myself heard, and in about an hour, they had my hearing aids adjusted and back in my ears. I called another cab, and this cab driver sounded worse than the first one, and he was an American!

"What fight you . . ."

"What fight am I going to?"

"What *flight?*"

"Oh, what *flight*. Any fucking flight. I don't care. Just drop me off at the airport and put me on the fucking luggage rack." I was depressed. If the best place in the world couldn't help me, then who could? Then I thought maybe I'd be better off half deaf. Think of all the bullshit I would never hear.

Just when I had given up, someone sent me to another top hearing specialist, this one in California. These people wanted five thousand dollars up front, and they had to tell me three times. The woman doctor there fitted me for two hearing aids. This time, I took a good look at them right there in the office. Stamped on the back was the name of the Midwest company.

"Excuse me," I said. "I just came from that place. I already did them."

"Well, yes," she said. "They're a wonderful organization."

"I couldn't hear shit with that hearing aid. I couldn't hear the cab driver from India, and I couldn't hear the American one. What makes you think I'm gonna hear the cab drivers on Sunset Strip any better?"

"Well, you have to give it a chance."

"Wait a second," I said. "You people knew where I went before, because I gave you all that information. And I was told that you people are the best on the planet. How the hell are you the best on the planet if all you do is order the hearing aids from where I just was? In fact, these here may be the same ones I got rid of at the airport!"

This sort of thing went on for years. I spent ten, twenty, thirty thousand dollars, and all I could hear was the change coming out of my cash register. Maybe that's how I developed tinnitus, which is a constant ringing in the ear. I considered surgery. One doctor wanted to operate on me and claimed there was a ninety-five percent chance he would cure everything. I said to him, "I'm seventy-three and you want to drill a hole in my fucking ear? You sick bastard. Go drill for fucking oil." And that wasn't all. He explained that for the rest of my life, in order to hear, I'd have to wear a box by my tits. I told him I preferred a box up my ass.

So I went back out shopping for hearing aids. Soon they knew Mr. Pat Cooper in every hearing aid place on the East Coast, the West Coast, and in between. I put together a collection of hearing aids so large I could have opened up a service for airplane mechanics and ex-rock stars.

I became an expert in hearing aids. One was good for listening to a record, but not for going to a concert. Another was good for walking and talking, but once we stopped walking, it was shit. Another was great for Chinese, but I didn't know any Chinese. And the one I really wanted nobody made—one for hearing my wife in bed.

There we were. She was horny and I was horny and we couldn't communicate. She'd say let's try something, and it sounded like *blurblebeebop.* So I told her here's what we have to do. We'll make up a number system. Thirteen is missionary style. Forty-seven is doggie style. Twenty-two is we get naked in the kitchen. One night she called out "Sixty-six!" I told her, "Wait a second, I gotta go look that up." And I did. Sixty-six is we do it in a chair. Eighty-nine is a trapeze. We worked without a net.

The countless thousands I spent on trying to hear better were not a complete waste. Far from it. I've gotten more personal laughs out of being deaf than I ever got when I could hear perfectly. I've also avoided hearing hundreds of idiots and pretended not to hear hundreds more. I tell people everywhere who are hard of hearing not to worry about it. Avoid the politics and the rhetoric and the bullshit out there. Jump into bed with your husband or your wife and use numbers.

I don't blame all the doctors and technicians who have filled my dresser with dud hearing aids. Those things must have worked for someone else, just not for me. Most of their patients didn't perform at thousands of shows in Vegas and didn't have a mother like mine screaming, "DON'T TAKE SO MUCH SAUCE!" in their ear for twenty years. Besides, these people are in sales. They have to make a commission. And now I have to be committed.

These days, it seems like everybody is selling something. Nothing is off limits. When my wife came down with cancer and had to go through chemotherapy, I made a commitment. I would stay right by her side for as long as necessary. Nothing in the entire world was as important as my wife's health, and nothing would interrupt her recovery. Nothing, it turned out, except a sales commission.

I considered Fred Travalena a friend. He was a great comedian who could mimic everyone from Nixon to Elvis to Michael Jackson. He was one of the rare ones who didn't just get the voice and the facial expressions. He got the whole body language, too. I did many shows with him in Las Vegas and Atlantic City, and we always got along.

One day, when Patti was home and feeling nauseous from the treatments, we got a call from Fred. He heard Patti was getting chemotherapy. He told me that he'd been battling lymphoma and prostate cancer, and that he was in full remission. He beat cancer. I didn't even know that Fred had been sick.

"That's wonderful," I told him. "God bless you."

Then he told me it was all because of some organic shake he drank that had all the cancer-fighting agents in it. He called it a miracle that saved his life. Fred wanted Patti to have it. I thanked him very much and asked for the name of the stuff, but he told me not to bother. He would have it shipped right to my door. He kept insisting that it was going to save Patti's life. When I hesitated for a moment, he told me that it was the best thing that I could ever do for my wife.

Right there I knew the game. He got me. If I didn't order the stuff, it would look like I didn't care about my wife at best, and that I wanted to kill her at worst. So I told him to send some over if he wanted to. He wanted to. He also wanted my credit card number. I read it to him over the phone, twice, and I ordered a case of the shakes.

A week later, two boxes came to the house. Each box had a case of shakes. The first thing that struck me was that I ordered only one case. The second thing that struck me was the bill. It was a thousand dollars a case! Two thousand dollars for Yoo-hoo with seaweed. I said to myself, *Jeez, this guy is really in business.* Patti was in the next room throwing up, and I was feeling sick, too.

So I called Fred. "I ordered one case. You sent me two." He immediately told me that Patti would need two. I asked, "How do you know she'll need two if you don't even know she needs one?"

Once again, he insisted and told me to make sure Patti drank the shakes and kept drinking them. I tried. My wife took one sip and spit it out. She tried again but just couldn't swallow it. So I took the two cases down to the drugstore and told them they could have the stuff for free. Maybe someone there with an iron stomach and no taste buds could use it, especially if they didn't have cancer.

A couple years later, I happened to work with Fred Travalena in Florida. The show went fine, but I had to get something off my chest afterwards.

"Fred, I have to tell you this, because it's been bugging my ass. What a pair of balls you had to call me up and sell me that shit."

He became very defensive and said that he was only trying to help Patti.

"How?" I asked. "If you were really trying to help, you would have sent me a can of that shit and said to try it. If it don't work, throw it the fuck out. Instead you get me on the phone at the worst time and charge me two thousand dollars for something we never asked for."

He immediately accused me of just being concerned with the money, which really pissed me off. It was absolutely *not* about the money. I told him that I would have given him the money to leave us the fuck alone.

After calling me a prick, Fred insisted that the stuff was not bullshit and that it worked for him. "Oh, so now you're a doctor!" I said. "Just because you lived doesn't mean that stuff is what saved you."

When Fred Travalena had a relapse, nothing—including the shakes—could save him. I was sad to have lost a friend . . . for the second time. Sometimes it's your time to go and nothing in the world can save you. But love of money can kill people while they're still walking the earth. And it can kill all sorts of relationships.

When it was Patti's time to leave the planet, nothing could keep her here. She came into my life when I had nothing and gave me everything, including my masculinity. When you get older, you may not always get wiser, but if you have someone to laugh about it with, your age won't really hurt you. The only thing that can really hurt you is when you lose that person. That's when you suddenly feel your age. The wisdom comes from knowing what you lost.

16

Break a Legacy

Any good comedian has a style. I don't see my style—raving maniac—around much anymore. My style is not an easy one, but it pays the bills. Sometimes it gets a little hard to handle, a little out of control. But that's okay. Every couple of months I go in to get it adjusted. I check into a hospital and say, "Can you tighten it up a little?"

But here's a secret. When I'm standing in front of a microphone, I may seem angry, but I'm not in a hate mode. I'm angry because of the sadness. There's so much of it, and most of it is what we do to each other. When I'm ranting and raving up there, I'm releasing sadness. I'm saying that if we talk about it—or yell about it—maybe we can turn that sadness into laughter.

I don't rant and rave because I'm full of hate. I don't rant and rave to make money. I rant and rave because people bring that out of me. If you don't hurt me, I won't rant and rave. Here's one example out of a million. I had a close friend who was about to go down the toilet financially. For about a year, I helped him get back on his feet. Now he's on his feet and running around, which is great. I've never asked him to repay a nickel. I've never even hinted at it. But he doesn't want to speak to me. He doesn't return my calls. From what

I can gather, he doesn't like the fact that someone bailed him out. When he sees that someone or hears from that someone, it reminds him of the help he got, and that's uncomfortable. So he shuts the door. *That* is sadness.

I'm a human being. I have feelings. That might sound like the most obvious thing in the world, but it's not always so obvious and needs pointing out. A performer is just a human being who performs. I would ask any performer how many times they have wanted to cry a minute before going out on that stage. As for me, it's happened more times than I can count. I have the same personal problems as anyone in my audience. But when I step out onto that stage, those problems become something else. They become my act.

As far as I can remember, I've missed only one performance in my entire career, and that was because of a serious throat problem. More importantly, no matter what I was feeling, I never took it out on the audience. I think that's a cheap, self-serving thing to do—and believe me, I've seen it done. Kidding with members of an audience, even pushing them near the edge is fine. Using an audience for target practice is not. A comedian is a professional who is paid to *entertain*. When a comedian forgets that, *he becomes a comedian who forgets that his audience is human.*

To maintain your humanity, your dignity, you don't have to come up with new routines. You don't have to come up with new ways to heckle. You just have to learn how to become a better person. I have. For instance, I've definitely learned that when you lend money to a friend not to expect repayment—not in terms of money and maybe not even in terms of gratitude. You have to do it from your heart. And you also have to know that that feeling in your heart may be the *only* thing you get back.

I've learned things like that over a period of fifty or sixty years. I've had to relearn most of them at one time or another. But there is no question that I have become a better person and that I'm a work in progress. That's all you can ask of yourself. Sometimes when I ask the same of others, I'm called a prick. If telling the truth makes me a prick, then I'm a prick.

I'm more than just a prick, though. I'm a privileged prick. Comedians have been given the greatest gift in the world. As a comedian you're in a position to relieve pain. Maybe for a week. Maybe for a day. Maybe for just twenty minutes. Perhaps there's a man or a woman out there in the audience with a serious illness and they just want to laugh and forget about it for a little while. As a comedian, for those twenty minutes you're a saint.

For my sainthood, I went anywhere and everywhere. I did it all. I played little back rooms where water was dripping from a pipe in the ceiling. I played Carnegie Hall. Then I played little back rooms again. I did fabulous television shows like *Mike Douglas* and *Merv Griffin*. I also did cable access shows whose main audience was the host's mother and her bridge partners. I did radio that nobody heard. Radio waves went out, bounced off some walls, and bounced back.

But maybe a few waves never made it back. Maybe a few were absorbed on some given night by someone special. That's what I tell young performers. Don't turn anything down, because you'll keep getting better at what you do—and you never know who may be listening. If there's only one person listening and he's deaf, do it anyway.

I still live by those words to the degree that I can. If you're full of shit, you'll make excuses. If you're a comic, you'll do it. If you want me to open the show, I'll open. If you want me to close, I'll close. I'll close for Jesus Christ if you ask me. That's a tough act to follow, but I'll give it a shot.

These days, however, things are different. If you go everywhere and do everything, people say you're trying to be a do-gooder. I'm not a do-gooder. I'm just an honorable guy. I've made a ton of mistakes offstage, almost as many on, and I've learned something from every one of them. Every mistake is a medal for bravery. I'm not afraid of medals. I'm not afraid to fail. If you're afraid to fail, you're afraid to succeed. When I fall on my ass, my ass gets tougher.

You'll know you've come a long way when you fall on your ass but don't want the next guy to fall on his. I don't wish other people harm. That's always been my philosophy, and like my style, it needs a little tune-up every now and then. If you ever want to give me a real compliment, walk up and tell me that I really treat my opening acts well. Opening acts are abused all the time, and most of the time it's all because of ego.

It's amazing how little has changed over the years, but then again, it's not that amazing at all. When many insecure performers step on the act in front of them, they feel taller. Any minute, though, they'll be going down, too, whether they know it or not. When someone opens for me and brings the audience to its feet, I'm proud as if it's my son or daughter.

I would never rank myself as a comedian, but one person I would be proud to be compared to is Don Rickles. Rickles is the last of the great comedic soldiers. And here's a story that proves it. Many years ago when Rickles was starting out, he was doing a show in Massachusetts. There was a young lady sitting near the front, and he threw her a line. "Excuse me, madam, what are you doing with that ugly guy?" Her male companion stood up, hopped onto the stage, and punched Don Rickles in the mouth. Rickles fell down hard on the stage. The guy sat back down and the audience was silent.

Rickles managed to get back up and quickly gather himself. Without missing a beat, the first words out of his mouth were, "Maybe you didn't hear me, lady. What are you doing with that ugly guy?" The place went berserk with laughter. Even the guy who punched Rickles got up and gave him a hug. That guy knew what the audience knew. Here was something special. Here was quickness. Here was *balls*.

Some people might put Rickles in the category of an insult comic, but he's so much more than that—he's witty and he's fast. Always was and still is. Rickles was an innovator who broke down barriers by saying things that no one else had the audacity to say. In that sense, he was up there with George Carlin, Richard Pryor, and Robin Williams. We're still learning from these great performers.

But unlike Rickles, I would never let anyone touch me. If anyone threatens me, I always say, "Don't put your hands on me." I won't make it part of my act. I'll make it part of your last act. And I'm not just talking about people in the audience. I say the same thing to anyone. "Hit me and I'll own you." Nine out of ten guys who threaten to hit have a record. That's a fact. That means I have the advantage, not them. So I bait them. "Come on, hit me, you motherfucker. I dare you to lay a hand on me. I'll break your fucking head. You sick fuck, I'm a comedian! If you had any balls, you'd go after Mike Tyson!"

The cop-out is almost always the same. "I ain't gonna hit you. You're crazy."

"I'm crazy? The problem is you're a fucking coward."

But they're not crazy and neither am I. We both know if they hit me they're going to prison, and in some cases for the last time.

When people talk about the good old days as far as fighting is concerned, I tell them that these are the good old days. The *old* old days sucked. People today don't take any shit as far as violence goes, and they shouldn't. Many years ago in the old neighborhood, a bunch of us went out dancing. One of my friends was a little effeminate in his mannerisms. Some local bully walked up to him, called him a faggot, and said he wore bloomers. Well, my effeminate friend threw him a shot in the face, and this bully asshole was on the floor missing two teeth.

My friend was ahead of his time. My advice is not to fuck with anyone today, because you don't know who you're dealing with. That includes women. Women today go to grab-the-balls school. Some graduate with high testicles. They get black belts in ball-grabbing, and when they got you, you're at their mercy.

Anyone who loves the old days just because they're the old days has got his head up his ass. Although a lot of things were better, not everything was. I respect new eras. If you can't appreciate something from the era you find yourself in, it's time to die. Even when I see a comedian who doesn't make me laugh, I can appreciate the fact that he's making the audience laugh. He's successful because he's funny. Period. His era is here, and God bless him.

The fact that I'm not laughing doesn't mean that he wouldn't have been funny in my era. Because if he were coming of age in my era, he wouldn't be doing the same material. Would Joe DiMaggio have been a superstar in the twenty-first century? Absolutely. Would Derek Jeter have been a superstar in the 1940s? Of course. Talent adapts.

Comics were capable of being hypocrites in the old days, and they're just as capable of it now. I went to a book signing for my friend and comedian Lisa Lampanelli, who had just published *Chocolate Please: My Adventures in Food, Fat, and Freaks.* I opened my copy of the book and was flattered by what she had written to me: "To Pat— you are my inspiration." I'm not looking for accolades, but I thought that was pretty flattering. Really nice. Maybe she heard one of my albums thirty or forty years ago and said, "Hey, I can do that."

I wanted to read the book anyway, but after that, I wanted to read it even more. What did I say that inspired her? Which of my routines was her favorite? So I read. And read. And read. There was nothing about Pat Cooper. There was stuff about screwing black guys, stuff about eating cake, more stuff about screwing black guys, and not a word about Pat Cooper. There was plenty of stuff about other comedians, but nothing whatsoever about her "inspiration."

This was amazing, because in the book she talked about roasts that she and I did together. There she was on the dais with her inspiration, but she wasn't inspired enough to remember any of it. That includes the Jerry Lewis roast, where I killed, if I do say so myself. She discussed the roast and managed to leave out the prime rib.

As I read the last few pages of the book, I thought about how I was doing roasts before Lisa Lampanelli learned not to touch the stove. I thought about how Lisa and her comedian friends had to hire writers for these roasts and then read the jokes off a piece of paper. I thought about how Italians don't want to mention other Italians. Most of all I thought about how you don't tell someone they're your inspiration and then not mention them once in three hundred pages. It's like telling me you want to bang me, but I'm not allowed to get off!

As much as I appreciate comedy today, I'm usually less than impressed. There's no depth. Back in the day it was show business. Now it's more like "show off" business. Very few comedians really kill. Some don't even know how to kill themselves.

Artie Lange is a comedian and a friend of mine. He was the co-host of *The Howard Stern Show* for almost ten years. One morning, I got up and read that Artie had stabbed himself nine times. He lived. The reason he lived is because he didn't want to die. If he really wanted to die, he could have made it happen. That was something he needed to know if he didn't already. You should never bullshit yourself . . . or another comedian. So I wrote him a get well card like no other. It was an email:

> "Artie, I love you, and I'm going to give you a little advice. The next time you want to kill yourself, give me a call. I'll show you how to fucking die. You've got to hit your heart! The arm's no good. The leg's no good either. And only an asshole stabs himself in the ass."

It's true. They never go for the heart. They never go for the balls. They never go for the throat. If they need it to live, fuck, or eat, it's off the menu.

A good comic usually makes a good actor, but a good comedic actor usually does not make a good comic. With some capable directing, a good comic can take his spontaneity to the stage or the screen. But someone who is trained to be funny reading lines usually goes down the toilet when there are no lines to read. The 2010 Academy Awards is a good example. The hosts were Alec Baldwin and Steve Martin, two of the most brilliant comedic actors in the world. But the show sucked.

They both read other people's words, and when you read other people's words in a live situation, the audience gets a subtle but clear message: Go to sleep. In a venue like the Oscars, people want to see someone shooting from the hip, not reading a bedtime story. Steve Martin is a superstar, but he can't ad-lib a fart. Neither can Alec Baldwin. Alec, I know you're pissed off with the ex-wife, but don't let it bring you down. And do me a favor, do something about your face. You used to have a kind of Cary Grant quality. Now you have a Ulysses S. Grant quality.

The Academy should give me the job one year. I guarantee one thing—that would be an awards ceremony no one would ever, ever forget. In the opening minute of the show, I would walk out on stage and say, "Let's get the fucking awards out of the way right now. Russell Crowe, Best Actor. Julia Roberts, Best Actress. Okay, now we're done and we can start the show. We have the rest of the evening to do what we all came here to do—talk about some of the assholes out there."

I don't expect the call to do the 83rd annual Academy Awards, because I know they want to go on to do an 84th. This is a business. I still do plenty of business, but not that business. If you can't accept that this is a business in at least one corner of your brain, you won't do much business.

In this business, it's often not enough to have a manager or an agent. Sometimes you need a manager to talk to an agent. By the time the manager is done talking to the agent and agent is done talking back to the manager, the manager and the agent have twenty-five percent of your money. But that's okay. You all could be making nothing. Instead, you're making thousands and you're helping at least two families besides your own. You feel good about being that kind of an earner and that people depend on you. In other words, when it's someone you don't know, it feels like that someone is reaching into your pocket. If it's personal, it's all good.

With me, it's personal. And that has been my downfall many times. I've been ripped off by some of the best agents in the world. One in particular called me his brother. I know now that when an agent calls you his brother, you're going to get fucked. But I didn't know it then. When his daughter fell very ill in Las Vegas years ago, Patti and I rushed to the hospital, stood by her side, and made sure everything was all right. Over the years, we dropped her off and picked her up at the airport and did the kind of things you do for a friend's daughter. The kind of things you do for a niece.

When this agent was starting out, I worked at the Westbury Music Fair on Long Island as a favor to him. At the time, the place was a tent. But we were in on the ground floor together, and every year the venue and the pay got better. Other people in the business told me to stay away from him, but my answer to them was that we all make mistakes.

This guy didn't make mistakes. He made tragedies. Eventually, I found out he had been ripping me off all along for twenty-five years. Our relationship ended when he made an inside deal with the manager at Westbury to give another performer my spot. Suddenly after a quarter century, at age seventy-nine, I was out. That was okay. I didn't need the job. What was devastating to me was knowing how long he had played me and with such a straight face. I had to look back and refigure every year and every booking. I couldn't figure out how a man like that could look in the mirror. But the awful truth was—*he could.*

I couldn't. I'm the opposite. I have sympathy for people who are down in the dumps, because I was once down in the dumps myself.

I've lived well above the dumps for a long time. I appreciate it, and for me, there is hardly a nicer feeling than being able to help somebody else. When I say I'm going to change, I'm kidding myself. I'm going to get ripped off again some way, somehow, by somebody I'm helping out, and then I'm going to do it all over again. That's who I am. It's too late to fight it. On the positive side, no matter what kind of family or professional problems I have, when I take my shorts off at night, I sleep like a log.

I admit that I could do a better job of listening to people around me who are trying to show me something that I refuse to see, even though it's the size of a camel. I have four eyes, but none of them are in the back of my head. But there is one area where I won't take advice. When some schmuck comes up to me and says, "Hey, here's what you should have said when you closed that routine," I say, "Shhh. Please. I don't tell a butcher how to cut meat. And when the plumber comes in to fix a leak, I shut my fucking mouth. So please, don't tell me how to *comede*."

It's fine for them to sit there with the remote and flip through three hundred channels. They pay for that privilege. But don't come up to me and claim to be an expert in assessing talent. William Morris couldn't do it. William Morris has been one of the top talent agencies in the world dating back to the Marx Brothers. In the early 1960s, when I was starting to do well, I wanted them to represent me. They refused. But a simple refusal wasn't enough. A big rep from the agency pulled me aside and told me the best move would be for me to get out of the business while I still had a chance to do something else with my life. "This business is not for you, son," he said.

Two years later, William Morris signed me. If I had listened to the idiot who said this business wasn't for me, I'd be cleaning fish, now. Which isn't bad if you're making a living, plus it smells better than some of the places I worked back then.

But in the end, of course, the people are the experts. I'll know when it's time to get out of the business. When people don't come to see me anymore, then it's time. In that case, I wouldn't take a hundred dollars or a hundred thousand dollars from a venue. But in the meantime, please, don't tell me how the fuck to do my act.

If you put yourself out there for many years—whether as a comedian, a fisherman, or a plumber—you're going to make mistakes. If you turn around and help people all your life, you're going to get screwed now and then. But if you're lucky, you'll have one day in your life when all the good things you tried to do for people come back to you. Once in your life, if you're fortunate, over a thousand people, including your closest friends and associates, will all get together in a room and insult you for hours on end.

That happened to me. On October 19, 2007, the Friars roasted me. But the roast wasn't held at the Friars Club. When fourteen hundred people come to insult you, they have to hold it at the New York Hilton. In the audience were celebrities like Joy Behar, Al Roker, and Tony Robbins. There were also dozens of unknown people who have been my friends for fifty years. Many of these people flew in from Texas or California on their own dime just to watch Pat Cooper get fried. There were also plenty of people I would have expected to make the trip who didn't bother. All I can say is fuck them.

The host was Lisa Lampanelli. You know, the fat chick who bangs black guys by the dozens. The one who calls Pat Cooper her inspiration and then doesn't mention him once in the three hundred pages of her book. She certainly mentioned me that night.

Lisa, do you by any chance remember saying, "We may be honoring you today, Pat. But you couldn't get it up with a pump and the clapper." Or what about, "Even though Pat Cooper can't get it up anymore, he still has an active sex life. Every night he fucks an audience out of fifteen bucks apiece."

Doesn't ring a bell? How about, "Pat Cooper actually showed me his penis backstage. I haven't been so disappointed since the last episode of *The Sopranos.*" Or "He had a tough childhood. Not only did his mother beat him. She forced him to look in a mirror."

Lisa, darling, can you recall this mini-epic that you read off a sheet of paper? "Two important events occurred in 1929. The stock market crashed and Pat Cooper was born. One was a catastrophe that resulted in years of suffering and misery for an entire nation. The other was a stock market crash."

Lisa, honey, what about when you had this to say about your inspiration, "To some people he's known as Pasquale Caputo. To others he's known as Pat Cooper. To most people he's known as 'Who?'" Do you remember saying, "Those glasses. Why the fuck do you wear those things? It's not like anybody is sending you scripts to read." I'll admit that one had me laughing. Too bad right after the show you came down with amnesia.

You might remember Richard Belzer from way back performing at Catch a Rising Star or from the cult classic *The Groove Tube*. You might remember him doing his act in a nightclub in *Scarface* moments before they opened fire on Al Pacino. You might remember Richard Belzer from hundreds of episodes of *Law and Order: Special Victims Unit, Law and Order: Not So Special Victims Unit,* or *Law and Order: Who Gives a Fuck.* I remember him as the guy who said these things to me:

"Before we begin, are you absolutely sure that you're not dead? Pat calls what he does an act—barking and cursing. It's like Tourette's al dente. Pat Cooper is as much a part of the Friars as bland overpriced food served by waiters who don't wash their hands. Pat Cooper and Freddie Roman's television careers were shorter than Jack Ruby's." And with that, Richard Belzer almost became another Jew who got shot on camera.

The next Jew to almost get shot was comedian Jeffrey Ross, who took care first to insult all the Italians in the room. "There haven't been this many Italians behind a microphone since the Valachi hearings. This isn't a roast, it's a grease fire." There were, in all likelihood, numerous Italians in the room that day packing heat, but too many witnesses. So Jeffrey Ross went after the Italian of the hour. "What's with the glasses? You look like Elton John. The only difference is you just suck at comedy. We love Pat Cooper at the Friars Club. We recently soundproofed a room in his honor and we named a drink after him. It's called Career on the Rocks. All bitters. In the '60s, Pat put out two comedy albums. They both went vinyl. Pat has a very rare form of Alzheimer's. He only remembers grudges."

Then came another Jew. We had a minyan that night, and the rabbi was the great Robert Klein, a five-tool comic from the old school who happened to go to Yale. Klein began by mixing vaudeville with the Ivy League. "I first met Pat when we were students at Yale together. I reached into my pocket for my student ID card and we shook hands." Then Klein showed he could get down and dirty with the rest of them. "Pat once had an erection that lasted more than four hours and did not seek medical attention. He fucked Totie Fields instead and is actually the father of Lisa Lampanelli." And I thought I was just her inspiration.

Robert Klein showed the room why he's a professor of comedy. Why he's not just an Ivy Leaguer but in a league of his own. "Pat Cooper went on to do wonderful movies. Beautiful movies. *The Sun Also Rises. The Fountainhead. Meet John Doe. High Noon. Pride of the Yankees.* What the fuck am I talking about? That's *Gary* Cooper!" Klein crumpled up his notepaper and threw it into the audience, who were screaming. If you ever happen to see the DVD and look to Klein's right, that's Pat Cooper cracking up, not Gary Cooper. Pat Cooper didn't see that one coming till the punchline, and that's something special.

Then Jim Norton put me on a spit and turned it slowly. Norton is the third mic on the *Opie and Anthony* show. He's good enough that the show should be called *Opie, Anthony, and Jimmy,* and on this night he proved it again. "Pat Cooper is a man who lives with a few simple mottos. Motto number one: Success—who the fuck needs it? Motto number two: When in doubt, scream 'Fuck you!' Motto number three: Never wait till a bridge is behind you. Burn that motherfucker while you're standing in the middle of it." What Jim Norton doesn't know is that I've blown up a few tunnels in my time, too.

Comic Greg Fitzsimmons, whose father let him hang around the Friars Club when he was still a little kid, went right for the jugular. "I've seen crack whores make better career choices than Pat Cooper. How do you not get a role on *The Sopranos?* That must tear the ass out of you. The show was on the air so long they were booking Native Americans ahead of Pat Cooper." Greg Fitzsimmons may not know that although they never let me on *The Sopranos* in person, they referenced Pat Cooper a total of twenty-two times. I did better than Al Capone and John Gotti combined.

Then Fitzsimmons let go of the jugular and hit below the belt. "The reason I'm in the business is because of guys like Pat Cooper. When I was ten, Pat Cooper would always take the time to give me advice and answer my stupid questions, and then he would put his fingers in my asshole. 'You see, this is what it is. Comedy is pain.'"

And with a routine like that, he ought to know.

Near the end of the roast, Artie Lange got up, which, if you're Artie Lange is very hard to do. Artie calls himself an Italian, but we just call him fat. Artie gained about five pounds during the roast, and then he took a dump on the audience. "Pat says he's still on tour. The only tour he's on is Lipitor. A friend helped me write jokes about Pat last night, which was hard, because we were both born after 1911. Pat, you were in *Analyze This.* You know your career's on the fast track when you get your SAG card at seventy-five."

Or when your weight hits three hundred and seventy-five! This was before Artie tried to stab himself, but he still managed to do a lot of damage with the silverware.

A Friars Club roast is a tradition. Part of that tradition is to say a few kind words about someone after roasting them. It's more like a sauté. And the wonderful thing is, the same way you know instantly if the roast is good, you know if the sauté is good. Comedy that isn't sincere isn't any good, and neither are kind words that are full of shit. The kind words I received that night not only completed a meal. They completed a life.

Richard Belzer, hard as nails, said softly, "Pat knows I love him. I met him many years ago. And when you first start in the business, you look up to other comics. And Pat was one of the early comics who was very supportive of me. Always encouraged me. Always had a kind word. And there's never been a time when I've seen him onstage when I haven't laughed till I cried. I love you, Pat. You're the best."

Robert Klein came down from his ivory tower and up from the gutter as only he could. "My mentor was Rodney Dangerfield 'cause we're so much alike. He knew who was funny and who wasn't, and he used to say, 'I'll tell ya, Pat Cooper is fucking funny, okay?' And you are indeed. And anyone who can last this long being a toreador, which is what being a stand-up comedian is, deserves our honor."

Jim Norton couldn't burn a bridge with me if he wanted to, but he built an extra one right to my heart. "Pat, in closing, I gotta say, you are, as a comedian, exactly what I would like to be. You are brilliant, and you're brutally honest, and you're unapologetic. And it's unfortunate that those things have lead to virtual anonymity. But as a comedian, I am in awe of your balls and how funny you truly are. Thank you, and I'm honored to do anything for you."

Just promise me you'll do my roast when I turn a hundred. I won't be there, but promise me you will.

I'd say the same for my friend Artie Lange, but first he has to make it to fifty. Artie tried to show his sensitive side, but all we could see was his fat ass. "Pat, let me tell you something, buddy. You're a good man. I'm Italian, you're Italian. I'm proud to say I'm of the same gene pool as you. My whole family loves you. I love you. And I say this from the bottom of my heart. Go fuck yourself."

Same to you, Artie.

Some acts are hard to follow. The hardest act to follow is yourself. My friends captured Pat Cooper that night. What the hell was left to say? I tried though.

"But what's important? The important thing is I gotta pee. Ladies and gentlemen, I swear to you, God as my judge, I'm not a religious guy. I thank Jesus Christ that I can pee. My prostate is enlarged. And I never touched it before Thursday. That's what life is all about."

My heart was touched, too. For a couple of hours it was impossible to be sad. It was impossible to be a raving maniac.

Epilogue

The original title for this book was *How Dare You?* But that wasn't good enough. People say "How dare you?" all the time, and that's usually the end of the story. For me, it's just the beginning. "How dare you?" should start a conversation—the very kind of conversation people have stopped having. I'm only too happy to tell you exactly how and why I dare. But then the next question has to be, "How dare *you* say how dare *me*?" I'm not asking because I don't think you have an answer. *I'm asking because I think you do.*

I don't mind the question, so please don't mind the answer. To enjoy other people, to understand other people, you have to be willing to take a good look at yourself. As I've said a million times, I couldn't be prouder of my culture. To some people that means you're too proud to poke fun at it. Those people have it all wrong. When you get a vaccination, you get a small harmless sample of something much worse. That vaccination protects you for life. That vaccination makes you stronger. But if you can't take a little needling you're going to wind up very sick one day.

I believe in getting things out of my system. As I told the audience at my roast, my big thrill now is peeing. When I used to get laid, I went, "Ahhhh!" Now I pee and I go, "Ahhhh!" People are spending thousands of dollars on drugs to get laid. Peeing gives me the same satisfaction in the end, and it doesn't cost a dime. And when I travel, I don't need to go to Italy or China for a thrill. When I go from the bedroom to the bathroom, I'm going somewhere. That's traveling. That's adventure.

My father had it right. He told me, *"Patsy, you don a just go to the bathroom. Because what a you do is communicate with nature. You go in a there and you bring a the newspaper and you say, 'Please a God, let it a happen.' And when you communicate with a nature, when it a happens, that means a the engine is a working."*

He was in there every day at six in the morning and he wouldn't come out until nature told him to come out. The rest of us saw what a wonderful trip he was taking and fought to get in there.

The trip back from the bathroom to the bedroom wasn't as good for my father and those of his generation. Italian old-timers didn't believe in things we believe in today, like pleasuring a woman. If you even came close to mentioning something like that to an Italian old-timer, you'd get the neck movement. The neck movement was a quick little jerk of the head that said, *"Ay, whatsamatter? Don a bother me with a that!"* And we sure as hell didn't.

Not too much bothered my father. He always wore a hat, and the hat always stayed on. There could be a thunderstorm and the hat stayed on. There could be a wind storm and the hat stayed on. The neck moved and the hat stayed on. He lived to ninety-one and never complained about a pain in his neck, though he divorced one. And when the obituary for Michael Caputo appeared, my mother made sure that her name and my three sisters were listed, but not Pasquale or Pat or Patsy. Even when he left the planet, she wouldn't let him take his hat off even once to me—and then she probably pawned the hat.

At eighty and climbing, not too much bothers me, either. My equipment may be a little soft and my neck may be a little stiff, but the good thing is my leg is still going. My leg has been going since 1929. Patti would turn to me in the middle of the night and complain that my leg was moving around. I told her that was my comedic energy. That was my performer's heart. I told her when the leg stops moving, call the coroner because I'm dead.

These days, I take my leg onto the subway. That's how I get around New York, and it's a thrill. I got a MetroCard recently, and it was a bigger thrill than playing the Flamingo. When I saw my picture on that card, it was like getting an Oscar. I looked at it and thought, *Mother of God, someone at the MTA likes me.* Because I'm a senior citizen I get onto the subway for only a dollar a swipe. I figure if I get on and off enough, I can do four, six, eight swipes in a day, no problem. And I don't need anywhere to go. One day I told the engineer, "I'm so happy that I'm only paying a dollar a swipe." He said, "You better close the door, son. I'm working in here."

Some people need a bigger thrill. My daughter is sending my grandkids, fourteen and fifteen years old, to Italy for a couple of weeks. Why? Because they're so smart. Because they got wonderful grades. I told my daughter she was just looking to spend five grand because she had it. She told me I was being unfair because I've been to Europe. I explained to her that there was nothing over there they needed to see. Just bedbugs and a guy named Aldo—and make sure those kids don't bring either home. Better yet, save the five grand. The kids can ride the subway with me for two weeks. I have a friend at the MTA.

I argued with my own parents, and my own mother got too absorbed in money herself. But that generation got at least one thing right—the simple pleasures in life are the greatest. I'm not saying this because I managed to scrape some money together and now I'm above it all. Trust me on this one thing, and don't wait till you're eighty to find out for yourself.

Every day I pick up the paper and read about someone who has

---

absolutely everything, but is absolutely miserable. I recently read about an heiress who overdosed and died in her posh New York apartment. She was rich, she was beautiful, and she was miserable. She had the freedom to do anything in the world, and what she did was kill herself. It doesn't take a Nobel Prize winner to see that the people with seven cents in the world are often the happiest people. I don't have all the answers, but I know that we are clearly missing something.

That heiress was thirty years old. This struck me above and beyond the obvious tragedy. When I look back on my life, I see that it really just began at thirty. Before then, things were very difficult for me. I would gladly do it all over again, but if I could have my way, I would be born at thirty. I didn't know this young lady, but my guess is she probably felt that life was over for her. She probably believed it was too late for her to turn things around. I wish I could have told her that if she tried, she definitely could have turned things around, if not at thirty, then at forty; and if not at forty, at fifty. People can be reborn at sixty or after. I've seen it happen. I've had it happen.

Of course if I was actually born at thirty, I'd be a hundred and eleven now and I'd really have trouble peeing. There's a reason we go through hell, but it usually takes a very long time to look back and even begin to understand it. Being the odd man out in my own family was no fun, but it gave me more than just a lot of great material. It gave me . . . me.

I know a lot of comedians, and I don't think I know one good one who breezed through their early years. Maybe that kind of life is great for becoming a doctor or a lawyer, but for becoming a comedian it's the kiss of death.

If you look at the best art ever created—books, movies, and music that will live forever—most of it is not about fitting in. Most of it is about being a misfit and dealing with it. Making shit into Shinola is the stuff of epics. When it's done right no one can look away, because just about everyone has been there somehow. I was lucky to get the shit I did as early as I did, and even luckier to have the tools to make the Shinola.

To this day that's what I try to bring to the stage. That's what I try to bring to the performance of life, right down to a conversation in a crowded elevator. It's not "Look at me!" It's "Look at us!" It's not "Look what I've done!" It's "If I've done this with two weeks of high school, what can you do if you put your mind to it?" Hard work never gets old.

Another thing that never gets old is giving. Takers get old and givers stay young. I've tried to be a giver. You can't give everything to everyone all the time or you'll wind up a taker. You have to have a philosophy on giving. Mine has always been that it's great to give a hundred dollars to a church, but I'd rather give that same hundred to a family that's having trouble feeding their children. You know where that money is going and you can see the results. You just have to remember to give without taking away a person's dignity in exchange. Give and call it a payment. Call it a loan. Call it anything you want. Just don't call it in.

When people ask me what I do with my time, I tell them I rehearse dying. I lie down like I'm in a box and I ask my friends, "Do I look good this way or that way?" And people misunderstand me. They think what I mean is I'm retiring. They think I'm giving up. I'm not. How can I possibly retire with all this energy? What am I going to do with my fucking leg? And please, don't ask me if I'm getting a boat like half my retired friends. Gilligan got a boat and look at the trouble *he* got into.

When I say I rehearse dying, it's my way of saying I'm ready to go if I have to. I've had a great life. I'm still having it, and I'm not afraid. Cremate me and put me over macaroni. There's nothing to be scared of. The hard part is living, and I've already gone through just about everything a guy can go through.

Death can be beautiful. Death can be peaceful. I have some family members who have been shown the future but can't let go of the past for even a second. When I'm gone, I won't have to hear it anymore. And that alone is something to look forward to.

In the meantime, don't waste your time trying to hurt me. There's nothing wrong with not liking a person. There's nothing wrong with staying away. But I say to those people of the world who enjoy being cruel, don't bother spreading your anger and your jealousy and your venom my way. People couldn't seriously hurt me when I was much younger, and now that I'm over eighty, Kryptonite won't do it either. I tell people if they still want to give it a try, they're only going to hurt themselves. I tell people not to wake up the dead.

We're all going to die, and we're all basically the same. I know people who think they are something special, who think they walk on water, but they are no better than anyone else. If you *really* want to be special, try apologizing for something you did wrong. It works for me.

And we can all do one better than that. We can stop pushing people aside. One day you might need me to save your life. One day you might need my blood to pump into your ass. And I'm the first one to say that I might need you. And if the whole world got over itself and saw how much we needed each other, we could all go out and give each other a hug and a kiss, get laid, and have a dish of macaroni together. That's what it's all about. *Ba-da-bump-bump.*